979 Merry Xmas to Bob, We hope you enjoy this. love Lorraine & Stephen.

CANADIAN D... ...ITY OF TORONTO

NTO

TORONTO

by Bruce West

A CHANGE OF PACE
TORONTO

TORONTO

Bruce West

DOUBLEDAY CANADA LIMITED, TORONTO
DOUBLEDAY AND COMPANY, INC., GARDEN CITY, NEW YORK
1979

ISBN: 0-385-02625-0

To my daughters and my grandchildren, with the hope that they will find as much to love and admire in the Toronto of tomorrow as I have found in the Toronto of yesterday and today

ACKNOWLEDGMENTS

I would like to express my deep appreciation for the use of the following photographs: to the Toronto Public Library for 6, 8, 10, 11, 13, 14, 16–18, 27, 29, 30, 33, 39, and 61 from the John Ross Robertson Collection; also 3, 4, 7, 9, 12, 15, 20–22, 24, 25, 31, 32, 34–36, 46, and 49. To the Ontario Department of Industry and Tourism for 19, 23, 41, 52, 62–65, 67–71, and the back endpapers. To the Toronto Transit Commission for 28, 42–44, 48, 50, 53, 54, and 56. To the City of Toronto Archives for 51 and 55 from the James Collection. To the Confederation Life Collection for 1, 2, 26, and 37. To the Cadillac Fairview Corporation Limited for 66 and 73. To the *Globe and Mail* of Toronto for 45 and 47 from the Galbraith Collection; also 5, 38, 40, and 57–60. To Ontario Hydro for 72. To Roy Nicholls, photographer, for the Royal Bank, 74. To Stuart Connolly for 75.

To the Canadian Department, Royal Ontario Museum, University of Toronto for the front endpapers.

My thanks to the University of Toronto Press for permission to use material in Chapters 1, 2, and 3 from *Toronto During the French Régime 1615–1793* by Percy J. Robinson.

B.W.

PREFACE

I suppose it should be stated at the outset that this book is not intended to be a formal history of Toronto. Although I have tried to preserve its accuracy, I have set down in it the events in the Toronto story which most appealed to me, without worrying much about whether one or the other of the prominent figures in Toronto over the years has received too much or too little attention. Such personages as John Strachan, Jesse Ketchum, John Beverley Robinson and others only briefly mentioned here, are worthy of whole volumes and some of them have been so honored. But this is the biography of a city, not that of any individual who lived in it. William Lyon Mackenzie, who was Toronto's first mayor, does receive a good deal of attention here because he and the events which surrounded him must surely make up one of the most exciting parts of the city's story.

One of the more striking aspects of this story, it seems to me, is the manner in which Toronto continued its steady progress from a muddy backwoods village to a great and throbbing metropolis while enduring many derisive jibes from other parts of Canada and even from visitors from outside the country. Needling Toronto has become such a national pastime in Canada that even the residents of the city—most of whom came to it from other sections of the country—will surely feel a little lost if the day ever arrives when Toronto achieves such undeniable stature that even Montreal will stop making jokes about it.

During more than four decades in which I have worked in Toronto as a newspaperman, I have developed an abiding affection for the city that sometimes reminds me of a gangling and somewhat uncertain youth who is still a little bashful and not fully aware of his true importance in the Canadian scheme of things. Torontonians, as a group, have in the past been inclined to be almost apologetic about their city, as though it somehow needed to be defended in the rest of Canada. But this attitude is rapidly changing to one of great confidence and pride, and I hope this book will help speed this desirable process.

Prior to about 1950, Toronto was more a group of different villages—so far as the thinking of most of its residents were concerned—than an integrated city. There were the East Enders and the West Enders and the

North Torontonians and those who thought in terms of the numerous suburban communities and it sometimes seemed that their only common ground was right downtown in the traffic jams. But this feeling has largely changed now and the idea of one big city has made a distinct difference in the attitude of Torontonians. The arrival after the Second World War of so many hundreds of thousands of new residents from the Old Lands has also helped bring about a marked change in the city's personality. The newcomers contributed a fresh vitality and character to the city, in everything from its arts to its eating habits. And certainly, in a physical way, by their sweat and toil, they have contributed hugely to the building of the new Toronto. Already they have shown in many ways their great pride in their adopted town and I hope this story of what went on before they arrived will help increase it.

I should like to acknowledge here my deep debt of gratitude to Miss Edith G. Firth, head of the Canadian History and Manuscript Section of the Toronto Public Library, who helped, in so many ways, with unfailing courtesy and even enthusiasm. Her two books containing selections of various early documents concerning the founding and development of the community—*The Town of York, 1793–1815*, and *The Town of York, 1815–1834*—are veritable gold mines of information for any one preparing a work such as this. For selecting and publishing these interesting documents alone, I would owe her a great debt. But she helped in other personal ways, including the reading of that part of my manuscript which dealt with the very early days of York and Toronto. Mr. Wallace Bonner of the Toronto Public Library photographic department was tirelessly cheerful in providing me with reproductions of a great number of old Toronto sketches from which many of the illustrations in this book were made. The *Globe and Mail*, the Ontario Department of Tourism and Information, the Toronto-Dominion Centre, and the Toronto Transit Commission were also extremely helpful in the task of collecting illustrations for this work.

I hope this outline of Toronto's past and present will arouse in the reader enough interest in the city's great story to cause him to go searching in some of the more exhaustive works dealing with special aspects of it. If this occurs, I shall feel amply rewarded for the effort which went into preparing this book, because I am sure he or she will then join me in the growing ranks of the extremely proud Torontonians.

CONTENTS

TORONTO

Chapter 1

1615

The Explorer

The long portage. The ancient trail. Etienne Brulé camps at mouth of Humber. A rough adventurer.

It might have been gratifying to be able to record here that the first white explorer to set eyes upon the site of the metropolis that would someday be renowned as Toronto the Good and the City of Churches was a God-fearing man of stainless character and exceedingly high principles. It would also probably have been nice, for those who were later to paint or describe this historic event, had he worn some heroic kind of raiment at the time and was standing on the deck of a ship scanning his latest discovery through a telescope, after the fashion of John Cabot sighting Cape Breton Island from the rail of the *Matthew* or Christopher Columbus peering across the waves from the *Santa Maria* at his first sight of the New World.

But the discovery of that part of Canada which was to become Toronto was not, alas, surrounded by any of these noble and romantic circumstances. From its very beginnings until the present, as we shall see, Toronto had to grow into one of the most exciting cities of the continent while living down various rather embarrassing circumstances concerning its birth and rise to great stature.

Etienne Brulé, who is credited with being the first white man to visit the place where the Humber River flows into Lake Ontario, is said to have been a rough and vulgar adventurer with little or no morals who finally committed the crowning sin of his iniquitous life by turning traitor against his own countrymen and guiding an English expedition up the St. Lawrence in 1610 during an attack upon Quebec. A particularly sorry aspect of this treachery was that Brulé had been a servant of the great Samuel de Champlain, the governor who had to accept the humiliation of surrender to the English ships which Brulé had helped to guide to the foot of Quebec's crumbling fortress.

And yet, Etienne Brulé, who now has a park named for him along the lower banks of the Humber River, was one of the New World's greatest explorers and had he been a man of higher education and character his name might stand today among the most honored in the early recorded history of this continent.

He was the first to find the route up the Ottawa and across to the Mattawa, following its course to Lake Nipissing and the French River, opening this important route to the Huron country. He was the first to set eyes upon Georgian Bay, making his way through the Inner Passage to Lake Huron. In fact, it is believed that he was the first white man to see each of the Great Lakes, with the possible exception of Lake Michigan.

But he was a rough man of the hard breed of the *coureurs-de-bois*, who took no notes and drew no maps as he made his way through the vast wilderness with his Indian companions, living and sometimes even looking like one of them. He was a powerful man who often went about stripped to the waist, his skin as bronzed and weathered as that of the savages with whom he liked to live.

He changed Indian wives as rapidly and as frequently as he changed his horizons in his restless roaming across the land. Father Gabriel Sagard, who was his friend, is quoted as sadly admitting that Brulé was "much addicted to women."

But perhaps the most damning description on record of Toronto's first white man is that of Father Du Creux, who wrote of him as follows:

> It is clear that Brulé was a bad man, and guilty of every vice and crime. He had served as interpreter for the French among the Hurons, and the wretch had not been ashamed to disgrace himself by betraying the French and passing over to the English when they took possession of the citadel of Quebec.
>
> Champlain taunted Brulé with this perfidy, and pointed out how disgraceful it was for a Frenchman to betray King and country, and for an orthodox Catholic to ally himself with heretics, share their foul intoxication and eat meat on days when, as he well knew, Catholics were forbidden to do so.
>
> The impious man answered that he knew all that, but since a comfortable future was not before him in France, the die was cast and he would live with the English.
>
> Brulé returned to the Hurons. It cost him nothing to give up his country. Long a transgressor of the laws of God and man, he spent the rest of his life in vile intemperance, such as no Christian should exhibit among the heathen. He died by treachery; perhaps for this very reason, that he might perish in his sins. Deprived of those benefits by which the children

of the Church are prepared for a happy issue from this mortal life, Brulé was hurried to the Judgment Seat to answer for all his other crimes and especially for the depravity which was a perpetual stumbling block to the Hurons, among whom he should have been a lamp in a dark place, a light to lead the heathen nation to the Faith.

Such was the harsh appraisal of the character of Toronto's discoverer, the once dashing and daring explorer who, after being turned away by his own people following his betrayal of Quebec, lived a drunken life among the Indians who finally turned upon him, beat him to death and ate him.

But on the autumn day, believed to be September 8, 1615, when Etienne Brulé first set out along the 28-mile trail that was to lead him over the Toronto Carrying-Place from the west branch of the Holland River to the mouth of the Humber and Lake Ontario, he still had many beckoning and mysterious horizons before him.

He was on a mission for Champlain, who was then camped at the northern outlet of Lake Simcoe preparing to set out with the Hurons upon an expedition against the Iroquois. Champlain had sent Brulé, his interpreter, with twelve Hurons in two canoes, to summon aid from the Carantouans or Andastes to the south in the Susquehanna.

On this September day, some of the great trees of the forests must have begun to take on their autumn coloring. The river that is now called the Humber was clear and sparkling then and along its banks huge pines reared above the maples, beeches, oaks, and cedars.

The trail was well worn, because no one knows how many generations of Indians had used this short cut from Lake Ontario to Lake Huron before the white man arrived. The long procession of travelers over the centuries must have included war-painted braves on their way to battle, or returning with their miserable prisoners from successful raids into the North. Many hunters traversed it during sorties into the rich fur country of the Northwest.

Approximately where Riverside Drive now runs was part of the trail which knew the soft tread of the Hurons and the Iroquois, the Ottawas and the Menominees, the Shawanoes, the Sacs, the Foxes, and the Mississaugas.

Such was the pathway followed by Brulé and his twelve Hurons as they stepped along smartly, intent upon reaching the shores of Lake Ontario before darkness fell. Their bark canoes must have been heavy to be borne over such a long portage, but Brulé was carrying his full share of the load because he had by now been living with the Hurons for some five years and to be accepted by them a white man had to bear equal burdens with them and have the same strong grip on the paddles as his Indian companions.

These were the days of the real outdoorsmen when, as a trapper once remarked, the *voyageurs* at nightfall "pulled a cloud over their heads" and slept the just sleep of men who had labored long and well from the first gray light of dawn.

The sun was just beginning to set below the western horizon when Brulé and his party emerged from the woods and stood at last at the mouth of the Humber where it enters the great lake. It was September 9 and, after their long day of sweating toil, the travelers were thankful for the cool, clean breezes off the lake which wafted against their moist faces.

Now there would be a night of sleep and on the morrow there would be miles of paddling ahead which, wearisome though it might be as the big canoes were driven along, would still be preferable to the strain and back-breaking toil of hauling heavy loads up and down the hills of the long portage trail over the Toronto Carrying-Place.

The broad body of water which they now surveyed was to bear many names throughout the years—Tadenac, Lac Contenant, Lac St. Louis, Lac des Entouhonoronons, Lac des Iroquois, Cataraqui, Contario, Lac Ontario, and Lac Frontenac.

As has been said, Brulé was a man of the wilderness, not given to dreaming or note-making or map-drawing. On that historic evening his mind was probably occupied with the routine job of setting up his overnight camp and planning the next leg of his journey around the western end of the lake to its southern shore.

Even had he been a romantic and a prophet it is not likely, as he made camp that evening on his first visit to the site of Toronto, that in his wildest dreams he could have pictured what would someday come to pass there.

How could anyone have foreseen that three and a half centuries later great vessels from far-off Europe would sail over these very waters to a huge inland seaport a few miles down the shore? Or, that rearing up behind the piers where they discharged their cargoes would stand the lofty spires of great towers of commerce, shattering with a million lights the darkness where now flickered only the small camp fire surrounded by the rugged wanderer Etienne Brulé and his twelve Huron companions.

Chapter 2

1617–1650

TORONTO—FRENCH OUTPOST

The first small trading post. Bitter rivalry between the English and the French traders. A community binge. Competition from Oswego. Firewater for the Indians. The second French trading post and fort.

In the years following Etienne Brulé's first brief visit to Toronto, the southern portage terminal rapidly grew in importance. Both the French traders, from Quebec and Montreal, and the English and Dutch from such points as Albany on the Hudson, were journeying into Lake Ontario and Lake Huron to compete with each other for the rich fur trade.

The term Toronto Carrying-Place came to refer to all of the pass which extended between the mouth of the Humber and the mouth of the Severn River. Even the present Lake Simcoe was for a time known as Lake Toronto.

By making this portage it was possible to cut out from the journey into Lakes Huron, Superior, and Michigan the long haul across the Niagara portage to Lake Erie and thence along Lake Erie for most of its length to the waterways connecting it with Lake Huron.

Strange as it might seem in today's conception of travel, the trail from Lake Ontario *northward* over the Toronto Carrying-Place eventually became part of the route to the Mississippi followed by such explorers as La Salle. After crossing the Toronto portage to Lake Huron they continued on through the Straits of Michilimackinac into Lake Michigan and found their way from this great body of water into the headwaters of the Mississippi.

In 1678, by which time the Iroquois had established their villages along the north shore of Lake Ontario, there was an Indian settlement near the mouth of the Humber called Teiaiagon, at which the famed explorer-priest Father Louis Hennepin once spent several weeks.

It was protected by a stout palisade, well guarded against possible attacks from the north. Nearby were some cultivated fields and within the compound stood the typical long houses of the Iroquois. Naked children played in the narrow streets and the women gossiped or performed their tasks while the young men gambled in the shade of the great maples or the old men smoked their tobacco.

Although Indian villages had a way of moving about at fairly frequent intervals, there are reasons to believe that Teiaiagon might have enjoyed a little more permanence than some of the other settlements.

For one thing, it was conveniently located at the foot of the important Toronto Carrying-Place. For another, the then clear and sparkling waters of the Humber provided a bounty of salmon during the annual runs and was a considerable source of food supply for the village.

It is a matter of sad record, in the early history of Toronto the Good, that one of its first groups of white visitors was a party of La Salle's men from Cataraqui (now Kingston) who, in the 1670's, staged a drunken debauch in the village in which they were joined by the Indians themselves.

This disgraceful community binge is recorded in an ancient tract entitled *Histoire de l'eau de vie en Canada:*

> The Carnival of the year 167– six traders from Katarakuy named Duplessis, Ptolemee, Dautru, Lamouche, Colin, and Cascaret made the whole village of Taheyagon drunk, all the inhabitants were dead drunk for three days; the old men, the women and the children got drunk; after which the six traders engaged in the debauch which the savages called *Ganuary*, running about naked with a keg of brandy under the arm.

It is also mentioned that two women were stabbed in Teiaiagon as a result of a drunken brawl which probably occurred during the same memorable blowout.

On several occasions La Salle made use of the Toronto Carrying-Place on his journeys to and from Lake Ontario and the upper lakes, with the French and Indian members of his expeditions hauling over the long portage their huge canoes, 20 feet long and three feet wide. It was said that each of these great craft was capable of carrying about 1200 pounds of freight and on one occasion it took La Salle and his men more than two weeks to move all of their goods over the trail that led from the mouth of the Humber toward the present Holland River and Lake Simcoe.

All the while the rivalry for the fur trade in the rich country along the northern shores of Lake Ontario was growing more keen between the French from Quebec and the English and Dutch traders who were coming up from their settlements on and near the Hudson.

"In America both the French and the English accused one another," writes Percy J. Robinson, in his scholarly work, *Toronto During the French Régime*. "Dongan [the Governor of New York] maintained that the French intended to confine the English to the coast, and the French in their turn were convinced that the English were already plotting to confine New France within the territory bounded on the West by the Ottawa and the South by the St. Lawrence and that in the event of war between the mother countries the French would be excluded from America."

But it was not until 1720 that the French decided to tighten their hold upon Lake Ontario by establishing a small trading post at the foot of the Toronto Carrying-Place.

It was little more than a branch of the one that had already been built by the French at Niagara and the infant settlement of Toronto was to remain a mere offshoot of the community on the south shore of the lake for some years.

The first *Magasin Royal* is believed to have been built by Captain Alexandre Dagneau, the Sieur Douville, on the east bank of the Humber not far north of its mouth, perhaps near the site of the Indian village of Teiaiagon.

A description of the goods offered by Toronto's first commercial establishment lists them as including buttons and shirts and ribbons and combs, knives, looking-glasses and axes; flour, lard and pepper, prunes, raisins and olive oil; tobacco, vermilion, powder and shot and caps of various sizes.

Once they had established their western posts, the authorities of New France took steps to see that all possible profits from the enterprises should go to the King rather than being drained off by the furtive efforts of the English from New York or the unlicensed *coureurs-de-bois* from Quebec. In 1726 Intendant Claude Begon issued an order which read as follows,

"Concerning the illicit trade in the neighborhood of the posts on Lake Ontario and Lake Erie pertaining to the King—Being informed that several private individuals are carrying on trade in Lake Ontario, Lake Erie and other places to the prejudice of that carried on for the King at Fort Frontenac [now Kingston] at Niagara, at the foot of Lake Ontario [Toronto] and elsewhere, we forbid all persons to trade in the aforesaid lakes Ontario and Erie, in their environs or anywhere else, on pain of confiscation of canoes, merchandise and the peltries with which they are laden, and a fine of five hundred *livres*, to which the said traders will be liable as well as those who outfit them . . ."

For a while the efforts of the French to monopolize the fur trade on Lake Ontario were fairly successful and at New York the profits of the

northern barter declined by almost one-half. But the English were not
long in accepting the challenge. In 1726 they erected a fortified stone
house across the lake at Oswego. This first English settlement on Lake
Ontario marked the beginning of the end of the French sway over the region.

Soon after the establishment of the competing post at Oswego—called
Chouaguen by the French—it became necessary to lower the price of the
King's goods in the French posts. Not only were the English giving much
better value for the Indians' furs, but their trading stocks included a liberal supply of firewater, which could not then be obtained at the French
posts.

The post at Toronto was finally leased to a private individual and then,
midst wrangles concerning the rates he was paying for it and the manner
in which he carried on trade, the establishment seems to have languished
and for some years there is no further mention of it.

The English post at Oswego, on the other hand, continued to flourish,
because the region was rich in furs. It was partly to offset this success of
their rivals that the French decided in 1750 to establish a fort at Toronto,
a project planned along more ambitious lines than those of the original
small trading post which had experienced such a struggling existence.

It was a symbol of the tightening of grips between the French and the
English in the wrestle for the fur trade on Lake Ontario. Included in the
trade goods of the new fort would be the rum and brandy which had formerly been available only at Oswego.

In a document entitled *Memoire sur le Canada*, the situation is described as follows:

> The English had built upon the south shore of Lake Ontario a fort which
> they called Oswego . . . The situation of the place was very advantageous,
> for it was in the midst of the country of the Five Nations and it attracted
> them to it and kept them in check. For though we had Niagara on the
> same side of the lake and Frontenac on the other, these two forts were not
> sufficient for the needs of the savages; they did not find the *eau-de-vie* and
> the rum which they were accustomed to find at Couaguin or Chouaguin
> and this was a very great disadvantage. The priests had made the sale of
> liquor a matter of conscience, and had placed it among sins that incur ex-
> communication.
>
> They had the Governor on their side so that it was a crime to sell it.
> This was a good rule in the towns where the savages might indulge in li-
> cense and so stir up trouble; but it was quite a different matter at the
> posts. It is the liquor which attracts the Indians and thanks to the drink
> Chouaguin had maintained itself and we had against us the tribes who
> resorted there.
>
> The Governor thought that the re-establishment of Fort Toronto would

catch all the Missisaugas and the tribes of the North who passed that way on their road to Chouaguin . . .

The strategic purpose behind the re-establishment of a more ambitious post and fort at Toronto is also described in a note to the French Colonial Minister, Antoinne Louis Rouille, from the Governor, the Marquis de La Jonquiere, and the Intendant François Bigot, dated at Quebec on October 6, 1749:

> On being informed that the Indians from the north generally stop at Toronto on the west side of Lake Ontario 25 leagues from Niagara and 75 from Fort Frontenac on their way to Chouaguen with their furs, we have felt it would be advisable to establish a post at this place and to send there an officer, fifteen soldiers and some workmen to build a small stockaded fort. The expense will not be great for there is timber at hand and the rest will be brought by the Fort Frontenac boats. Too much care can not be taken to prevent the said Indians from continuing their trade with the English and to see that they find at this post all that they need as cheaply as at Chouaguen.
>
> Instructions will have to be given to those in command at Detroit, Niagara and Fort Frontenac to be careful that the traders and shopkeepers in these posts furnish goods in future at the same price as the English for two or three years. In this way the Indians will lose the habit of going to Chouaguen, and the English will be forced to abandon the place. If anything else occurs to us likely to hasten the downfall of Chouaguen, we shall act.

In the spring of 1750 instructions were given to proceed with the construction of the new fort. The project was commenced under the supervision of M. Pierre Robineau, the Chevalier de Portneuf, an ensign in the marines who had been on duty at Fort Frontenac.

In less than two months a small palisaded enclosure had been erected and a modest storehouse had been built in which to keep the goods which had been shipped by bateaux down the St. Lawrence. Although there seems to be some doubt about the exact location of the first Fort Toronto, it is believed that it may have stood on the high ground on the east bank of the Humber near what is now known as Baby Point.

The new fort, which now included liquor among its wares, did a booming business and it was soon decided that a second and larger one should be built. Accordingly, Jonquiere dispatched another letter to the Colonial Minister in Paris:

> My Lord,
> I have learned by your honoured letter of April 15 last that you approve the proposal which I made to you in the letter signed by myself and the

Intendant on the 9th of September last for the establishment of a post at Toronto. I have the honor to submit an account of the trade there.

To avoid expense to the King I undertook to instruct the Sieur Chevalier de Portneuf, ensign on duty at Fort Frontenac, to report to Toronto with a sergeant and four soldiers. He set out from the said fort on the 20th day of May last, and at the same time a clerk appointed by the Intendant left Montreal with the goods necessary for the said trade for the King.

On his arrival at Toronto, the Sieur de Portneuf had his men build a small stockaded fort and a small house for the safe-keeping of His Majesty's effects. He remained there with the said clerk until the 17th of July last. The said Sieur de Portneuf then left to rejoin his garrison and the clerk-trader went down to Montreal with the bales of furs.

They traded with most of the tribes who called at the said post. This trade has not been altogether bad; they made seventy-nine bales valued at eighteen thousand *livres*.

The trade-clerk assures us that he would have made more than 150 bales if he had had more cloth, *eau-de-vie* and bread for the Indians, and this would have been provided had we expected such success.

Since the tribes from the north have promised the said Sieur de Portneuf to come next year in much greater numbers and to give up the English altogether, it is very essential, my Lord, to profit by their friendliness and to establish the said post firmly.

The house which the Sieur de Portneuf had built is too small and it might have been feared that the King's effects would not have been safe in as much as the large numbers of Indians of various tribes who will probably go there to trade next year (most of whom have been guilty of the worst conduct during the late war) could easily overpower the Sieur de Portneuf and plunder all the goods.

To avoid any risk, I shall have built a double-staked fort with curtains of eighty feet not including the gorge of the bastions, with a lodge for the officer on the right side of the fort, and a guard-house for twelve or fifteen soldiers on the left.

The warehouse will be along the curtain facing the entrance; the trade-clerk will lodge there; a bakery will be built in one of the bastions.

It is important that the fort should be finished early in the year so that the Sieur de Portneuf can move there in the month of April with his party. It is certain that the trade will be best if we are there early. In view of this the Intendant and I have despatched a carpenter with three men to cut and square the timber. The trade-clerk has gone with them, also a baker, a tanner and five or six hired men to help him in the trade which he will be able to carry on during the winter with about ten Indians who are good hunters and live in the neighborhood of the said post.

During the autumn I shall have delivered by ship planks from Fort Frontenac and by *bateaux de cent* the provisions, merchandise, liquors and other necessaries, so that there may be no lack at the said post.

In this way the said fort will be built without trouble and there is room to hope that this establishment will be in every way profitable. My Lord, I beg your approval, for my naming it hereafter Fort Rouille. Your honoured name will attract in great numbers all the tribes and will give it the importance we should wish.

In fact all the tribes from the north who go to Chouaguen and pass the said post will be stopped there; and finding in abundance all that they need and especially *eau-de-vie* and cloth, they will naturally do their trading there and not go to Chouaguen.

The English will be deprived of the visits of these Indians and will find from that time a great decrease in revenue which they have been accustomed to draw from their furs. This might help hereafter to make them give up the said post which would become useless.

Besides, if we succeed in making these tribes trust us and have nothing to do with the English, on the one hand we shall be quiet and nothing will hinder the French in their trade in the north; and on the other hand it will be very easy to persuade these tribes that it is in their interest not to allow the English to have the post at all beside them because they are enemies always at hand to harm them; and little by little we shall be able to make the Indians decide to destroy Chouaguen by force of arms. They are malicious, and once they form a decision, they are sure to carry it out.

The destruction of Chouaguen is a powerful motive for which I neglect nothing to accomplish its downfall one way or another. I am in earnest about this, but in time of peace I can do no more than try to bring over to our side the tribes loyal to the English.

I venture to assure you, my Lord, that if unhappily we should have a new war with them, Chouaguen would have to be well defended to prevent my becoming master there, having devoted myself to find out all I can about this post.

Chouaguen, or Oswego, was indeed destined to fall to the French. But so, alas, was Niagara to fall to the English a short time later, and with its fall the French flag would be lowered at the brave new fort at Toronto, never to rise there again.

Chapter 3
1651–1787

FORT ROUILLE

*Business improves for the French. An unhealthy location. The fall of
Oswego. Capture of Fort Niagara by the British. The burning of Fort
Rouille. Rogers' Rangers visit Toronto. The Toronto Purchase.*

The third post and last fort to be established by the French in Toronto
was completed in the spring of 1751 and was located approximately at the
foot of Dufferin Street on a spot which now lies within the grounds of the
Canadian National Exhibition. Although it was officially referred to as
Fort Rouille, the residents and most of those who visited it continued to
call it Fort Toronto. This was not to be the last time that officialdom was
to be balked in its efforts to give Toronto a name other than its ancient
Indian one which, according to some authorities, meant "place of meeting" and according to others was a term referring to "trees in the water."

In his report to the Colonial Minister in the fall of 1751, the Marquis
de La Jonquiere expressed great satisfaction with the new and larger fort.

It was a certainty, wrote the Governor, that the high prices being obtained from the Indians for the goods at Fort Rouille would soon pay for
the expense incurred in erecting it. Tribes in the region who had formerly
gone to trade at the hated English post across the lake at Oswego were
now doing their dealings exclusively at Toronto.

"The inhabitants of Toronto have had at heart the establishment of the
fort," wrote Jonquiere to the Colonial Minister. "One can only attribute
their docility to the protection with which you honour the colony, in
which protection they profit especially. They even sent messages to their
allies and to the other tribes to divert them from Choueguen (Oswego)
and to invite them to go and trade at Fort Rouille. They did more; they
refused their canoes to several Indians from the Upper Country who

wanted to buy them in order to go to Choueguen. This secured us their peltries."

But conditions within the brave little fort were not at all times as happy as the Governor had reported in his letter to his Minister. Writing to the commandant at Niagara the young Sieur de Portneuf told of the maladies which were inflicting his fort.

"The sickness we have had here for a long time compels me at last to have recourse to you to beg you to be so kind as to send us your doctor for a few days. If it had been possible to have our numerous invalids conveyed to you I should have done so," he wrote.

"But of all the garrison and all the employees we have only three soldiers left who are well and the three Canadians by whom I am asking you to aid us in our present need.

"You will oblige me for I myself will be ready to get cured since I am not at all well myself again after the fevers which left me some days ago. There must be some bad air to contend with, for the strongest are among those struck down among the first comers.

"If you have the soldier, sir, in your garrison who knows how to cook, I beg you to send him to us till ours recovers; he and his wife are very sick."

The Abbé Picquet, when he visited Fort Rouille, reported that both the wine and the bread there were better than those which were offered at some of the other posts. But he criticized the manner in which the trading post was carrying on its dealings with the Indians.

The main purpose of the fort, said he, was to provide enough competition to drive the English interlopers out of Oswego. Yet the English were still giving the Indians far better value for their furs.

"We should have imitated the English in the matter of the trinkets which they sell to the savages, such as silver bracelets, etc.," he wrote. "The savages compared them and weighed them . . . and it was found that the bracelets from Choueguen weighed as much and were purer silver and more attractive and cost them only two beaver skins, while they wanted to sell them for ten skins at the King's magazines. So we were discredited and these silver articles remained a dead loss in the magazines of the King. The French brandy was better liked than the English; but, that did not prevent the savages from going to Choueguen."

The Abbé Picquet, however, did not think much of any of the forts from which the French carried on their trade with the Indians. He believed that the sharp practices of the traders turned the savages against the French and that only through the more benign efforts of the missionaries could the Indians be won over to the service of God and the King.

He reported that during his visit to Toronto some of the more pious Indians in the settlement complained that in their village the French had given them only a brandy shop instead of the church they so earnestly desired. (A strange commentary indeed upon the beginning of a community which would someday be renowned throughout the land for the abundance of its churches and the dry dullness of its Sundays.)

There was good reason for the Abbé to look with disfavor upon the liquor-peddling activities in Toronto. The Indians, who had not known strong liquor until the white man's arrival, did not believe they were enjoying its proper effects unless they were utterly and completely drunk and had either been injured or had injured someone else.

When they traded their furs for a keg of brandy or rum, their squaws gathered from the lodges everything which could possibly be used as a weapon and stole off to spend the night in the woods. And even then the drunken braves sometimes managed to tear down lodgepoles and beat each other with them.

But the liquor business went merrily on, despite the objections of the missionaries.

"I beg you sir," wrote the commandant of Fort Rouille to his superiors at Niagara in April of 1752, "to be so good as to give orders to send us a cooper from your fort . . . we are almost out of kegs and consequently almost out of business."

In 1756 the post at Oswego, which had for so long been a thorn in the sides of the traders at Toronto and other French forts on Lake Ontario, fell to a French expedition under Montcalm and the English were routed or taken prisoners.

But the exclusive French rule of Lake Ontario and its fur trade was not to last for long. In 1758 the English descended upon Fort Frontenac and destroyed it. In July of 1759 they attacked and took the French fort at Niagara, of which Toronto's Fort Rouille was a dependency. When it became apparent that Niagara could not withstand the English attack, a French schooner standing offshore scurried across the lake to Fort Rouille with the bad news.

Shortly after the tidings from Niagara had been received, a plume of black smoke arose from Fort Rouille as its buildings were put to the torch to prevent them falling into the hands of the English.

Thus ended the days of Toronto as a French outpost on Lake Ontario. Little remains now to remind us of it except a plaque on a stone pillar in the Grounds of the Canadian National Exhibition marking the site of Fort Rouille. Perhaps a footsore visitor to the "Ex" occasionally rests against one of the cannon at the base of the monument to eat a hot dog or drink his pop, without even bothering to read the inscription.

When a scouting party from the British forces at Niagara reached Fort Rouille a few days later to reconnoiter, they found only five heaps of charred timbers and planks, with a low chimney stack of coarse brick standing on the shattered flagstone floor. In this final chapter of French rule in Toronto, the flimsy little fort's four pitifully small guns had never had a chance to fire in its defense.

The Indians, whose loyalty to Fort Rouille and the French had been so warmly praised by Jonquiere after the establishment of the last and largest Toronto fort, lost no time in pledging their allegiance to the English.

Shortly after the fall of Niagara and the subsequent burning of Fort Rouille, an Indian chief named Tequakareigh from Toronto visited Sir William Johnson, commander of the victorious British forces. The meeting took place at Niagara and Sir William welcomed the chief with a string of beads and two belts of wampum.

"I recommended hunting and trade to them, which would be more to their interest than quarrelling with the English, who have ever been their friends," wrote Sir William righteously in his *Journal*.

"To which he answered and said it gave him great pleasure to hear our good words and was certain it would be extremely agreeable to all of the nations with whom he was acquainted, who, with his, were wheedled and led on to strike the English, which he now confessed he was sorry for and assured they never would again; and that, should the French, according to custom, ask them to do so any more, they would turn them out of the country . . . He also desired I would send some person to the Mississaga town, near where Toronto stood, to hear what he would say to their nation, and to see that he would deliver my belts and message honestly . . . I clothed him very well, and gave him a handsome present to carry home; and then took from about his neck a large French medal, and gave him an English one, and a gorget of silver, desiring, whenever he looked at them, he would remember the engagment he now made."

On September 30, 1760, the famous American frontier soldier, Major Robert Rogers, and two hundred of his Rangers arrived at Toronto in the fifteen whale boats they had brought up the St. Lawrence from Montreal into the Great Lakes to take formal possession of the forts abandoned by the French.

"We passed a bank twenty miles in length, but the land behind it seemed to be level, well timbered with large oaks, hickories, maples and some poplars," reads an entry in Rogers' *Journal*. "No mountains appeared in sight. Round the place where formerly the French had a fort that was called Fort Toronto, there was a tract of about 300 acres of cleared ground. The soil here is principally clay. The deer are extremely plentiful in this country. Some Indians were hunting at the mouth of the river, who ran into the woods at our approach, very much frightened. They came in, however, in the morning, and testified their joy at the news of our success against the French."

Three years after the French had abandoned Fort Rouillé there was again sporadic trading taking place at Toronto and once more the demon rum seems to have been one of the principal items of barter.

"Complaints have been made from Michilimackinac that the traders of Toronto debauch the Indians from those quarters by selling them rum," testily wrote General Thomas Gage from Montreal to the commandant at Niagara, a Major Wilkins, in October of 1762.

The English traders, who now came frequently to Toronto, were worse than the French in their treatment of the Indians and their willingness to provide them with liquor.

But, although the French flag had disappeared from Toronto, it was yet to hear the last of the French language or French names among its permanent inhabitants because, in 1780, St. Jean Rousseau, a trader from Montreal, set up a post near the mouth of the Humber in what may have been the buildings of the first small Fort Toronto, which are believed to have been spared the torch when the larger Fort Rouillé to the east was burned after the fall of Niagara.

In 1787, apparently impressed by the strategic importance of the area which lay at the foot of the Toronto Carrying-Place, the British authorities decided to purchase it from the Indians. On September 23, a meeting was held at the Carrying-Place on the Bay of Quinte between Deputy Surveyor John Collins from Quebec, acting for the Crown, and three chiefs of the Mississaugas, to discuss the terms. On August 1, 1788, HMS *Seneca* entered Toronto Bay laden with 149 barrels of presents and provisions for the Indians. Her cargo included such varied items as "24 brass kettles . . . 200 lbs. Tobacco 47 Carrots . . . 10 dozen Looking Glasses . . . 1 Hogshead containing 18 pieces Gartering . . . 24 Laced Hats . . . 2000 Gun Flints . . . 1 Bale flowered Flannel . . . and 96 Gallons of Rum." Such goods, amounting in all to a sum of about £1700, were the price His Majesty's Government would pay for an area of about 500 square miles which included roughly one-third of the present County of York. Although it may not have been as favorable a deal as that obtained by the Dutch when they bought Manhattan Island from the Indians for $24, it did turn out to be quite a bargain in the light of later events.

Lord Dorchester, Governor General of Canada, arrived at Toronto a few days after the *Seneca* had anchored. With Sir John Johnson, Superintendent of Indian Affairs and Colonel John Butler, of Butler's Rangers, he formally completed what came to be known as the Toronto Purchase. It was not until 1805, however, that the final details of the deal with the Indians were worked out during a third meeting between them and government officials at the mouth of the Credit River.

Chapter 4

1793

The Birth of York

Arrival of the Simcoes. Their first shelter in the tent of Captain Cook. Mrs. Simcoe visits the Island and a shore she names Scarborough. Toronto named York. The first winter.

Although traders and travelers continued to come and go at the foot of the Toronto Carrying-Place during the years following the burning of Fort Rouille—and St. Jean Rousseau had established a small permanent post there—the real turning point in the transition of Toronto from a rough French outpost to a budding British community took place on July 30, 1793.

On the previous evening, after waiting some hours for favorable winds, Lieutenant Governor John Graves Simcoe and his family had boarded at Niagara His Majesty's schooner *Mississauga*, a topsail of 120 tons, mounting six guns and carrying a crew of fourteen under command of Captain Jean Baptiste Bouchette. The capital of Upper Canada was then situated at Niagara, but Simcoe was considering a new site for the seat of government.

On deck the band of the Queen's Rangers played jaunty military airs and there was an optimistic mood of expectation aboard the *Mississauga* as she hoisted sail, because Simcoe, although he had made a brief exploratory visit to Toronto during the spring, was now actually on his way to establish residence there.

At this time he had no intention of making Toronto the capital of Upper Canada. He had his heart set, in fact, upon establishing for this important purpose a new London on a new Thames, then called the River Tranche. His study of maps in England and after his arrival in Canada the previous year had indicated to him that Toronto might be an ideal spot for the location of a naval base and arsenal situated at a more comfortable distance from the Americans than Kingston or Niagara and containing a harbor with topographical features which were ideally suited for adequate fortification. His visit during the spring had confirmed this opinion.

He wrote to Major General Alured Clarke, Lieutenant Governor of Quebec, who was then acting as Administrator of Canada during the absence in England of Lord Dorchester, the Governor in Chief: "I lately examined this Harbour accompanied by such officers, Naval and Military, as I thought most competent to give me assistance therein; and upon minute Investigation I found it to be without comparison the most proper situation for an Arsenal in every extent that the word can be met in this province.

"The Spit of Land which forms its entrance is capable of being so fortified with a few heavy guns as to prevent any vessel from entering the Harbour, or from remaining within it. From the diversity of the Sand Banks any small point of ground is sufficiently strong to be selected for the present purposes, and which as Circumstances shall require, may be occupied to the widest extent. At the bottom of the Harbour there is a Situation admirably suited for a Naval Arsenal and Dock Yard, and there flows into the Harbour a river [the Don] the Banks of which are covered with excellent timber."

On the morning when the *Mississauga* arrived at Toronto, men of the Queen's Rangers, who had previously been sent ahead in a number of bateaux, were already hard at work clearing ground and building the huts they would occupy during the coming winter.

At the rail of the *Mississauga*, eager for her first sight of the spot where she was going to make her wilderness home, was the Lieutenant Governor's young wife, Elizabeth Posthuma Simcoe, a wealthy heiress who had married her husband at the age of sixteen. Her peculiar middle name had been given her because her father had died seven months before she was born and her mother had died in childbirth.

With her aboard the *Mississauga* were her three children, Sophia, Francis, and Katherine. Katherine, who had been born at Niagara in January, was destined to die in York during the following spring.

Mrs. Simcoe, a lively and talented young woman who liked to write and sketch, was enchanted with the appearance of her new home. On hand to pilot the *Mississauga* into the harbor was St. Jean Rousseau, the French trader. It was somehow symbolic, in view of Toronto's past as a French outpost, that a man with such a name should guide into its harbor the ship bearing those who would found the new British community.

Later that day, while the men of the Queen's Rangers prepared to erect the "Canvass House" which would shelter Simcoe and his family, Mrs. Simcoe took the first of many rambles in the vicinity which she was later to describe in her diary. The large tent was one which Simcoe had purchased in England from the effects of the renowned explorer Captain James Cook. It was now being erected, once more, in a spot far from the distant Pacific isles which had been frequented by its previous owner.

"The Queen's Rangers are encamped opposite the ship," wrote Mrs. Simcoe of that first day in Toronto. "After dinner we went on shore to fix on a spot whereon to place the Canvass House, & we chose a rising ground divided by a Creek from the camp—which is ordered to be cleared immediately, the soldiers have cut down a great deal of wood to enable them to pitch their tents, we went in the Boat 2 miles to the bottom of the Bay & walked thro' a grove of fine Oaks where the town is intended to be built, a low spit of sand covered with wood forms the Bay & breaks the Horizon of Lake which indeed is very pleasing, the water in the Bay is beautifully clear and transparent."

Although there was considerable wind and rain during the next few days, Mrs. Simcoe continued her little strolls of exploration. She also visited the peninsula, which is now the Toronto Island, and noted that the trees were mostly poplar mixed with some pines and discovered on the ground some "everlasting Peas, creeping in abundance, of a purple color, I was told they were good to eat when boiled, & some pretty white flowers like lillies of the Valley."

In the small boat of surveyor Lewis Grant, she was taken on another short voyage of discovery along the lakefront east of the harbor where "the shore is extremely bold & has the appearance of Chalk Cliffs but I believe they are only white sand—they appeared so well that we talked of building a summer residence there & calling it Scarborough."

On August 26, little more than three weeks after Simcoe's arrival, a momentous General Order was posted at Toronto by Major Edward Baker Littlehales, Simcoe's military secretary:

"His Excellency the Lt. Governor having received official information of the success of his Majesty's arms under His Royal Highness the Duke of York, by which Holland has been saved from the invasion of the French Armies; and it appearing that the combined Forces have been lately successful in dislodging their Enemies from an entrenched camp supposed to be impregnable, from which the most important consequences may be expected; and in which arduous attempt his Royal Highness the Duke of York and his Majesty's Troops supported the national Glory; It is his Excellency's orders that on the raising of the Union Flag at Twelve O'Clock tomorrow, a Royal Salute of Twenty-one Guns is to be fired to be answered by the shipping in the harbour, in respect to his Royal Highness, and in commemoration of the naming of this Harbour, from his English Title, York."

Once more the ancient Indian name of Toronto was being discarded for that of a dignitary far across the sea, but it would return to the community for good a few years later.

Next day, as the guns aship and ashore boomed out their first Royal salute in the new settlement of York, the smoke of their firing hung low and trailing across the waters of the bay. Fluttering proudly, the British flag was raised to the top of its rough-hewn mast. During the firing of the guns, an Indian picked up young Francis Simcoe to allow him a better view of the ceremonies and grinned delightedly when the youngster appeared to be undisturbed by the thunder of the cannon.

Young Francis seemed to hit it off well with his new Indian friends from the very first. They made him a chief and provided him with Indian costumes, which he wore with great pride.

"Francis shakes hands with the Indians in a very friendly manner," wrote Mrs. Simcoe, "tho he is very shy and ungracious to his own countrymen."

Francis was to lose his life at the age of twenty-one while serving with the British forces as an officer in the Peninsular War.

The Indians were highly impressed by the celebration of the supposed victories of the Duke of York and that evening some of them met with the newcomers in the trading post of St. Jean Baptiste Rousseau.

Present from Niagara were Chief Justice William Osgoode, Attorney General John White and Major Littlehales, along with "several other gentlemen." Although the major's description of this meeting puts into the mouths of the supposedly savage red men some rather fancy words and phrases, it does give an idea of the friendly mood of the occasion:

"There were present," he wrote, "22 Indians, principally Chiefs, and a Lake Huron Chief of consequence . . . The Lake Huron Chief, addressing himself to Major Littlehales—'Father—Some time ago a great man came to this place and kindled a fire. He soon went away to our great surprise and never returned, we earnestly hope that the great man now here will rekindle the fire that the chimney be strong, that it may never be extinguished.

" 'My good Father—Our young men are very much in want of spear to kill their fish with, they are under the necessity of making use of wood, which by no means answers the purpose, & indeed they cannot procure subsistence, we therefore hope you will order us a blacksmith.

" 'Father—We trust you will prevent our being injured by any white people, we understand that you are sent here by the King our father to protect and take care of us . . . we hope that all our father's chiefs present have paid attention to our words, & we implore the great Spirit to protect them.

" 'Father—As we are in want of some little provisions, we hope you will give us some to carry to our homes, and we also wish to have a walking stick to remember that we are supported by our father the great man near us; we also solicit a small quantity of tobacco.' "

Major Littlehales assured the chiefs that some provisions would be given them from a supply ship which was expected to arrive hourly and that Lieutenant Governor Simcoe himself would meet with some of them on the morrow.

"Children and Brothers," said he, "the King, your father's representative, will take care of your interests, will guard and protect you, and prevent you being injured by any white person."

The chimney at York had indeed been built strong and would not be extinguished, because from that day York and later Toronto continued its steady growth.

But in this autumn of 1793 the budding settlement certainly did not present an impressive appearance. On a visit from Niagara, Peter Russell, then Receiver General of Upper Canada, called upon the Simcoes in their flimsy dwelling in the former tent of Captain Cook. For the official residence of the Lieutenant Governor of Upper Canada and his family, it was indeed a mean abode, as Mr. Russell reported in a letter to his sister, Elizabeth Russell:

> The Governor & Mrs. Simcoe received me very graciously. But you can have no conception of the Misery in which they live—The Canvas house being their only residence—in one room they lie and see company—& in the other are the Nurse & Children squalling &c—an open Bower covers us at dinner—& a tent with a small Table and three Chairs serves us for a Council Room . . .

But Simcoe was engrossed in the establishment of his settlement and his wife was enjoying the wild new country and the sights and sounds as the sturdy men of the Queen's Rangers labored at the job of building the foundations of the new town of York. She found the salmon from the waters of the Humber and Don very tasty.

". . . an Indian named Wablé Casigo supplies us with Salmon which the Rivers & Creeks on this shore abound with," she wrote in her diary. "It is supposed they go to the Sea with such velocity with which fish move makes it not impossible & the very Red appearance and goodness of the Salmon confirm the supposition—they are best in the month of June—I brought a favorite White Cat with grey spots, with me from Niagara, he is a native of Kingston, his sense & attachment are such, that those who believe in Transmigration would think his soul once animated a reasoning being—he was undaunted on board the Ship, sits composedly as Centinel at my door amid the beat of Drums and the crash of falling Trees, with as little fear as a Dog would do—there has been a fever at Niagara, this place is very healthy & I think it probable we shall spend the Winter here . . ."

As the autumn wore on and the breezes in York became more chilly, Mrs. Simcoe appeared to lose none of her enthusiasm for her new home. She continued her rambles, making note of the butternut trees "the nuts are better than Walnut," sampling the wild grapes and gathering the berries "of Cockspur Thorns." Sometimes she rode her horse along the peninsula, to which she had developed a great attachment.

"My horse has spirit enough to wish to get before the others—I rode a race with Mr. Talbot [Thomas Talbot, Simcoe's private secretary] to keep myself warm . . . we dine in a Marquee today, it is become too cold in the Arbour—the Canvass House we use as a bed Room but the other is going to be erected for winter dining Room. I have gathered most beautiful White berries with a black Eye from red stalks—I cannot find out its name.

"At this season of the year," she wrote in her diary in November of 1793, "there is usually a fortnight of foggy weather; the air is perfectly dry and hot and smells and feels like smoke; it is called Indian summer. I have never heard these fogs well accounted for . . . We dined in the woods and ate part of a raccoon; it was very fat and tasted like lamb if eaten with mint sauce."

Meanwhile, in the capital across the lake, the activities of the Simcoes in the upstart community of York were being eyed with some wonder and disapproval.

Sniffed Mrs. William Jarvis, in a letter from Niagara to her father:

> The Governor & Family are gone to Toronto [now York] where it is said they Winter—and a Part of the Regiment—they have or had not four days since a Hut to Shelter them from the Weather—in Tents—no means of warming themselves, but in Bowers made of the Limbs of Trees—thus fare the Regiment—the Governor has two Canvass Houses there—Every Body are sick at York—but no matter—the Lady likes the Place— therefore every one else must—Money is a God *many* worship . . .

In spite of what must have been the great discomfort of her first winter in York in a makeshift home, Mrs. Simcoe found interesting things to do. In January of 1764 some youngsters had set fire to the dry reeds of the marsh at the edge of the bay, creating a spectacular but harmless blaze.

"I walked below the bay and set the other side of the marsh on fire for amusement," she wrote. "The Indians have cut holes in the ice, over which they spread a blanket on poles, and they sit under this shed moving a wooden fish hung to a line in the water by way of attracting the living fish, which they spear with great dexterity when they approach.

"The Governor wished me to see the process; we had to walk a half mile to the place. There was no snow on the ice and we were without cloth shoes. The Governor pushed a large limb of a tree before him which kept him steady and with the assistance of Mr. Talbot I reached the spot where they were catching maskalonge, a superior kind of pike, and pickerell. I was almost frozen from looking on, tho' the apprehension of falling kept me warm while I walked."

That February Governor Simcoe promised his young wife that he'd take her to Detroit for a visit in March and hinted to her that their stay would be more of a holiday and a sample of the comparative pleasures of that town, than a business mission.

"The weather damp, mild and dirty," she wrote in her diary on February 9. "When will the end of March arrive. I am quite impatient to set out for Detroit."

At the beginning of March, York was still in the miserable grip of winter.

"The weather extremely cold," wrote Mrs. Simcoe. "Tho' I wore three fur tippets, I was so cold I could hardly hold my cards this evening."

Later in the month the Governor told her that they'd have to delay their visit to Detroit, but by now it was maple syrup time in York and Mrs. Simcoe had made another discovery: "This is the month for making maple sugar; a hot sun and frosty nights cause the sap to flow most. Slits are cut in the bark of the trees and wooden troughs set under the tree, into which the sap—a clear sweet water—runs."

She bought thirty pounds of maple sugar from the Indians for $3.

It it a curious fact that, although her youngest child Katherine died in York that spring, Mrs. Simcoe makes no mention of the tragedy in her diary. It is probable that she felt the tragedy was a too deeply personal thing to record in the diary, which might have been written to describe the sights of early York for later publication.

She did, however, reveal some of her heavy burden of sorrow in a poignant letter to a friend in England:

"It is with pain I take up my pen to inform you of the loss we have sustained & the melancholy event of our losing our poor little Katherine, one of the strongest healthiest children you ever saw, every person admired her as an extraordinary fine handsome child. She had been feverish two or three days cutting teeth, which not being an unusual case with children I was not alarmed; on good Friday she was playing in my room in the morning, in the afternoon was seized with fits, I sat up the whole night the greatest part of which she continued to have spasms & before seven in the morning she was no more. Our own surgeon was absent & the one present had certainly less ability. She was the sweetest tempered child imaginable, just beginning to talk & walk, & the suddeness of the event you may be sure shocked me inexpressably . . . to enhance the misery the Governor was in Detroit; he returned within a fortnight in good health but at his landing from Lake Erie was told of the loss of his Child & that I was not expected to live, on which latter alarm he rode 18 miles of bad road in two hours & was coming on instantly without settling his business at Niagara, but at Niagara he learnt that my illness was slight . . ."

Chapter 5
1793–1796

FAREWELL TO THE FOUNDER

Simcoe builds York's fortifications. He plans Legislative Buildings.
Castle Frank. The opening of Yonge Street and Dundas Road. The
blockhouse on Gibraltar Point. Departure of the Simcoes.

Throughout the first long, hard winter of 1739–94 in the infant settlement
of York, Simcoe kept his Queen's Rangers busy at the job of clearing the
townsite and cutting roads. He was bursting with plans for the new community, not because he envisaged it as the future capital of Upper Canada, but because the possibility of an attack by the United States was always on his mind and he hoped to make Toronto an impregnable fortress
on Lake Ontario should the only two other British settlements on the
lake, Kingston and Newark (at Niagara), come under assault from across
the nearby border.

Simcoe has been described by some as a man of broad vision who might
have worked miracles of settlement in the wilderness of the new colony
had he enjoyed more co-operation from his superiors and more time to
carry out his plans. Lord Dorchester, the Governor in Chief at Quebec,
viewed many of Simcoe's ambitious proposals with suspicion because the
two had developed an animosity during their service with the British
forces at the time of the Revolutionary War in the United States.

Dorchester was still rankled by the fact that Simcoe had been selected
in England as Lieutenant Governor of Upper Canada instead of Sir
William Johnson, the man who had routed the French at Niagara and
was Dorchester's choice for the job. The Governor in Chief considered
Simcoe to be a subordinate. Simcoe regarded his post as an independent
one and he sometimes carried this view to the point of corresponding with
London over Dorchester's head.

Dorchester wanted Kingston to be the capital of Upper Canada when the time came to shift the administration from Newark, a move that was inevitable when the day arrived for the United States to take over the east side of Niagara from the British under the terms of the Treaty of Paris. Perhaps because of his dislike of Dorchester, as much as any other factor, Simcoe opposed the selection of Kingston and held out for his dreamed of capital in the second London on the Thames. Meanwhile, Little York, the proposed naval base and arsenal, received top priority because of Simcoe's preoccupation with the possibility of warfare on Lake Ontario.

He was a stern man, in many ways, with a liking for spit and polish among his Queen's Rangers, as though they might have been on a parade ground in the green softness of England rather than toiling in the hard wilderness of Upper Canada.

The cat-o'-nine-tails was often swung upon the naked backs of Simcoe's soldiers when they were convicted of some minor breach of military discipline and deserters who fled into the trackless wilderness were hunted down like wild animals by the Indians and brought back to face the harsh consequences of their folly. It is said that one soldier who deserted his sentry post at Fort Erie while serving under Simcoe was court-martialed and made to kneel upon his own coffin while a firing squad carried out the death sentence.

Again and again Simcoe's requests for what he considered to be the bare essentials for setting up a satisfactory fortress at York were turned down by Dorchester, but he was a hard man to discourage. Although Dorchester approved the development of the townsite, he did not share Simcoe's enthusiasm for the idea of immediately providing it with ambitious fortifications. It was only in pitiful dibs and dabs that the armaments arrived with which to equip the tiny settlement that Simcoe hoped to make a British stronghold in Upper Canada.

"I am truly sorry that Your Lordship does not approve of any Fortifications being at present erected at this most defensible and important Spot . . ." wrote Simcoe in a dispatch to Dorchester in the winter of 1793.

Simcoe's York was, from the first, what might be described in modern parlance as a planned community. It did not grow in the comparatively haphazard manner of such older settlements as Kingston. It was thoroughly surveyed and marked off with designated areas for specific purposes before the axes of the Queen's Rangers echoed in the woods at the new townsite.

Writing in 1793 to Isaac Todd, a fellow mechant in Montreal, Richard Cartwright, of Kingston, had this to say about Simcoe's new town at the western end of the lake:

> . . . the Governor is at present at Toronto where he has laid out a town plot which he has called York, and where I am told he intends to pass the winter in his Canvass House, for there is no other built, nor preparations

for any. His regiment is also to hut themselves there. This situation for the Capital unites many advantages, as it will contribute to the more speedy settling of the vacant lands on both sides of it, and be a means of sooner uniting the settlements above the Bay of Kente [Quinte] & below the head of Lake Ontario; and also it lays at the entrance of a communication into Lake Huron by Lake La Claye [Simcoe] which may bye and bye be found practicable and useful. But, not withstanding this he does not scruple to say that he has his eye on the River Tranch [Thames]; and though he may for a while put up with the Town of York, and the River Humber, he seems determined to be satisfied with nothing less than another Thames & a second London—You will smile perhaps when I tell you that even at York, a town lot is to be granted in the Front Street only on the condition that you shall build a house of not less than 47 feet front, two stories high & after a certain order of architecture; in the second street they may be somewhat less in front, but the two stories & mode of architecture is indispensable; and it is only in the back streets and allies that the Tinkers and Taylors will be allowed to consult their own taste and circumstances in the structure of their habitations upon lots of 1/10 of an acre. Seriously, our good Governor is a little wild in his projects.

While the building of his town continued, Simcoe kept calling upon the other government officials at Niagara to move their offices and homes to what was still considered to be only the temporary new capital of Upper Canada. But these worthies had a hundred different excuses, worded in the most polite and formal ways, to explain to the Lieutenant Governor why it was not possible, at the moment, to move to the muddy little settlement of York. Some of them had considerable investments in their homes in the older community across the lake and were loath to give up Niagara's comparative comforts for the raw pioneering life of the new village.

Considering the uncertainty of Simcoe himself concerning the future of York, they could hardly be blamed for their hesitation to give up their Niagara homes and build new ones in the little settlement. In a letter to Lord Dorchester, Simcoe said:

. . . I have given information to the Civil officers of Government that York, for the present, is to become the seat of Government, and in consequence, I am preparing to erect such buildings as may be necessary for the future meeting of the Legislature; the plan I have adopted is, to consider a future Government House, as a Center and to construct the Wings as temporary offices for the legislature, purposing that so soon as the Province has sufficient Funds to erect its own Public Buildings, that they may be removed elsewhere.

But should the seat of Government be ultimately established on the River Thames as in my opinion every public consideration and the King's

Service requires, the *Wings* now erecting with the Lands appropriated for the Government House, may hereafter be sold, so as materially to lessen if not liquidate the Sums expended in their erection.

In a letter written at the same time to Bishop Mountain in Quebec, Simcoe suggested that the buildings of the House of Assembly could be made into a church "should, as I hope for the King's interest the seat of Government be only temporary at this place."

But, today's Board of Trade in Toronto should have a picture of Mrs. Simcoe hanging above the head table at all of its dinners, because she was undoubtedly one of the first and most enthusiastic boosters of the infant community. In her diary she wrote page after page of praise for the climate and the exciting life in York, describing her rides along her beloved peninsula and her jaunts up the Don, upon one of the high banks of which she selected the site for a summer residence which was eventually built and called, half-jokingly, Castle Frank, after her son Francis.

In the winter there had been the sleigh rides and the fascinating experience of watching the Indians spear fish by torchlight through holes in the ice of the bay and the big bonfires which sent their sparks leaping upward into the frosty winter skies while a jolly gathering toasted venison on sticks.

"The ladies did not catch cold & were delighted with the novelty of dining in the air in winter," she wrote. "Francis has a small sleigh which the servants have taught a goat to draw. He is the handsomest goat I ever saw & looks very well in the harness—it is a very pretty sight to see Francis drawn in this car—they used the animal to draw the sleigh by making him draw it full of wood, at first he was very untractable."

There is the occasional mild complaint in her diary about the mosquitoes in the summer and the cold in the winter, but running in through all of her remarks is the indication that this wealthy and aristocratic young Englishwoman was enjoying what were perhaps among the happiest days of her life when she was sharing with her husband the rugged times in the rough little settlement overlooking Toronto's bay.

"I persuaded the Governor to ride this evening," she wrote in her diary on May 2, 1794. "We had not ridden a mile before there came so violent a shower that we were wet through in three minutes, and the claps of thunder were so loud as to make the horses start. After changing our clothes we sat down to tea and agreed with Mr. Talbot that the rain had been the pleasantest mode of taking a shower bath."

She was pleased with Castle Frank when she and her family moved into the little log retreat for a visit in April of 1796.

"The Porticos here are delightful pleasant & the room cool from its height and the thickness of the logs of which ye House is built," she wrote in her diary. ". . . we rode there thro those pleasant shady Pine Plains, now covered with Sweet scented Fern—there is no wood under the pines so it is good riding."

Meanwhile, under the supervision of Simcoe, the hard-working Queen's Rangers and civilian laborers were cutting a road northward from the town toward the Holland River and westward toward the Grand River. The road to the north had been named Yonge Street, after the Secretary of War, Sir George Yonge, and the one to the west bore the name of Henry Dundas, the British Home Secretary, under whose direction colonial affairs were at that time administered.

Secretary Dundas approved of Simcoe's plans for York: "I agree with you that the place upon the River Thames which You have marked for the Scite of London, is well situated and judiciously chosen for the future Capital," he wrote to Simcoe, "but as the defence of the Colony is the first object, if that defence should be Maritime, it follows that the Settlement of York is the most important for the present, not as the future Capital, but as the Chief place of strength and security for the Naval force of the Province."

A sawmill had been erected on the Humber and a number of round log huts had been set up as quarters for the troops. "Two row gun boats with oars, rudders and masts" and mounting "six-pounders in their bows" had been built "for the purpose of transporting Troops with facility to whatsoever place they might be required."

A blockhouse had been constructed on the tip of the peninsula at a spot that was then called Gibraltar Point (now Hanlan's Point). On the mainland work had gone ahead on the construction of a barracks and other military installations close to the site which is now known as Old Fort York, one of the most popular tourist attractions of modern Toronto. At that time Fort York was situated close to what was then the shore line of Lake Ontario, but land reclamation projects have since then moved it well back from the present water's edge.

Simcoe had by this time collected, from various sources, his pitiful assortment of artillery. These arms included some condemned 18-pounder cannon (Simcoe believed in making his fortress *appear* to be well-defended even if he couldn't obtain all of the pieces he required); five 18-pounder carronades and ten 12-pounders. In addition, said he when he wrote to the Duke of Richmond, Master General of the Ordnance in England, he had acquired "an excellent medium twelve-pounder intended for a gun boat."

But acquiring proper equipment was a slow and trying task. Even in a modern age government red tape can be an exasperating thing, but Simcoe is deserving of special sympathy when it is considered that in those

1. Etienne Brulé says farewell to Champlain as he leaves on journey south from Lake Simcoe which will bring him to the sight of Toronto.

2. Lord Dorchester completes the Toronto Purchase from the Indians in August, 1788.

3. John Graves Simcoe, founder of York and Toronto.

4. Elizabeth Posthuma Simcoe.

5. Fort York during the winter of 1803.

6. Toronto's first jail was situated on the south side of King Street at Leader Lane.

7. Ice-boating on Toronto Bay in the early 1800s.

8. Jordan's York Hotel on the south side of King Street between Princess and Berkeley Streets. Legislature met here after Americans burned down Parliament Buildings.

days it sometimes took a letter six months to travel from far-off London to the isolated town of York. Many of Simcoe's military plans for York were wise ones and the apathy of his superiors in providing him with the means to carry them out must have been disheartening as he strode about his new town trying to make it ready for the war with the United States which he felt was in the almost immediate offing.

So certain was he of the imminent outbreak of war that when he received word in 1796 that a United States force under General Anthony Wayne had attacked a British outpost in a minor skirmish, he concluded that the war was already under way, and moved his family from York to Quebec to ensure their safety. Later in that same year the Simcoes sailed to England, never to return to Canada, although York's founder did for a time retain his office of Lieutenant Governor while living overseas. He resigned his appointment in 1798.

July 21, 1796, was a sad day for Mrs. Simcoe, who had loved the rough little settlement from the first moment she arrived there. In her diary for the date she wrote:

". . . took leave of Mrs. McGill & Miss Crookshanks. I was so much out of spirits I was unable to dine with her, she sent me some dinner but I would not eat, cried all that day—the Governor dined with Mr. McGill & at 3 o'clock we went on board the *Onondaga* [a sister ship of the *Mississauga*, which had brought her to her new home] under a Salute from the vessels, little wind, soon became calm . . ."

When the wind did pick up later in the day to fill the sails of the *Onondaga*, Mrs. Simcoe for the last time watched the shores of her beloved wilderness home fade in the little schooner's wake.

So far as can be ascertained by the remarks written in her diary, the high spirited young woman of aristocratic background had greatly enjoyed virtually all of her three-year stay in the tiny pioneer community of York. She seemed to relish the adventurous experience of living in the backwoods. She admired the Indians and once remarked they looked like something painted by one of the Old Masters. Her enthusiastic comments upon the flora and fauna of the country indicated a lively interest in the things of nature she found in her wilderness home.

One writer of the time remarked: "Mrs. Simcoe is a lady of manners, highly interesting, equally distant from hauteur and levity. Accustomed to fashionable life, she submits with cheerfulness to the inevitable inconvenience of an infant colony. Her conduct is perfectly exemplary & admirable, conforming to that correct model, which ought to be placed before a people, whom a high pattern of dissipation would mislead, of extravagance would ruin . . ."

It seems likely that, as well as enjoying the backwoods life, she also appreciated her position as the Governor's lady and social leader of the little community. Evidently not all of the other women in Mrs. Simcoe's sphere held her in affectionate regard.

Mrs. William Jarvis seemed to take particular pleasure in using an acid pen while mentioning Mrs. Simcoe in letters to friends.

After the Governor had given two public balls at which Mrs. Simcoe did not appear, Mrs. Jarvis remarked in a letter: "Mrs. Simcoe has been ill on both occasions—the first in childbirth the second in Fevor as *reported* . . . I'm sorry the Governor did not come out solo as the people seem not to like Petecoat Laws . . ."

When the Simcoes left, Mrs. Jarvis wrote: "I hope they will detain him in England and his Wife also—let us have a Man who is fond of Justice . . ."

Socially, Upper Canada was a small place and it is not unlikely that some of its women harbored small spites. But, if we are to judge by what is left for us to read concerning what they said and did, none was more vivacious than the first First Lady of the York that became Toronto.

Chapter 6

1797–1799

THE GROWING VILLAGE

The first newspaper. An early court trial. The "Stump Act." The hog pound. The first shops and schools. The first church services. Some affairs of honor. The first hanging in York. The slaves.

In 1797, four years after Simcoe had established his rough little settlement, the population of York had reached 212. Some of them were Loyalists from the United States who had applied for lots in the new town, others were government officials who had moved somewhat reluctantly from their homes across the lake at Niagara, some were new immigrants from Britain, and many were former members of the Queen's Rangers, who had helped carve the little community out of the wilderness and had decided to stay on as settlers.

Life, it seems, was anything but rosy in the new town. For one thing, there was a shortage of food and other supplies in the settlement. In the spring of 1798, Ensign William Peters of the Queen's Rangers wrote from York to a friend: *I reached this Metropolis last Saturday and found all the inhabitants starving, as they say, but not quite as bad as that . . .*

But the inhabitants weren't so discouraged that they couldn't stage "a ball & supper" when King George III's fifty-ninth birthday came along on June 4 of that year. Invited to the soiree were fifty-two of the town's leading citizens, who consumed seventy bottles of wine and three bottles of brandy. Seven dollars was paid out for "musick By Order" and several drinking glasses and a window pane were broken during the festivities.

By this time, in the absence of Simcoe, the direction of York's affairs were in the hands of Peter Russell, who was President of the Executive Council and Administrator of Upper Canada. Although Simcoe had founded the tiny community, it remained for Russell to carry out much of

the actual development of York during the first faltering years of its existence.

Under his supervision the two small buildings were completed which
eventually housed the first sessions of a legislature in York. They were
originally built to serve as the wings of a fine new Government House
planned for the location.

Russell was highly enthusiastic about the town when he wrote in September of 1798 to William Osgoode in Quebec:

"You would be pleased to see this place now that it is really beautiful
and makes a very different appearance from what it did when we were
here about this time six years ago," he said. "I have a very comfortable
house near the Bay, from whence I see everything in the harbour and entering it . . . I have about 700 acres two miles from the town, on which I
have out a farmer on shares, in hopes of supplying my table without
searching the Country for Provisions . . . The Chief Justice is building
here a very fine house which will cost at least 4000 pounds—so I presume
he does not look for removal—The Expence of living is most enormous—
Beef 1/—Mutton & Veal 1/6—fowls a dollar a couple—Flour 7 dollars the
Cwt—laborers 12/—& Artificers 16/—per day—& no likelyhood of a fall in
anything."

York's first newspaper, the *Upper Canada Gazette or American Oracle*,
had followed the government officials across the lake from Niagara, where
it had originally been published. Its first issue in its new location was published on October 4, 1798. York's first newspaper bore the Royal Arms and
the initials G.R. on its title page, indicating the official nature of this early
publication. It was often a trifle late with the news. When, on January 5,
1799, it published the report of Lord Nelson's victory over the French
fleet at the Battle of the Nile—five months after it had happened—the
residents of York joyously placed burning candles in the windows of their
homes to join in the "general illumination" called to celebrate the historic
event.

By this time York was growing so briskly that it was deemed high time
that a small log jail should be constructed, along with some stocks in
which to place minor disturbers of the peace. While the jail was still in
the building six culprits were hauled before the justice of the peace in
York's first recorded trial. William Hawkins, James Williams, John
McLean, Mathew Dunn, Joseph McCarthy, and Joseph Thompson were
accused by tavernkeeper Elisha Beman of stealing from him "an Iron Tea
Kettle—a cooking Kettle an axe a Tea Cannister—a Hat and three Gallon
Kegg, with about two quarts of brandy therein & sundry other articles."

Williams was pardoned when he turned "approver" and McLean,
Thompson and Dunn were acquitted, but their two companions in what

would today be considered a fairly petty crime were the recipients of the stern justice handed out in York in those pioneer days for relatively small offenses. McCarthy was sentenced to be burned on the hand, a penalty that was carried out right in the courtroom before the spectators. He was probably branded with the letter T for thief with an iron heated in the courtroom stove. Hawkins was publicly lashed in the market place, an event which, according to the custom of those days, undoubtedly attracted a large gathering of onlookers.

Even common drunks, in York's early days, received a particularly humiliating kind of sentence. It is recorded that they were usually ordered by the court to spend a certain period helping to remove the countless stumps from York's busier thoroughfares. These obstacles were considered to be a menace to any one returning home after dark—especially if he happened to be a little drunk.

One of those who is reported to have been constantly inconvenienced by this particular law—jokingly called the "Stump Act"—was a Captain Peeke of Duffin's Creek, who shipped lime to York in his own sailing vessel. It seems that Captain Peeke, whose crew was a thirsty lot, was often vexed to find most of them digging out stumps when he tried to round them up in the morning for the return voyage after an overnight stop at York.

Civic pride in York was growing and the *Upper Canada Gazette* remarked: "The public are much indebted to Mr. John McDougal, who was appointed one of the path-masters at the last town meeting, for his great assiduity and care in getting the streets cleared of the many and dangerous (especially at night) obstructions therein; and we hope by the same good conduct in his successors in the like office, to see that the streets of the infant town vie with those of maturer age, in cleanliness and safety."

It should perhaps be noted here that in York's early days many of the minor public offices, such as that of path-master or fence-viewer, were handed out in a manner which made it extremely difficult to turn down the honor. If a citizen were appointed and refused to accept the job, he was taken before the magistrate and fined. This process was repeated until some one eventually accepted the office, at which time, in addition to his other small remunerations, he was given the fines collected from the previous reluctant appointees.

In keeping with York's growth of civic spirit, it was ordered that the Pound Keeper should receive the sum of five shillings for "each and every Hog he shall take up and empound."

No longer, after this order, would the townspeople of York be allowed to let their livestock wander about the streets with impunity.

Although, up until the beginning of the nineteenth century, York's business establishments had been the kind which stocked only the bare necessities, some of the more genteel shops began to appear around 1800.

The *Upper Canada Gazette* of May 25, 1799, carried the following advertisement,

Evean Eavens
Taylor and Habit-Maker
(From London.)

Having taken a room in a small building belonging to Mr. Willcocks, for the purpose of prosecuting the duties of his trade; begs leave to inform the ladies and gentlemen of York, that he has commenced the above business; and to those who may honor him with their commands, he flatters himself from his experience, to afford satisfaction.

The first hairdresser to advertise in the new village didn't have a name like Antoine or François but he was stylish enough to use only one name in his announcement, which read as follows:

Rock
Hair Dresser, from London

Begs leave to inform the Ladies and Gentlemen of York and its Vicinity, that he will open Shop on the 25th inst. in Mr. Cooper's House, next to the Printing Office. All orders left for him at said place will be punctually attended to. N.B. Shop customers, and others will be dressed on the most reasonable terms.

Along with these offers of services designed to bring finer attire and better grooming to the residents of the primitive little settlement, there also arrived at about the same time those who were willing to provide more refinement to the minds and souls of York's pioneer inhabitants.

In the *Upper Canada Gazette* William Cooper begged leave "to inform his Friends and the Public, that he intends opening a school at his house in George Street . . . for the instruction of youth in Reading, Writing, Arethmetic, and English Grammar. Those who chuse to favor him with their Pupils, may rely on the greatest attention being paid to their virtue and their morals."

Although the people of York appeared to take quite well to the opportunity of sending their youngsters to school, it is another embarrassing fact, in the history of the city that would some day be called Toronto the Good and home of the Blue Sunday, that those who first tried to bring them some religion had a rather discouraging time of it.

"I believe," wrote the Reverend Nathan Bangs, a Methodist circuit rider, "I was the first Methodist preacher that ever attempted to preach in

Little York . . . and I preached in a miserable half-finished house, on a week-evening, to a few people, for there were not over a dozen houses in the place, and slept on the floor under a blanket . . . I was then attempting to form a circuit on Yonge Street, a settlement west of Toronto, and I was induced to make a trial in this new little village, the settlers of which were as thoughtless and wicked as the Canaanites of old . . ."

The stern battle of the Reverend Mr. Bangs against the particularly active Devil who seemed to lurk in the vicinity of York sometimes appeared to be an uphill one all the way. At one point of his circuit, a few miles up Yonge Street, Lucifer had evidently enlisted even a fiddler to confound the good works of the Methodist preacher:

"There was a great awakening among the people," wrote the Reverend Mr. Bangs, "but an inveterate fiddler seemed set on by the great adversary to contest the victory with me inch by inch. He had earned considerable money as the musician of the winter-night dancing parties of the settlers; but he was now willing to fiddle for nothing, if they would meet to dance and frolic rather than to pray. He contrived every possible method to keep the young people from our meetings. For some time he carried matters with a high hand, and the war was at last fully opened between us.

"One Sabbath morning, however, I fairly caught him. I was preaching on Galatians v. 19–21, and when I came to the word 'revelings' I applied it to his tactics and said, 'I do not know that the devil's musician is here today; I do not see him anywhere.' But he was sitting in a corner out of my sight, and he now put out his head and cried out, 'Here I am, ha! ha! —making the place ring with his laughter. 'Ay,' said I, 'you are there, are you?' and turning to him I addressed him in language of rebuke and warning. I finally told him that if he did not cease to allure the young people into sinful amusements I would pray God either to convert him or take him out of the way, and I had no doubt God would answer my prayer. The power of God evidently fell upon the assembly; a divine influence seemed to overpower them. The guilty man began to tremble all over like a leaf, and turned deathly pale. He finally got up and rushed out of the house. He went home, burned his fiddle, and we were henceforth rid of his interference with our meetings and his opposition in the community."

The Methodists of the day who *had* been won over by such prophets as the Reverend Mr. Bangs were indeed devout. In a book called *Old Time Primitive Methodism in Canada*, Mrs. R. P. Hopkins describes an incident which gives an insight to the religious attitude of some of the families who cleared the land around York:

"Father, mother and all the professing Christians in the house were expected to take their turn in leading worship. We had a man named Tom

Smith. He never was hurt with religion, but father and mother tried to think the best of him. He had come out in the revival services and joined the society.

"It was his turn to read and pray in the morning. He got the place, and coming to the words 'there shall be weeping and gnashing of teeth,' he halted and said, in a solemn voice: 'I suppose them that has no teeth will have to gum it.' There was no reply; no countenance changed its expression, but no doubt Tom would hear a little on the subject privately from mother."

There might have been some bias in the Reverend Mr. Bang's appraisal of York's godlessness, because in those days the Anglican Church worked closely with the government, and its ministers in Upper Canada were, in fact, paid and assigned by it. The Anglicans, therefore, had the inside track in the new settlement of York and a Methodist, Baptist, or Presbyterian minister would probably have had a hard time mustering much of a congregation in the town itself, although he might have had more success among the settlers up Yonge Street, who were not so predominantly English as the residents of York.

The first Anglican minister to reside in York was the Reverend Thomas Raddish, who held his services in the Government Buildings. One winter was enough for him, and he returned to England. He did, however, acquire during his brief stay some 4700 acres of choice land in the new town, part of which he promptly sold to Chief Justice John Elmsley. As was mentioned earlier, the Church and the State worked quite closely in those days—even more closely, in fact, than during Toronto's period under the French regime.

Meanwhile, great efforts were being made to equip York with better lines of communication, befitting a community which had become the capital of Upper Canada in spite of the derision which had been directed upon the mushrooming little settlement that had started off as a merely temporary site of the government. Rough as they were, Yonge Street reached through the bush to the north and Dundas Street extended through the wilderness to the west. Both of these roads had an encouraging number of settlers along their lengths.

A great deal of construction in York and much of the work on opening Yonge Street north of the village on the Bay was carried out by a contractor named William von Moll Berczy, who had been born in Saxony and came out to North America in 1791 as an agent of the Pulteney Associates in supplying German settlers in the Genesee country in what is now the state of New York. He left this settlement and in 1794 came to Upper Canada with about sixty German families. He was granted Markham Township for settlement and promised a personal grant of land on condition that he open Yonge Street past his community, which was located about twenty miles northeast of York. He suffered heavy financial losses in establishing his settlement and for various reasons was unable to carry out all of the conditions concerning the opening of Yonge Street. His lands were therefore taken from him in 1797. The engineer and architect who erected many of York's first buildings left Upper Canada in 1797 and went to Montreal, where he earned his living as a painter.

In 1799 Peter Russell ordered the commencement of a new road to the east which would eventually connect York with the Bay of Quinte. The contract was let to Asa Danforth, who undertook the job on the agreement that he should receive $90 a mile and that each of forty workers who were to be recommended by him should be granted 200 acres of land alongside the right-of-way.

At about the same time the *Upper Canada Gazette* announced a splendid new means of connecting the isolated capital with the rest of the province:

"The Toronto Yatch, *Captain Baker*, will, in the course of a few days, be ready to make her first trip. She is one of the handsomest vessels, of her size, that ever swam upon the Ontario; and if we are permitted to judge from her appearance, and to do her justice, we must say that she bids to be one of its swiftest sailing vessels . . ."

Two days after the New Year of 1800 the little frontier community of York was shocked by the tragic results of the first affair of honor, between two of its leading citizens. The duel resulted from an altercation between the wives of John White, Upper Canada's Attorney General, and John Small, Clerk of the Executive Council. Mrs. White claimed that Mrs. Small had publicly slighted her during one of the legislative assemblies and her infuriated husband was imprudent enough to make some remarks about the character of the woman who had insulted his wife. The content of these remarks evidently reached the ears of Mrs. Small and she demanded that her husband seek satisfaction from Mr. White.

During the argument which followed between these hot-blooded gentlemen, Small challenged White to a duel and they proceeded to the field of honor. Small was seconded by Sheriff Alexander McDonell and White by Baron Frederick de Hoen, a former German officer who had migrated to York.

When the opponents finished walking their required number of paces and wheeled to fire, White slumped to the ground, mortally wounded, and died the next day.

President Russell wrote his condolences to Sergeant Sheppard in England:

I take up my pen under the deepest affliction to inform you of the death of your Brother in Law, Mr. White, who was shot in a Duel with Mr.

Small, Clerk of the Ex. Council of this Province, in the morning of the 3d Instant, and expired at my house in the evening of the next day. Tho under the most excruciating torture he retained his senses and understanding in their fullest force to within an hour of his death and wanted for nothing with the tenderest affection of my sister and myself with the best medical aid to be found here could possibly supply. But the wound was mortal from the first, the ball having entered the right side between the two lowest short ribs and striking the spine, probably dividing some of the bundles of nerves that pass from the vertebra, causing an instant palsy of the lower extremeties and the most painful spasms. Knowing his dissolution to be inevitable, he submitted to his fate with a most pious and Christian resignation to the divine Will and forgiveness of all his enemies . . .

Small was tried in York's court and acquitted.

At the same session of the court which acquitted the Clerk of the Executive Council for the slaying of his adversary in an affair of honor, a more humble prisoner did not fare so well. Humphrey Sullivan stood charged with uttering a forged note for three shillings and ninepence. The actual forgery, it seems, had been done by someone else. Sullivan's only crime was that he had attempted to pass the note. Upon the completion of his trial, the judge ordered him to stand, and sternly addressed him as follows:

"Sullivan, may all who behold you, and who shall hear of your crime, and of your unhappy fate, take warning from your example. But, although your crime is great, it does not exceed the boundless mercy of God! to pardon through the all-sufficient atonement of His Son. I therefore recommend you to the mercy of God for pardon and salvation, through the merits of His Son; and do recommend to you to employ the few days that shall be allowed, of a life spent in wickedness, in humble and fervent prayer to almighty God, that He would give you a realizing sense of your sins, and misery, true contrition of heart for, and a genuine repentance of them; and that He would enable you, by His grace, to be wise in His Son the Lord Jesus Christ unto eternal salvation."

At the conclusion of these pious remarks, he harshly pronounced the death sentence upon the hapless prisoner who, on May 16, 1800, for a crime involving less than a dollar, was the first man to be hanged in the new town of York. Unable to find an executioner to carry out the sentence, the authorities finally obtained one by granting full pardon and twenty guineas to another Irishman named McKnight, who happened to be in the jail serving a term for robbery.

". . . it fulfilled the old adage—put an Irishman on the spit and you will get another to turn him," wryly observed Joseph Willcocks, a prominent Irish citizen of York, in a letter to his brother in Dublin.

At the beginning of the nineteenth century, many of the gentlemen of York kept slaves. Peter Russell himself, who shares with Simcoe the honor of fathering the community, ran an advertisement in the *Upper Canada Gazette* during this period in which he offered two slaves for sale.

> To be sold:—a Black Woman named Peggy, aged forty years, and a Black Boy, her son, named Jupiter, aged about fifteen years, both of them the property of the subscriber. The woman is a tolerable cook and washerwoman, and perfectly understands making soap and candles. The boy is tall and strong for his age, and has been employed in the country business, but brought up principally as a house servant. They are each of them servants for life. The price of the woman is one hundred and fifty dollars. For the boy two hundred dollars, payable in three years, with interest from the day of sale, and to be secured by bond &c. But one-fourth less will be taken for ready money.

One reason Mr. Russell was anxious to sell Peggy was that she had developed the habit of going away from his home without leave and on one occasion, before he offered her for sale, he ran an advertisement warning the people of York of the possible legal consequences of harboring her. Mr. Russell's sister, Elizabeth, once presented a slave named Amy Pompadour to the wife of Captain John Denison as a gift.

Advertisements offering a slave for sale or seeking to purchase one were quite common in York's newspaper. One such ad read as follows: "Wanted to purchase, a negro girl from seven to twelve years of age, of good disposition." Another offered for sale "a healthy strong negro woman, about thirty years of age: understands cooking, laundry and taking care of poultry. N.B.—She can dress ladies' hair."

There were many among York's upper class, however, who must have had some misgivings about the custom of keeping slaves, because Robert I. D. Gray, a Solicitor General of Upper Canada, made provision in his will that upon his death one of his slaves, "a faithful black woman servant, Dorinda," and her children should be granted 1200 pounds and their freedom and that two servants named Simon and John Baker be given their freedom and 200 acres of land each.

By an ironic quirk of fate the slave Simon missed his legacy and his liberty by dying with his master in a shipwreck on Lake Ontario, but John lived on as a free man until his 105th year, when he died in Cornwall after drawing for fifty-seven years a pension for wounds he received while fighting for the King in the War of 1812.

Chapter 7

1800

AN EARLY ELECTION

A hectic voting day. A dubious victory. A new election and a different member.

In 1800 York had its first election, and it was an uproarious one. Prior to this time, the town was represented by the member for Durham, York and the First Riding of Lincoln, a constituency which extended from just east of Port Hope all the way westward to the Grand River. But in 1800 the separate East Riding of York was created and the people of the town and surrounding district were at last able to select one of their own residents to represent them.

Lofty indeed were the flights of oratory and the written exhortations in the *Upper Canada Gazette* as the various candidates and factions took sides. This first political skirmish in the frontier town was to set the tone for many other passionate campaigns which were to be waged in York and later Toronto in the years to come.

Whatever else might be said about Toronto, there are few who could dare to say that it never had any lively election campaigns, and its first was as hectic as any of them. A correspondent writing under the pseudonym Cato to the *Upper Canada Gazette* on behalf of a candidate named Henry Allcock, set out to inform the electors how they should go about the job of selecting their representative. Present day politicians might blanch nervously upon reading the high qualifications demanded by Cato of the man who dared seek public office:

"Nothing," he wrote, ". . . can be more true, than that the primary wish of every elector is to see himself represented in his country's legislature by an *honest, upright man.* Honest and upright indeed, ought that man to be, who is entrusted with so *high a charge.* A charge, gentlemen, of such magnitude and so sacred, that no one should assume it without mature examination of the eventful and interminable consequences. A solemn and unprejudiced review of the duties encumbent on the representative, of the powers vested in his hands, of the many whose rights he binds himself to support, should, methinks, deter the unwary from aiming at it—and the unequal to it—from wishing it, should establish this prominent, though neglected truth, that something more than plebian honesty, than rugged uprightness, is necessary to qualify an individual for the dignified station. A station, gentlemen, to which is attached duties so various and so sacred, so extensive and so complicated, that he who has a just sense of them, will not enter on their discharge but with conscious fear and trembling. The subject, gentlemen, is a field on which volumes might be written, then could not the weight of the awful charge be sufficiently impressed on the minds of mankind.

"I shall confine myself in this place, to opening to your views, a few of the needful qualifications—the efficient qualities and more striking duties of the legislator. At the same time I pause to admire, and gratefully contemplate, that noblest fabric of human wisdom, the *British Constitution* . . . The representative more particularly, who stands so high in this general order, should look abroad and ask: What are my duties? What my necessary qualifications? What my necessary knowledge? I answer: Your duties are, to enact wise and beneficial laws for yourself and your constituents—your country and posterity. You are not only to be the guardian of their rights and liberties, but you are to be the guardian of their morals. You are to guard against encroachments from superior orders, and to restrain every symptom of license and licentiousness in the body which you represent. You are to promote and establish such wholesome regulations as effectually to secure, a free and uninterrupted course to civil and moral order. Regulations which will benefit and harmonize the present age, and entail to you the blessings of the yet unborn!

"The qualities you should possess to warrant your claim to this preeminence are, honesty, independence of spirit, penetration, an intimate knowledge of the true interests of your country, and an acquaintance with its existing laws. You are not blindly to be led astray by what may be of temporary advantage, yet militate to the incalculable injury of posterity. At no time, will this country stand more in need of men of abilities than at the present. You are, as it were, now laying the foundations of its future consequence and its happiness—its dearest interests are involved—its welfare and existence are in a manner submitted to your care and guidance.

"Your knowledge of governments and the constitutions of empires should be general . . . And here let me assert it, no earthly consideration, whether of interest or friendship, should influence the elector . . . Yet let me conjure this last description of men, for the love of God! for the love

of their country, for the love of themselves, for the sake of their credit, for
their modesty, for the sake of their families, and lastly for the sake of not
violating nature, forever to renounce, the idea of obtaining seats in
Parliament—of imposing on the country, or like Falstaff's shadows, of
filling up the muster roll."

In spite of Cato's awesome warning concerning the duties and godly
qualifications expected of York's first member of Parliament, four candidates did have the temerity to stand for election. They were Henry Allcock, the paragon who evidently fulfilled Mr. Cato's formidable requirements, William Jarvis, John Small, and Samuel Heron.

The poll of York's first election opened quietly enough at ten o'clock on
the morning of Thursday, July 24, 1800. The voters trickled in until two
o'clock in the afternoon, when the poll was closed for the day. Next morning at ten o'clock the poll was opened again and as each voter stepped forward he was carefully checked by scrutineers for the various candidates, including a lawyer by the name of William Weekes, who was doing a
particularly energetic job on behalf of candidate Allcock. Although the
other scrutineers were also doing a fairly conscientious service in checking
the voters, lawyer Weekes was making it extremely hot for all those who
signified their intentions of voting for candidates other than his man Mr.
Allcock.

"Mr. Angus McDonnell acted the part of advocate also," says a description of the events at the polling booth. "His interogatories were general,
but in that mild way which characterizes the man: perhaps his fee was
smaller; for the eloquence of Mr. Weekes seemed invariably to prevail."

Although Baron Frederick de Hoen had been sent up to Markham with
supplies of bread and rum to seek support for candidate Allcock among
the German settlers in that area, Mr. Allcock was chagrined to find when
they arrived at the poll that they had decided to vote for candidate Heron.

This was thought to be particularly ungrateful, considering that Mr. Allcock had promised the Markham farmers that he would make the merchants of York pay more for their produce if he were elected.

Shortly after the German settlers from Markham arrived on the scene, a
group of soldiers appeared to cast their ballots. It was at this point that
the fight broke out. A drunken bystander at the poll objected loudly to
the presence of the soldiers, maintaining they were not allowed to vote.
Candidate Allcock, who was confident that the soldiers intended to vote
for him, evidently forgot the noble words of his supporter, Cato, in the
Upper Canada Gazette, and ran over to the protesting drunk and shook
his fist in his face. He then called upon the constables to arrest the dis-
senter, which was duly done.

But the crowd didn't like this way of running an election and rushed over to rescue the drunk from the law. When a William Allan complained about this interference with the work of the law, one of the voters threatened to knock him down with a cudgel.

During the ensuing turmoil the polling was hastily adjourned for the day, but the wily lawyer Weekes, realizing that his man Allcock now had a majority of two votes, persuaded the confused returning officer to close the poll completely and declare the election finished.

Although most of the other candidates were struck speechless by this turn of events, candidate Heron did manage to protest, but was shouted down by lawyer Weekes.

"The poll for the Election of a Member to serve in parliament for the East Riding of the County of York, was closed yesterday, when Henry Allcock, Esq. was declared to be *duly elected*," reported the *Upper Canada Gazette* later. "The election terminated sooner than was expected by consequence of a daring Riot instigated by persons inimical to Peace and good Order, and to the *pure excercise* of that valuable privilege of the subject—the *elective franchise*. After the Returning Officer closed the poll, conformably to precedents established in such cases—he called upon the Magistrates to check any further outrage, and by their spirited exertions tranquility was in the course of the evening restored.

"It was a matter of much regret to a large majority of those who were sensible of the advantages to be derived from the election of a character distinguished for talents and virtue, that they were prevented (by the acts of the riotous and disorderly) from enrolling themselves among the number of independent electors who supported Mr. Allcock—they have, however, in common with the public, to rejoice that the majority of the poll has secured to the country his services, and enabled them to look with confidence, to a faithful and independent representative."

A considerable portion of the populace of York, however, did not see Mr. Allcock's highly dubious two-vote victory in the same light as did the mealymouthed editor of the *Gazette*. An investigation of the election was held in the House of Assembly in June of the following year.

"For singularity of unfairness, this election is scarcely to be equalled," remarked the more independent *Niagara Herald*, in commenting upon the results of the investigation, which found that Mr. Allcock had not been legally elected and demanded that he withdraw from the House.

Mr. Allcock, determined to hang on to office as York's first member of Parliament, declared that he would not withdraw from the House unless "they throw me out, neck and heels." He finally did give up, however, when a writ was issued calling for a new election.

In the second and more orderly proceeding Angus McDonnell, a former Clerk of the House of Assembly, was elected by a comfortable majority, receiving 112 votes as against 32 for his opponent.

"I stoop with Reluctance, gentlemen," said the happy Mr. McDonnell, in his election address, "to animadvert upon some puny Fabrications, circulated to mislead your Judgment, and alienate your Favor. It has been said that I am Canvassing a Seat elsewhere; No, Gentlemen, the Satisfaction, the Pride of Representing that Division of this Province, which, comprehending the Capital, is consequently the Political Head, is to me too captivating an Object of Patriotic Ambition for a moment, by the prospect of any inferior Representation; be assured, therefore, Gentlemen, that I shall not foresake my Post, until You or Life shall have foresaken me."

As it turned out, life did forsake Mr. McDonnell before the electors because he was serving his second term as a member of Parliament when he was drowned in the foundering of the schooner *Speedy* while en route from York to Presqu'ile three years later.

Chapter 8

1800–1813

The Frontier Life

When bears and wolves came right into town. The fine salmon-fishing. The demon rum. The militia drills. Disappearance of lawyer Weekes. He loses a duel. The Ridout-Jarvis duel. Night life in York. Fox hunt on the Bay. York's first fire engine.

At the beginning of the nineteenth century the town of York consisted of a fairly narrow fringe of buildings running along the shore of the bay between Jarvis and Parliament Streets. Some of these structures were frame buildings, others were of log construction and a very few, including the two used for the meetings of the upper and lower houses of the legislature, were built of brick.

During wet weather, the streets of York were seas of mud, a characteristic which soon won for the little settlement the scornful name of "Muddy York" among those who ventured to visit it during the damp days of spring and fall or at other times when it had been deluged by rain. Although the town had self-consciously assumed its almost accidental role as Upper Canada's capital, instead of being merely a naval arsenal and shipyard, as Simcoe had intended, it was still a rather woebegone frontier village. It possessed all the telltale marks of a raw townsite which had been carved quickly out of the wilderness in a few years, instead of undergoing the slow and more graceful kind of growth—like that of Kingston or Niagara—which might have presented a more refined and mellow picture to the visitor's eye. It is hard to realize, in this day, that in the early 1800s York was "out West" so far as the rest of Canada was concerned. To the people who lived in the older settled areas along the St. Lawrence and the Atlantic seaboard, the primitive little settlement which grew into the sedate city of Toronto must have appeared to be almost like a Canadian version of the romantic Dodge City of the American West.

Lord Selkirk, when he visited the town in 1803, reported that it contained about sixty or seventy houses.

The roads called streets are famous and almost impassable, he wrote. *The whole appears very ragged from the stumps.*

There was an unhealthy marsh of about a thousand acres near the mouth of the Don, said Lord Selkirk, and the party of soldiers stationed in the blockhouse near this area were "constantly affected by fever and ague" while those quartered in the garrison on a dry bank two miles to the west remained quite healthy through the winter.

Bears and wolves often entered the town to make raids on the livestock which grazed in the grounds of York's homes and sometimes wandered through the streets when they found holes in the fences.

There was great depradation committed the night before last by a flock of wolves that came into this town, wrote Joseph Willcocks in 1800 to his brother in Dublin. *One man lost 17 sheep, several others lost in proportion. The perpetrators escaped with impunity. We let loose a pack of hounds after them, but from their scattering after the different scents we had no diversion. But when the snow comes we will have fine fun tracing them and the deer of which there are a great abundance. I assure you that as for the wild ducks and pigeons they surpass any mention I could make of them. Fish of all kinds are in the Lake. We will get salmon at 20lb weight as good as ever killed at Island Bridge, for an Irish shilling, frequently less. You may think this underrating the matter, but I assure you it is a fact. The Indians spear them . . .*

The thoroughfare which is now called Bay Street was then a road called Bear Street because some horses had been attacked by a bear in a nearby pasture. Considering that this street eventually became the center of the city's financial district and stock market activities, it seems a shame that the ancient name wasn't allowed to stand, with perhaps a Bull Street running into it near the stock exchange.

One visiting bear which entered the town was killed by a Lieutenant Fawcett of the 100th Regiment, who split its skull with his sword when he encountered it on George Street. Although incidents of this kind constantly reminded the inhabitants of the new capital of Upper Canada that they were situated deep in the wilderness, York had shown such dazzling progress in so short a period that its growth sometimes amazed those who beheld it.

"The advancement of this place to its present condition has been effected in the lapse of six or seven years," marveled Deputy Postmaster General George Heriot, "and persons who have formerly traveled in this part of the country are impressed with sentiments of wonder on beholding a town, which may be termed handsome, reared as if by enchantment in the midst of the wilderness."

Over in Niagara, from which the government offices had been moved to York, there was no such enthusiasm over the growth of the upstart community which had become the new capital. When, in an address of welcome to the new Lieutenant Governor Peter Hunter, the term "We, the inhabitants of the Capital" was used by an orator in York, the *Constellation* at Niagara couldn't resist an impulse to use the editorial needle.

"This fretted my pate," said the *Constellation*'s sarcastic writer. "What can this be? Surely it is some great place in a great country was my conclusion; but where the capital is, was a little beyond my geographical acquaintance. I had recourse to the books, all the gazettes and magazines from the Year One I carefully turned over, and not one case, among all the addresses they contained, afforded me any instruction."

The *Constellation*'s wit then admits that he was astonished to discover that the capital referred to was indeed York! This drew him to the derisive conclusion that whenever the term "We, the inhabitants of the Capital" was encountered, it should be translated to read: "We, the inhabitants of York assembled at McDougall's over a glass of grog . . ."

Tippling did indeed provide one of the major recreations of the people of York in these early days of the tiny settlement's birth. Ely Playter, who helped run one of the town's six taverns, makes frequent mention in his diary of the prodigious thirst of his fellow townsmen.

". . . The little snow that had fell brought people to the town from the country, and it look quite lively," reads one entry in February of 1802. "We had four or five sleighs in the yard that stayed all night. It was 12 O'clock before I got to bed and just after J. Hunter knocked at the door. T. White not being in bed let him in and he plead for some time for me to get up and let him have a pint of rum, but I answered him very determined that I would not, and he went off. Sometime after I had got to sleep, A. Cameron wakened me knocking at my window wanting a pint of rum. I tried to put him off but he resolved to have it and I got up and supplied him and sent him off."

One night a meeting of the town council at Mr. Playter's establishment ended on a rather high note:

". . . we spent the evening very pleasant with Songs and Toasts until the wine began to operate," Mr. Playter records, rather ruefully . . . "We were all, in fact, quite intoxicated. Mr. Howard, being more able to bear liquor, was capable to see Mr. Boyd home. The wine taking its usual effect on me, I turned very sick and staggered off to bed with Mr. Ward's assistance. He desired me to go into the Parlour and take a cup of tea. I knew enough, drunk as I was, not to expose myself—and tumbled into bed whare I lay and slept sound till morning."

Mr. Playter, who seems to have been an observer full of zest and good humor, gives many intimate glimpses in his diary of life in York during these rugged and boisterous times when it was still a backwoods outpost. At this period, all males in York between the ages of sixteen and sixty were obliged to devote a certain amount of their time to their drills in the militia and were, of course, subject to immediate call-up in the case of an attack upon this portion of the King's domain. These drill sessions, however, were more social occasions than military exercises and were treated in extremely casual fashion. Perhaps, had York's part-time civilian soldiers known that in a very few years they would be facing Yankee shot and shell in the new-born community, they would have been a little more serious in their approach to their military training.

Mr. Playter describes in his diary a typical muster of York's citizen soldiers for one of their regular drills:

". . . Hurried to the alarm post to join the Company. The men attended pretty generally and we marched into Town and joined the Battalion in the Park. The men looked very well. We went through no exercise, only formed the Line. The Captains gave in their returns to the Colonel and he dismissed us, offering a beaver hat to the best marksman with the smoothe board guns and another to the best with their riffles. We fired at the target by turns in the Companys—Mr. Hale got the first hat and Mr. P. Mills the other . . . the Town of course was full of people and a great number drunk, whare was restling, jumping, boxing and the like all the evening. The House was full of all kinds of people . . ."

Mr. Playter may have had a little trouble with his spelling, but he was an excellent reporter as well as a busy bartender. He tells, for instance, about an event which may have been York's first mystery thriller. It seems that lawyer Weekes, the aggressive advocate of Mr. Allcock at the poll during York's first election, disappeared one day under extremely suspicious circumstances. The town was in an uproar, wrote Mr. Playter, because no one had seen lawyer Weekes for twelve days nor appeared to know what had become of him.

Finally a man named Samuel Whitesides and Mr. Weekes' housekeeper, who is unnamed, where arrested on the charge of murdering him. After the pair had been thrown into jail, the word got around that they had confessed to their crime.

"I felt low-spirited and dejected," wrote Mr. Playter, "at the thought of such heinous crimes being committed in so new a settlement as York . . ."

Two weeks later some bones were discovered which were accepted as being the last mortal remains of poor lawyer Weekes and arrangements were made to bury him. But on the very day the sad ceremony was to take place, a traveler arrived from across the lake with word that lawyer Weekes was alive at Niagara, where he had ended up after being lost for many days in the woods. Although the mourners were pleased to hear that lawyer Weekes was still alive, they were naturally keenly disappointed over the prospect of calling off the funeral, so it was decided to go ahead with the service anyway. Mr. Playter put it this way:

". . . these people thought proper, as the Bones were found and known to be human bones, to bury them, and had a full and handsome coffin made and intered them about sunsett that evening."

Although Mr. Playter does not say so, it can be assumed that Mr. Whitesides and Mr. Weekes' housekeeper were promptly released. Lawyer Weekes returned to York a few days later. Mr. Weekes, who later became a member of the legislature, seems to have been a hot-tempered man who was frequently the center of some turbulence in the lusty little town of York. Joseph Willcocks, in his diary, records an altercation he had with the peppery lawyer.

Willcocks had made a call on Weekes one evening and before long their conversation became heated.

"He said that I was in the pay of the Government as their informer and used many other approbious imputations," wrote Willcocks. "I gave him the lye. He said I should fight him tomorrow. I agreed to fight, but not so soon . . ."

After departing from Mr. Weekes on this prudent note, Mr. Willcocks went home. But, next morning, Baron de Hoen, the aristocratic former German military officer who had been second for the late unfortunate Mr. White in his duel with Mr. Small, called on behalf of Mr. Weekes. The Baron, who seemed to be as eager to hold coats as Mr. Weekes was to get into fights, desired to complete with Mr. Willcocks the arrangements for a time and place for the duel.

"I told him 6 next morning at the point of the Don," wrote Mr. Willcocks. "I then went to Mr. Ruggles to get him to be second. He agreed to lay with me that night—the hour was changed from 6 to 5."

A four o'clock next morning Willcocks and his second arose, dressed, and proceeded through York's chilly mists of dawn toward the spot that had been chosen for the duel. Somehow, however, the Sheriff had got wind of the affair and was on hand to intercept Willcocks and his second before they reached the rendezvous. He promptly placed them both under arrest and later Magistrate William Jarvis put Willcocks under bond to keep the peace for six months. No mention is made of what legal action, if any, was taken against lawyer Weekes, who had issued the challenge for the duel in the first place.

But the hot temper of Mr. Weekes finally brought him to a sad end. During his appearance as counsel in a court case at Niagara, five years later, he was reprimanded for his language and behavior by a fellow lawyer named William Dickson. Although lawyer Weekes didn't appear to be much upset by lawyer Dickson's remarks at the time, he evidently took to brooding over them that night while discussing the case with some fellow members of the legal profession in one of Niagara's taverns. Someone suggested that he should demand satisfaction from lawyer Dickson and next morning Weekes challenged him to a duel. Lawyer Dickson won, and the fiery lawyer Weekes was carried away feet first from the field of honor, near the old French Fort Niagara.

In spite of the obviously quarrelsome nature which led lawyer Weekes to his doom, the *Upper Canada Gazette* of October 11, 1806, contained the following eulogy:

It is with sentiments of deepest regret that we announce to the public the death of William Weekes, Esq., Barrister-at-law in this Province; not only from the melancholy circumstances attendant on his untimely death, but also from a view of the many virtues this Province is deprived of by that death. In him the orphan has lost a father, the widow a friend, the injured a protector, society a pleasing and safe companion, and the Bar one of its ablest advocates. Mr. Weekes was honest without a show of ostentation. Wealth and splendour held no lure for him; nor could any pecuniary motives induce him to swerve in the smallest degree from that which he conceived to be strictly honorable. His last moments were marked with that fortitude which was the characteristic of his life, convinced of the purity of which, he met death with pleasure.

A few years later another celebrated duel took place between young John Ridout and Samuel Jarvis, members of two of Toronto's most prominent families. The adversaries met on a dismal and rainy dawn on a farm located near the present corner of College and Yonge Streets. So murky was the light on the field of honor that the parties took shelter in a barn to await the end of the showers and an improvement in the visibility. When the weather had cleared enough, the principals faced each other at a distance of about eight yards, with instructions to fire at the count of three. Ridout hastily fired at the count of two, and missed. He apologized for his mistake and asked for another weapon, but the referee decreed that, according to the dueling code, he must now stand to the fire of Jarvis. This he did, and, taking careful aim, his opponent shot him dead.

Young Jarvis was tried before Chief Justice Powell but, as was the custom after these affairs in those days, the jury took only a few minutes to acquit him.

As has already been mentioned there wasn't much—except for the frequent gatherings in York's small and crudely built pubs—to liven up the evenings in the little wilderness settlement. It was perhaps for this reason that the jovial Ely Playter and his pals entered with such enthusiasm into the business of staging a "shivierie" for the bride and groom when, in 1802, a York belle by the name of Eugenia Willcocks married a dashing Frenchman named Augustin Boiton de Feugeres. It was a memorable affair that went on for three nights in a row. Playter wrote the following description of the boisterous event in his diary:

> York 12th. Oct. 1802 . . . the young beaux of the town, remindful of the happy occasion and the French Custom of Shivierieing the Parties, a number of them in disguise assembled and made a great noise about the old Esquire's house, till the Esquire, his Son and Doctr. Baldwin came in a great passion with their guns and threatened to shoot if the disguised Party did not disperse, some run off, one frenchman was taken, the guard that was in the town was sent for, the Constables call'd, and the noisey Party soon were all gone. About 10 o'clock, all was quiet and we went to bed.
>
> Wed. 13th . . . The weather was wet in the evening a small company of wild rakes gathered to keep up the Shivierie, but the night being rainy and dark they soon gave it up . . .
>
> Thur. 14th . . . after Tea all was prepared for continuing the Shivierie and such noise with drums, Kettles, Cowbells and Horns was never before heard in York. They keep'd it up till Past Midnight, round the town, but the old Esqr. nor none of his family made their appearance. Some of the parties, in the appearance of Indians, went to McDougall's, calld for Liquor and danced in the House. Then to A. Macdonnell's, Pull'd him out of bed made him treat, danced all over the House and stayed cutting capers till 2 o'clock in the morning.

Mr. Playter was always ready for a "shivierie." He notes that on another occasion "we heard a shivierie going on in the town occasioned by the marriage of Miss Fisk. Mr. S.H. and me could not be easey without being with them which we were in a short time and, well disguised, we rallied the House—the old man shott at us 3 times and then came with his sword —we made some fun and dispersed."

So starved were the people of York for a little entertainment that Mr. Playter was eager to join the other townspeople in a visit to the Hinds Hotel to have a look at "a little animal called the Saigou Brown, a species of orangutang, a curious sight for which we paid one shilling."

It seems possible, however, that even in these early times there were forms of entertainment in York which weren't quite so innocent as quaffing a pint of ale or observing the antics of the Sagou Brown in Hinds Hotel. Mrs. Elizabeth Ellis and her husband Stephen were tried for keeping a disorderly house. Although her husband was acquitted, Mrs. Ellis was found guilty and sentenced to six months imprisonment and two sessions of two hours each on market days in the pillory opposite the market place.

Excitement ran high during York's first organized fox hunt, which was held on the ice of the Bay. The *Upper Canada Gazette* carried the story:

HOICKS!   HOICKS!   HOICKS!

On Thursday last, William Jarvis, Esq., entertained the inhabitants of this town with a diversion new in itself to many; and in some circumstances to all. About noon he caused a fox of full growth to be unbagged, near the centre of the fine sheet of ice which now covers the Bay, and when at a suitable distance, turned loose the hounds upon it. As previous notice had been circulated, the chase was followed by a number of gentlemen on horseback, and a concourse of the beau monde of both sexes in carioles and sleighs . . . a light coat of snow covered the surface of the shining plain, and contributed much to steadiness in driving and confidence in riding.

After the death of the unfortunate poulterer, his remains served as a dragg, to prolongue for several hours the sport. It seemed doubtful whether the horses in harness or in saddle had the advantage in running, as all indeterminately kept up with the hounds in a promiscuous novelty of group.

In common with most wilderness settlements—even those of today—there was constant fear in York of the outbreak of fire in the surrounding woods or the town itself. It was the custom to burn much of the brush left over from the clearing of lots or roads in the area and there was always a dread among the townspeople that a wayward spark might start a conflagration which would wipe out the little community.

In 1800 it was ordered that each householder should equip his premises with two fire buckets and two ladders, one of which must lead to the eave of the building and the other up the roof to a point near the chimney. The penalty for neglecting to take these precautions was a fine of five shillings. The citizens of York were also directed, in the same order, to clean up the piles of wood and stone which many of them had left lying in the streets in front of their homes.

But, in December of 1802, an event occurred which made the people of York swell their chests with pride and agree that their town was at last achieving considerable stature. The announcement of York's great good

9. Major General Sir Roger Hale Sheaffe, commanding British troops in York at time of American invasion.

10. Located near Queen and Yonge Streets, this building served as York's first courthouse in 1813.

11. The Bank of Upper Canada (York's first) in 1822.

12. The Red Lion Hotel on Yonge Street, just north of Bloor, in 1833.

13. Bishop John Strachan.

14. Toronto in 1834, looking west from the Gooderham Windmill.

15. New Parliament Buildings on Front Street, 1834.

fortune appeared in the December 18 edition of the *Upper Canada Gazette:*

> His Excellency the Lieutenant Governor has been pleased to give to the Inhabitants of York, the use of a Fire Engine, for which signal mark of his parental concern for the safety and welfare of the King's subjects, all ranks and descriptions of people seem highly grateful.
>
> As a very small token of their sense of this indulgence, a subscription was most cheerfully set on foot, which was immediately filled, for the erection of a proper building in the Town for the preservation of the Engine, and such measures will be immediately adopted as are best calculated to procure the most easy access to the Engine at all hours of the day and night.

In this subscription the grateful citizens of York donated a grand total of $30.50, which was evidently enough, in those days, to erect the town's first fire hall to shelter the engine that had been inspected and admired by virtually every man, woman and child in the community while it sat outside waiting for the completion of its new home.

Even with the elegant fire engine, however, many of York's buildings, which were mainly frame or built of logs, went up in smoke from time to time and the pioneer inhabitants were obliged to pitch in and help their neighbors build new homes.

But, gradually, York was growing up and in the process was saying farewell to the boisterous days of its youth and taking on some of the prim and proper character which would one day be derisively pointed out by visitors from livelier centers as one of the main features of the community. As early as July of 1802 the shadow of future events may have been cast during one of the regular General Quarter Sessions of the Peace, from which most of York's bylaws of the day emanated.

"The Grand Jury present," read the minutes of this meeting, "to the Worshipful The Justices in Session assembled, that it is proper to direct wardens appointed for the Town of York to visit the several Keepers of Houses of Public Entertainment therein and represent to them the indecency and impropriety of allowing people to drink intoxicating liquors and be guilty of disorderly behaviour during the hours of Divine Service, and generally on the Sabbath days—"

Barely nine years old, the future city of Toronto had already entered the era of the Blue Sunday for which it would one day be renowned from coast to coast.

Chapter 9

1804–1812

The Years Before the War

The first church. The Rev. George Okill Stuart. The wreck of the Speedy. The confusing currency. Quetton St. George's store. Joseph Cawthra starts a business. The "debtors' posts" on the streets of York. The first lighthouse on Gibraltar Point. The traveling entertainers.

In the decade before the American attack on York in 1813, there was small but steady progress in the little community, marked by events which brought both elation and sorrow. The town had not yet reached the full stride of its growth, but it had achieved certain milestones. For one thing, it had obtained its first church, an event which brought assurance to the residents that their town was at last emerging from its stage as a rough backwoods settlement and taking on some of the atmosphere of a more respectable place in which to live and raise families.

St. James Church was erected in 1806. It sat in a clearing, dotted with numerous stumps, on the site now occupied at Church and King Streets by St. James's Cathedral. It was a tiny frame building, measuring 50 by 40 feet and, at that time, its entrance faced Church Street. All round its grounds, in an area which is now close to the seething heart of the city, stood the forest. The first pastor of St. James was the Reverend George Okill Stuart, who conducted his services in the Parliament Buildings while awaiting the erection of his church.

Dr. Henry Scadding, in his book *Toronto of Old*, gives us a picture of the first pastor of St. James when, after moving to Kingston, he used to come back occasionally to his old pastorate to give a sermon:

". . . a very tall, benevolent, and fine featured ecclesiastic, with a curious delivery, characterized by unexpected elevations and depressions of the voice, irrespective of the matter, accompanied by long closings of the eyes, and then a sudden re-opening of the same. Whenever this preacher ascended the pulpit, one member of the congregation, Mr. George Duggan, who had had, it was understood, some trivial disagreement with the doctor during his incumbency in former years, was always expected, by onlookers, to rise and walk out. And this he accordingly always did. The movement seemed a regular part of the programme of the day, and never occasioned any sensation."

At first the Reverend Mr. Stuart found the task of converting York's boisterous people a somewhat unrewarding one, but he was hopeful.

The people had not yet contributed to his support, he wrote to his Bishop in 1802 . . . "pleading inability from the high price of labour and the necessaries of life. But they have subscribed to the building of a church . . ."

In 1804, he believed that he was at last making a little headway:

". . . he assures the Society of his continuing to discharge his duty," he reported, "and tho' sensible that religious impressions have been made upon several of his Congregation, yet he has cause to lament the general reluctance of the people to receive the Sacrament, tho' he has urged in his discourses the obligation, necessity and beneficial effects of observing that Institution of Love; which he rather attributes to ignorance than to prejudice and mistaken scruples. He therefore requests the Society to send him some religious tracts which may assist exhortations on that subject.

"The observance of the Sabbath . . . is not so much neglected as it has been and he flatters himself that the religious conduct and moral habits are gradually taking the place of irreligion and liscentiousness. That reformations should be gradual is to be expected among a great proportion of the inhabitants, the labouring class consisting almost wholly of disbanded soldiers, whose manner of life has been ill calculated either to improve, or preserve, their morals . . ."

In 1804, a curious tragedy hit York which removed from the town some of its leading citizens. An Indian named Ogetonicut had been charged with the slaying of a white man named John Sharp, who had been the factor at a trading post at Ball Point on Lake Scugog. Ogetonicut and his entire tribe, the Muskrat branch of the Chippewas, arrived one day at Gibraltar Point on what was then the peninsula enclosing York's harbor, where the accused man was handed over with due ceremony to the soldiers of the King.

Ogetonicut was lodged in the little jail at York but, before his trial could be held, it was discovered, during a land survey, that the spot where the crime took place was actually in the District of Newcastle. It was decided, therefore, to move the whole proceedings to the district in which the murder occurred.

Accordingly, on October 7, 1804, the prisoner and all of the officials of the court went aboard the schooner *Speedy* bound for Presqu'ile. Included among the twenty passengers and crew were Mr. Justice Cochrane; Robert I. D. Gray, Solicitor General and member of the House of Assembly; Angus McDonnell, advocate and member of the House of Assembly, and several other prominent citizens among the townsmen who formed the jury.

On the evening of the next day the *Speedy* was sighted off Presqu'ile, but a shift in the wind prevented her from entering the harbor and as darkness fell she was seen being beaten back into the open lake. It was the last time the ship and those aboard her were ever seen. Huge signal fires were lighted that night to guide the *Speedy* in case she should still attempt to enter the harbor in the darkness, but she never reappeared.

Although maritime disasters were not uncommon on Lake Ontario in these times, travelers preferred during the summer months to risk the perils of the inland seas in frail sailing craft rather than endure the discomforts encountered in travel over the atrocious roads which connected York to other parts of the country.

The *Gazette* of November 3, 1804, described the sad aftermath of the loss of the *Speedy*:

"The total number of souls on board the *Speedy* is computed to be about 20. A more distressing and melancholy event has not occurred to this place for many years; nor does it often happen that such a number of persons of respectability are collected in the same vessel. Not less than nine widows, and we know not how many children, have to lament the loss of their husbands and fathers . . ."

Although numerous factors, including transportation costs, made goods extremely expensive in the frontier settlement, there were several merchants in York at this period who were doing a brisk business. Much of their goods was sold on credit, some was exchanged in barter and a relatively small amount was sold for the bewildering kinds of cash which were in circulation at that time. There was no such thing as Canadian silver currency, and money of all kinds, including Mexican, United States, and English, changed hands in York. Prices were sometimes quoted in Halifax currency, United States dollars or English pounds sterling. Each merchant had to be his own currency expert, familiar not only with the going rate of exchange but also with the matter of whether a note, especially one of United States origin, was genuine or counterfeit.

Among York's more prominent merchants of this period was Quetton St. George. In an advertisement in the *Gazette* Mr. St. George tactfully let it be known that he had detected the mysterious absence from his counters of two pairs of boots and one book and obliquely suggested that if they were quietly returned no questions would be asked:

"Mr. St. George has just received by Captain Kendrick, L.P. Madiera Wine, Jamaica Spirits, Rappie Snuff, Nails, best Spanish Segars.

"Mr. St. George having missed two pairs of Suwarrow Boots, requests those persons who have purchased from him to let him know, as he is afraid he has forgot to charge them, or should they have been taken on trial, it is requested they may be returned.

"It is also requested that the Gentleman or Lady who has borrowed a Volume of the Revolutionaire, Plutarch, will return it immediately."

Those who think that the wide variety of goods now available in drugstores is a comparatively modern development, may be interested to read the announcement in the *Gazette* of Joseph Cawthra, founder of one of the early Toronto fortunes:

"J. Cawthra wishes to inform the Inhabitants of York and the adjacent country, that he has opened an Apothecary's Store in the House of A. Cameron, opposite Stoyle's Tavern, in York, where the Public can be supplied with most articles in that line. He has on hand also, a quantity of Mens', Womens' and Childrens' Shoes, Mens' Hats: also for a few days will be sold the following articles, Table Knives and Forks, Siscars, Silver Watches, Maps and Prints, Profiles, some Linen, and a few Bed Ticks, Teas, Tobacco, a few casks of fourth proof Cogniac Brandy, and a small quantity of Lime Juice, about twenty thousand Whitechapel Needles."

Credit was not too hard to obtain from the early merchants of York because defaulters could end up in debtors' prison. Although a man unable to pay his debts could be clapped into jail, he was in at least one respect given better treatment than that which would be received by a common criminal. He was occasionally released for an hour or two to take a stroll within a certain radius of the jail, the boundaries of which were indicated by white markers known as "debtors' posts." So long as he kept within these limits as he walked York's muddy streets, he was allowed his brief fling in the fresh air.

One of Quetton St. George's hard-up customers, a farmer named Timothy Nightingale, wrote the merchant the following anxious note from Whitby:

As Anderson has disappointed me about taking my farm I am like to disapoint you about the Money due you it is out of my power to pay you unless I sell my farm which is for Sale. I have offered to sell for three or four hundred Dollars less than the Value of it but if you know anybody that will buy it plese to send them and I will take the same that Anderson was to give in order that you may get your pay, or I will let you have it for twelve Shillings an Acre which is worth Double what I offer it to you for or I will deliver my farm to you and you may let it out till you get your pay. I can't offer anything more if I can't sell and you won't Comply with these terms to gaol I must go . . . N.B. You need not send no officer any

more only send a line and I will come up immediately and go to gaol if
you say so . . .

There doesn't seem to be any record of whether Mr. Nightingale finally
raised the money to pay his debts or ended up behind bars in York.

But Mr. St. George had other problems besides those of collecting from
customers who owed him. One of his suppliers in New York wrote to tell
him that he would be encountering an unexpected delay in replenishing
some of his stocks.

> I am sorry to inform you, *said the letter,* that last Wednesday I received
> letters by Capt. Monger from Montreal mentioning that the Ship John
> from Liverpool, bound for Montreal, with all your woolens and a number
> for others, was taken by a French Privateer . . .

The stern penalties imposed upon those who couldn't pay their debts
were hardly more severe than those applied to apprentices who grew weary
of their jobs and set out in search of greener fields. In those days a youth
who signed up to learn a trade was kept in bondage almost as strict as that
placed upon a Negro slave. Advertisments such as the following were
fairly common in the *Gazette:*

RUN AWAY

Ran away from the Subscriber on the 22nd Inst.—An Indented Apprentice to the Wheel Wright's Trade, about 19 years of age, and five feet five
or six inches high, with light hair and weak eyes; named John Brady. Had
on when he went away, a short blue Coat and Trowsers of the same, white
Vest, new fur Hat, and several other new articles which he obtained from
his Master's credit, without his permission, on the day previous to his leaving this place. All persons are therefore cautioned not to harbor or trust
him on his said Master's account, or employ him. From his want of good
qualities, industry and whatever else can make an apprentice valuable, the
Subscriber will not offer any reward for the expences of his apprehension.

The advertisement was signed by Lardner Bostwick, a wheelwright who
owned an acre on the southeast corner of Yonge and King Streets (which
he had purchased for $100).

In 1809 the town's first lighthouse was built on Gibraltar Point which
was then situated near the mouth of the western entrance to the bay and
harbor. (Shifting sands and reclamation projects have now placed this
spot some distance south of the Western Gap, but the original lighthouse
still stands and is probably one of the oldest York structures still in existence.) The lighthouse was constructed of limestone hauled from Queenston.

A study of the original maps of what was the "peninsula" in the early
days of York and Toronto and is now an island, shows that the shape of

this piece of land has changed drastically over the years. As far back as 1854, Captain Thomas Smith remarked upon these changes, brought about by wind, sediment, and currents:

"I have lived in Toronto for over forty years," said he, "and have been connected with sailing the greater part of the time . . . When the light-house was built by my grandfather and uncle the materials for building it were landed within 25 feet of where it stands; but land extends now over a quarter of a mile to the west of the lighthouse."

It was around 1809 that York began to be favored by the visits of small traveling theatrical troupes who were eager to provide entertainment for the good people of the backwoods settlement.

In February of 1809 Maria Jarvis wrote an excited letter to the Reverend Samuel Peters in New York:

> Well, my dear Grand Papa, what a surprising circumstance I am about relating. Will you believe that positively there was a play acted here last Night, and what do you think it was? Nay you don't know how much we admire your New York comic gentry for the happy display of their choice in choosing a comedy so applicable to this gay metropolis as the School for Scandal, well calculated, my dear Sir, to excite the risible faculties of some tho horrible faces in others . . . I am happy to inform you that many of the York scandal hunters were present . . . I have nothing to recount very material such as Coaches run away with, squeezing to death, fainting fits caused by the crowded audience and confined air . . . headlong tumbles from the Gallery's that to be sure I did not see owing I suppose to my not being very observing at the best of times—particularly at such a critical moment as that in which the most of the inhabitants of York were so ad-mirably depicted . . . Law what an exclamation and what an appearance of grandeur this sentence has—I am going to the Play, do you go? . . .

In the spring following this notable theatrical event in York an adver-tisement announcing still another entertainment treat appeared in the *Gazette*:

EXHIBITION
Messrs. Potter & Thompson
From London

Take the Liberty of informing the Ladies and Gentlemen of York and its vicinity, that they will perform at Mr. Miller's Assembly Room, formerly the Toronto Coffee House, (on Duke Street) on Monday the 7th instant,
Philosophical, Mathematical and
Curious Experiments,
many of which were never performed in America by any others but them-selves; Theatrical performance, consisting of Songs and Recitations and
Ventriloquism
In the course of the evening will be sung the following Songs, the Straw

Bonnet, the much admired song of the Cosmetic Doctor, or the man for the Ladies, Caleb Quotern or the Man of all Trades and Giles Crogans Ghost, by Mr. Potter, with an accompaniment on the Violin by Mr. Lyon. Tickets to be had at the performance. Front seats half a Dollar, back seats half price.

In another advertisement in the *Gazette* a week later Mr. Potter and Mr. Thompson offered a second performance with new songs and recitations and the reassuring promise that "Persons who honor the Exhibition with their company, need be under no apprehension of accidents by the future giving away of the Gallery, it having been secured under the direction of an obliging Gentleman."

Perhaps the shape of things to come in the field of Toronto entertainment was indicated in this theatrical notice which appeared in the *Gazette* of May 23, 1811:

Some Things Wonderful

The Public are informed that a gallant Display of various performances will take place on Monday Evening next, May 25, at Mr. O'Keefe's Assembly Room, which is fitted up on purpose, for the reception of the worthy Inhabitants of York and its Vicinity, when a famous Entertainment will be exhibited of various curiosities . . .

Thus did the people of York work and worry and laugh and play in the days immediately preceding the grim times which came with the War of 1812.

Chapter 10

1813–1814

THE FALL OF YORK

Arrival of the American fleet. The invasion. Death of General Pike. Retreat of General Sheaffe. The burning of the Parliament Buildings. Parson Strachan lays down the law to the intruders. A warning to the disloyal. The mysterious scalp. The return of the Americans. York's lost parliamentary mace.

In the late afternoon of Monday, April 26, 1813, watchers on the bluffs of Scarborough, gazing out across the waters of Lake Ontario, observed a startling and chilling sight which sent one of them running pell mell to saddle his horse for a dash to York. Outlined against the distant southeastern horizon stood a fleet of fourteen vessels flying the Stars and Stripes, their billowing sails touched with pink in the slanting rays of the setting sun.

The American invasion of York, which had long been feared by Simcoe, who had tried so hard to obtain proper armaments and fortifications for the little outpost, had begun.

Compared to some of the other, better-known battles of history, the American attack on York might seem a minor encounter, which local historical societies have tried in vain to glorify. In the frame of its place and its time, however, it was a short but bitter and bloody engagement, in which the British losses were at least 62 killed and 76 wounded and the Americans lost 55 killed and 257 wounded—no small casualty list for those days in a clash which lasted only a few hours.

The American fleet, which had sailed, after the break-up of the ice, from Sackett's Harbor, under Commodore Isaac Chauncey, carried 1700 soldiers commanded by General Henry Dearborn. Included in this expeditionary force was a hard-bitten brigade, made up of the 6th, 15th and

16th Regiments, under command of Brigadier General Zebulon Pike, the famed United States explorer for whom Pikes Peak was named.

Waiting ashore to meet the attack was a force of greatly inferior numbers, which might have been even smaller had not a group of British Regulars happened to be resting in York that day while en route from Kingston to the Niagara frontier. They were composed of some units of the Glengarry Light Infantry, the Royal Newfoundland Regiment, the 8th (or King's) Regiment and a bombardier and twelve gunners of the Royal Artillery. The rest of the forces were made up of members of the York militia and a party of Mississauga and Chippewa Indians under command of Major John Givins. The entire force available for the defense of York on this fateful day totaled only about 700.

In command of these troops was Major General Sir Roger Hale Sheaffe, who, only a few days before, had expressed in a letter to Earl Bathurst his fears that an American attack upon York might take place as soon as the spring navigation opened. Now, with the American fleet in sight, he began hastily mustering his meager forces for the approaching battle. This time, when the militia assembled in their makeshift uniforms, they knew it was not to be another social occasion, but a contest in which the prizes for good shooting would be far more important than a new beaver hat and the penalties of defeat might be the loss of their very lives and property. All able-bodied men from sixteen to sixty were subject to call and as the word spread of the impending attack they left their plows and their forges and their axes and their families to do their duty. Echoing through the tiny settlement, as the forlorn little army mustered for battle, drifted the thin but brave sounds of a few fifes and drums.

When night fell, while the men of York prepared to face their foes, the Americans dropped anchor three miles offshore and a meeting of the expedition's commanders, to draw up the final strategy for the morrow's attack, was held aboard the *President Madison*, flagship of the invading fleet.

Only the *President Madison*, a 24-gun corvette, and the *Oneida*, carrying 18 guns, were actually men-of-war. The other vessels were converted merchant ships fitted with armament. Commodore Chauncey had his eye on two attractive prizes when he sailed for York. One was the British cruiser *Prince Regent*, which had wintered there. But by the time the invading fleet arrived, the *Prince Regent* had already sailed for Kingston. The second and even more important prize was still there, however. The *Sir Isaac Brock*, a 30-gun man-of-war then under construction in York, would be the most formidable fighting ship on the lake when completed. Spies in York had informed the Americans that the *Brock* was nearly finished and Commodore Chauncey had brought along with him a party of ship's carpenters which, he hoped, would be able to make the vessel ready for sailing soon after she was seized. Once she was in American hands, they would most certainly control Lake Ontario, and there would then remain little chance of Upper Canada surviving as a British province.

When the small boats returned to their respective ships that evening, the invaders retired to await the coming of the dawn and what fortunes war might bring. The ships rocked gently in the light breeze. Many of those who slept within them that night would sleep next evening forever, on the ground they had set out to conquer. Ashore, other brave men waited, some of whom would also lie dead before the smoking ruins in the little settlement by the time another sunset had arrived.

At five o'clock on the morning of April 27, 1813, signals were hoisted in the stiffening breeze and the American fleet stood for shore. It was the original plan of Commodore Chauncey to land the invaders at a point near the present Exhibition Grounds, but the brisk and rising easterly winds drove them past this spot. When the ships finally dropped anchor about a half-mile offshore, the small boats carrying the landing parties were blown farther westward, by the strong winds, to a point approximately opposite the place where the Sunnyside railway station now stands.

It was by then about eight o'clock in the morning. As the boats carrying the first American landing parties approached the small clearing on shore, the only ones on hand to oppose them were Major Givins' Indians. The stiff winds, it seems, had carried the invaders along in their boats faster than York's main body of white defenders could make their way through the woods on foot. Briskly returning the fire of the Indians, the invading forces made the shore and mounted the bank to higher ground. (It must always be remembered, in trying to visualize the Battle of York, that the actual shore line of the lake was then some distance north of where it lies today. Fort York, which now huddles in the shade of the Gardiner Expressway, well back from the lake, was then situated near the water's edge.)

Offshore, the shallow-draft American vessels were laying down a murderous barrage of grapeshot to cover the landing of their troops. Suddenly, from the pale green of the spring foliage on the eastern boundary of the clearing, there appeared the crashing scarlet line of the men of the King's Regiment as they approached the invaders with bayonets fixed. Their charge momentarily checked the American advance, but the vastly superior strength of the invaders soon overwhelmed them and the other forces which shortly arrived to join them.

As the defenders retreated to the woods which lay between the clearing and the path to York, both sides were enveloped by the forest.

Nothing could be heard, later wrote Colonel Cromwell Pearce of the

American forces, *but the shouts of the rival combatants, the war-whoop of the savages, and the echo of bugles, mingling with the scattering reports of the musketry.*

As the boats continued to shuttle back and forth between the shore and the American fleet, reinforcements gradually swelled the strength of the invaders, and it soon became evident that the battle to save York had been all but lost. For a few minutes silence descended upon the scene, an eerie, fateful stillness, in which firing had ceased and only the low moans of the wounded and the dying broke the quiet tension which enveloped the field of battle.

Then the guns of the American fleet once more reopened their thunder as they bombarded the nearer of the two small batteries which lay between the American forces and the western approaches to York.

The first and most important of these was the Western Battery, situated approximately at the foot of what is now Strachan Avenue. It mounted two ancient 18-pounder guns which had been scrounged by the desperate Simcoe from Carleton Island at the head of the St. Lawrence after they had been condemned when their trunnions were knocked off. They had been "stocked" in the Western Battery by being clamped to logs, in the same manner in which a rifle barrel is attached to its stock. The second gun emplacement, known as the Half Moon Battery, was a feebly armed earthwork of little consequence. It was situated slightly to the east. Still farther to the east, in Fort York itself, was what was known as the Government House Battery, armed with two 12-pounders and possibly a pair of six-pounders.

Having covered the landing of the American troops, Chauncey's ships then beat back against the wind to engage in a duel with the defending shore batteries. It was just about one o'clock when, with a great roar, the Western Battery exploded, killing most of its crew and a number of infantrymen who had taken shelter in it. It was not put out of action by enemy fire, but was evidently blown up when a gunner in the crowded quarters accidentally allowed his portfire to come into contact with the powder in a portable magazine. One of the toppled 18-pounders was restored to action by the time the invading Americans had appeared, but it had been mounted high, for use against enemy ships, and could not be lowered rapidly enough to inflict much damage on the invading troops. What remained of its crew retreated and the way to Fort York was now clear to the Americans. They at last stood within 400 yards of the main powder magazine and in full view of the fort and the town beyond.

General Pike, who was commanding the shore operations while the portly General Dearborn (who was seasick) remained aboard ship with Commodore Chauncey, ordered his troops to halt, while artillery was

brought up with which to bombard Fort York. It was then that a shattering thing happened, which killed and maimed more Americans than all
the rifle fire of York's heavily outnumbered defenders. The nearby main
magazine, containing 500 barrels of powder, suddenly blew up with a tremendous, earth-convulsing roar that could be heard that day for many
miles. A huge billowing cloud of smoke boiled up high into the sky and
from it descended tons of stone which fell in a deadly hail upon invaders
and attackers alike. One huge boulder struck General Pike, crushing his
chest, and he fell to the ground mortally wounded. Thirty-eight Americans were killed on the spot and many of the 222 wounded died later.

"Some of the great stones," wrote Ely Playter, who was then a lieutenant in the militia, "sank deep into the ground as they descended with
terrific force.

". . . saw Captain Loring [General Sheaffe's aide-de-camp] a little distance from me, fall with his horse and Mr. Sanders also with one leg
mashed by a stone," he recorded in his diary. "Captain Loring escaped but
his horse was killed . . ."

Defense of Fort York had by now been abandoned and General Sheaffe
and the remainder of his Regulars had begun their retreat back to Kingston. The order to blow up the powder magazine had been given by General Sheaffe after he had made his decision to withdraw, although he had
no way of knowing at the time that its destruction would inflict such disaster upon the attackers. Before heading eastward, General Sheaffe's
defeated troops paused to carry out another task of destruction. The Sir
Isaac Brock and the stores in the naval dockyard (situated near where the
Union Station now stands) were put to the torch. Although the fine new
ship would be a serious loss to the British, she would not be a gain for the
Americans. The retreating British troops also burned behind them the
small bridge over the Don River.

General Sheaffe would later be highly criticized for his retreat and his
defense of York generally, but some military historians now believe that
he made a wise decision in quickly removing his outnumbered Regulars
from York instead of allowing them to be taken prisoners for the remainder of the war.

Members of York's rag-taggle militia, after laying down their arms, were
paroled by the Americans and allowed to return to their homes. Infuriated
by what they considered to be the treachery of blowing up the powder
magazine, the Americans burned many of York's public buildings, but it is
to this day a subject of lively argument among historians as to whether the
invaders actually did put the torch to York's little Parliament Buildings.
Certainly they did burn, but, as is pointed out by Canadian military historian Colonel C. P. Stacey, "one could write a historical whodunit entitled

'Who Burned the Parliament Buildings?'" There appears to be only one eye-witness account still in existence, and it was written by Major Joseph Grafton of the U. S. 21st Infantry, who related that on the third day after the American landing he saw "a column of smoke arising at a distance of 200 or 300 paces." He said he asked a group of bystanding citizens about the fire and they replied it was the Parliament Buildings but that they could not say what had started the blaze. Major Grafton said he did not see an American soldier at the time. Remarks Colonel Stacey:

"Note that Grafton says nothing about sailors."

Yet there does seem to remain a possibility that the buildings were burned by a spiteful jailbird released by the Americans, or by some other traitor.

In the evening of the day of the battle it began to rain, and the smoke from the ruins of York's public buildings rose to mingle with the lowering storm clouds which hung dismally over the little community that had been suddenly torn asunder so soon after is hopeful birth.

(A reminder of York's ordeal by fire can be seen to this day should you walk down Pennsylvania Avenue in Washington past the residence of the President of the United States. During a British raid on the American capital, the presidential mansion was set afire in retaliation for the burning of York's tiny Parliament Buildings. Only part of the building was destroyed and the charred walls of the remainder were whitewashed to cover the scorch marks. It was thereafter called the White House, the name it bears today.

Although comparative quiet appeared to reign over York on the night that followed the heat and the clamor of the short, fierce battle, Dr. William Beaumont, a surgeon with the U.S. forces, provides in his diary a glimpse which should dispel any modern illusion that the village's first enemy invasion was a comic opera affair. He describes his experiences as he worked frantically through the night to treat the soldiers who had been so horribly maimed in the explosion of the powder magazine:

"A most distressing scene ensues in the hospital. Nothing but the groans of the wounded and agonies of the dying are to be heard. The Surgeons wading in blood, cutting off arms, legs, and trepanning heads to rescue their fellow creatures from untimely deaths. To hear the poor creatures crying, "Oh, dear! Oh, dear! Oh my God, my God! Do, Doctor, Doctor! Do cut off my leg, my arm, my head, to relieve me from my misery! I can't live, I can't live!' would have rent the heart of steel, and shocked the insensibility of the most hardened assassin and the cruelest savage. It awoke my liveliest sympathy, and I cut and slashed for 48 hours without food or sleep. My God! Who can think of the shocking scene when his fellow creatures lie mashed and mangled in every part, with a leg, an arm, a head, or a body ground in pieces . . ."

Although most of the women and children of York had been removed to places of comparative safety among farm friends in outlying areas before the American troops had landed, at least one doughty housewife and her family refused to budge in the face of the invaders. Wrote Mrs. John Beikie to her brother, after the battle:

". . . We all have reason to be thankful to Providence, for never did I pass so awful a day as the 27th of April . . . I never prayed more fervently, or said that beautiful psalm ('He that dwells in the help of the Highest shall abide in the protection of the God of Heaven, etc.') more devoutly, since my father's death, than I did that day. It is a beautiful psalm, and He who strengthens the weak gave me more strength and fortitude than all the other females of York put together; for I kept my Castle, when all the rest fled; and it was well for us I did so—our little property was saved by that means. Every house they found deserted was completely sacked. We have lost a few things, which were carried off before our faces; but as we expected to lose all, we think ourselves well off.

"Will you believe it? I had the temerity to frighten, and even threaten, some of the enemy, though they had the place and me in their power. Poor William Swan was one of their majors, and behaved by no means like an enemy; he came without leave and stayed a night with us. I believe that through him we were treated with civility by their officers. Should he fall into our hands, I hope it will not be forgotten of him. They so overloaded their boats with the spirits of this place that I am told they have thrown great quantities of pork and flour into the lake . . ."

A mighty tower of strength to the bewildered and disorganized people of York was Dr. John Strachan, the lately arrived new pastor of St. James Church. He became the principal civilian spokesman for the town. Although it had capitulated to the American forces, there appears to have been some delay in the ratification of the surrender terms, during which time a considerable amount of pillage continued. This sent the courageous and stubborn Dr. Strachan into a towering rage and such a belligerent attitude that he might easily have been mistaken for a leader of the victors rather than the vanquished. Demanding a meeting with General Dearborn, who had by now recovered sufficiently from his *mal-de-mer* to come ashore, Dr. Strachan berated him as though he might have been a parishioner who had been caught with his hand in the poor box.

"We have been generally deceived already, sir," he roared, in his best fire-and-brimstone pulpit manner, "but we shall not be deceived and insulted. If the conditions are not complied with immediately there shall be no capitulation. We will not accept it. You may do your worst, but you shall not have it in your power to say, after robbing us, that you respected our property."

A strong man, Dr. Strachan, who would wield much influence in York, and later Toronto, for many years to come. General Dearborn promised that all looting of civilian property would cease, and it did.

Accounts of how the American soldiers behaved in York differ widely. Some praised their conduct, and others condemned them. Although opinions might naturally vary in relation to the personal experiences of those who expressed them, there was probably another factor which influenced the reaction of York's inhabitants toward the victorious Americans. There were some residents of the town, for instance, who almost openly welcomed the arrival of the invaders and others who took advantage of the confusion to loot the homes of their own countrymen. Wrote York Militia Sergeant Isaac Wilson, to his brother Jonathan:

". . . They [the Americans] used the people with great civility. They did not allow their men to plunder any property that could be prevented. In the night they put a sentry over every store, but they could not keep the inhabitants from it who made shameful work in some people's houses . . . Many Americans like the country very much and said they would come and settle in it if the war was over. It struck my mind very forcibly, the evening after the battle was over, to see men who two hours before were doing their utmost to kill one another, now conversing together with the greatest familiarity."

In those days, national identities and sympathies and even the border itself were not always sharply defined. Many of the residents of York, for instance, had only recently migrated from the United States, not, like the United Empire Loyalists, out of any particular love for the Crown, but simply because of opportunities to acquire better land and other material benefits. Recognition of the possibly fickle loyalties of some of the inhabitants of the town are contained in the minutes of a special emergency meeting of York's magistrates, held shortly after the invasion, while the American fleet still stood offshore:

"The Enemy's Fleet and Army lying in the harbour, all our Military defences at the Post destroyed, the inhabitants disarmed and on parole, it is obvious that measures of as much energy as our circumstances admit, should be instantly adopted to preserve order and prevent anarchy; to support and encourage the loyal; to surpress the disloyal and to confirm the wavering.

"It is therefore unanimously declared that by the irruption of the Enemy and temporary possession of this Post, no change has taken place in the relation of the subject to His Majesty's Government & Laws, except as to such who were parties to the Capitulation as prisoners of war, and are under parole of honor not to bear Arms until exchanged . . . That it is equally now, as before the invasion, high treason to aid, assist, counsel or comfort the Enemy . . ."

Although General Dearborn evidently tried to provide as much protection as possible for the private property of York's people, all stocks belonging to the public stores were seized and carried off. This loot included one thousand silver dollars found in the home of Donald McLean, Clerk of the House of Assembly, and a splendid scarlet and gold tunic which had been left behind, in his hasty departure, by General Sheaffe and was later snapped up for $55 by an American officer when it was auctioned off in Oswego. Also carried away was York's fine fire engine.

One particularly curious and mysterious trophy taken by the Americans in their looting of the Parliament Buildings was an item which, they maintained, was a human scalp they had found hanging in the Chamber. Later, in the United States, this incident was cited as an example of the barbaric nature of Upper Canada's parliamentarians, but these gentlemen stoutly denied the story and maintained that the object was probably the Speaker's wig. This would still leave some mystery as to why such an article could be mistaken for a human scalp, because such hairpieces must surely have been familiar to the Americans in those times. There appears to be some possibility, however, that it actually was a human scalp the looters had found, although it is unlikely that it was hanging in the place of honor where they said they had discovered it. It seems that at one time the clerk of the assembly had indeed been given a scalp as a souvenir and that the Americans may have found it stowed away in a drawer of his desk in the Parliament Buildings.

The invaders occupied the town four days. For three months after they departed the battered little community was left alone to make an effort to recover from this severe blow. But on July 31 an American fleet of twelve sails appeared once more. This time there was no fight. The United States troops were unopposed as they came ashore in small boats. After releasing some prisoners from the jail and again seizing some goods—mainly provisions—from public and private stores, the Americans sailed away. Among the articles carried off in the first raid was the crudely made little mace which had reposed in the destroyed Parliament Buildings. After resting for 121 years in the United States Naval Academy at Annapolis, Maryland, it was, by order of President Franklin D. Roosevelt, returned in 1934, during the celebration of the centennial of Toronto's incorporation as a city and may now be seen in old Fort York.

Chapter 11

1815–1836

ARRIVAL OF THE REBEL

Rebuilding after the war. The Old Town and the New Town. York's capital status questioned. Introduction of speed and traffic laws. "Little York" is touchy. William Lyon Mackenzie prints the Advocate. *The Family Compact. The raid on the* Advocate. *Mackenzie's election to Parliament. His ejections from the House. "Toronto" once again. Mackenzie becomes new city's first mayor. The tragedy at the St. Lawrence Market. The collision of wills between Sir Francis Bond Head and Mackenzie. Mackenzie's defeat at the polls.*

When, on February 15, 1815, news of the end of the War of 1812 reached York, its 700 inhabitants put aside the anxieties which had gripped them for so long and went about the job of restoring their little community. Although the town had had its share of hardship and peril, the war years had not really treated it so badly as they had some other areas. The Parliament Buildings, the bridges across the Don River and much of the garrison had been destroyed and the one church, St. James, and a few private dwellings had been damaged. The wear and tear on St. James occurred when it was used as a war hospital. Yet, the war had brought certain compensations too. For one thing, it had provided a considerable boost to the town's commerce and at least a few of its family fortunes had been founded upon the brisk business done at this period. The men of the town who had not been killed or wounded during the American invasion had also fared quite well because, after this attack, members of the militia were placed on parole by the victors and were thereafter exempt from further service on other fronts of the war.

Most of York's inhabitants, in the days immediately following the war, lived in what was called the Old Town, which lay south of Queen Street between Jarvis and Parliament Streets. But a district called the New Town had grown up in the area extending from Jarvis Street west to Peter Street, below Queen Street. Although it was more sparsely inhabited than the Old Town, the New Town soon became a keen rival of the original settlement, huddled close to the marshy and unhealthy land near the mouth of the Don. So intense did this rivalry become that gangs of boys from the two areas often held pitched battles along the common boundary.

King Street was the town's main thoroughfare and was a muddy road extending from the Don to Peter Street, containing most of York's seventeen shops. Although the wealthy merchant Quetton St. George had built a handsome brick house on the corner of King and Frederick Streets, most of the 114 residences in the town were modest frame cottages. Only thirty of them were two-story dwellings. Six taverns stood ready to serve the public. The largest of these was Jordan's York Hotel on King Street, in which both the legislature and the courts held their sessions after the burning of the Parliament Buildings during the 1813 invasion of the town.

One disturbing aftermath of the war was that York's occupation on two occasions by the American forces had raised grave official doubts about its suitability as the capital of Upper Canada. It had, after all, been selected by Simcoe to serve this role only on a temporary basis and this decision had largely been based upon its supposed defensibility and its comfortable distance from the American border. Yet Kingston, by now York's main rival for the honor of becoming the colony's permanent capital, had never even been threatened during the war, despite the fact that it was located so close to the American frontier.

It looked almost certain, then, that York would lose its proud position when Lieutenant Governor Francis Gore came back to York after a four-year absence with word that Lord Bathurst, Secretary of State for War and the Colonies, had definitely instructed him to remove the seat of government from York to Kingston. Although the leading residents of York, most of whom had a considerable stake in the community, praised its advantages as a capital, many visitors to the town obviously did not share their enthusiastic views.

Dr. William (Tiger) Dunlop, visiting York shortly after the war, described it as "a dirty straggling village containing about 60 houses." Even less flattering were the remarks of Lieutenant Francis Hall after he had made his initial visit to the town:

"York, being the seat of government for the upper province, is a place of considerable importance in the eyes of its inhabitants," he wrote. "To a stranger, however, it presents little more than about 100 wooden houses, several of them conveniently—and even elegantly—built, and I think one, or perhaps two, of brick. The public buildings were destroyed by the Americans; but as no ruins of them are visible we must conclude either

that the destruction exceeded the desolation of Jerusalem or that the loss
to the arts is not irepparable. I believe they did not leave one stone upon
another, for they did not find one. Before the city a long flat tongue of
land runs into the lake, called Gibraltar Point, probably from being very
unlike Gibraltar. York, wholly useless either as a port or a military post,
would sink into a village, and the seat of government be transferred to
Kingston, but for the influence of those whose property in the place would
be depreciated by change."

Another visitor, E. A. Talbot, offered some particularly scathing remarks
about the town's miserable location when he saw York a few years after
the war.

"The situation of the town is very unhealthy," he wrote. "For it stands
on a piece of low marshy land, which is better calculated for a frog pond
or beaver-meadow than for the residence of human beings. The inhabitants are, on this account, much subject, particularly in spring and autumn,
to agues and intermittent fevers; and probably five-sevenths of the people
are annually afflicted with these complaints. He who first fixed upon this
spot as the site of the capital of Upper Canda, whatever predilection he
may have had for the roaring of frogs, or for the effluvia arising from stag-
nated waters and putrid vegetables, can certainly have had no very great
regard for preserving the lives of His Majesty's subjects."

General Sir James Carmichael Smythe, heading a commission sent out
from England to survey defenses in the North American provinces of the
Crown, had this to say about York in his report to the Duke of Wellington:

". . . We cannot avoid expressing upon the subject of York our regret
that it should ever have been selected for the capital of Upper Canada. It
offers no advantages that we are aware of either of a Civil, Military or
Commercial nature. There can never be any Water Communication to it,
as we shall have the honor more fully of explaining to Your Grace when
we come to that part of our Report on the subject of the proposed Canals.
Kingston appears to us to be the natural Capital, in a Military point of
view, and being the point where the most important of the proposed Canals will meet, its commercial importance must proportionably increase. If
Kingston could be made the Seat of Government, the Civil, Military and
Naval Authorities would be more collected, and as appears to us, with the
happiest effects to His Majesty's Service."

Despite these low opinions of York and the objections by outsiders to
its role as the capital, the town's leading citizens, including the indomi-
table Parson Strachan, managed to persuade the colonial authorities to
change their minds about moving the capital to Kingston and Lord
Bathurst finally recalled his instructions to Lieutenant Governor Gore.

Although the Town Well had been provided in the market place (it is said that the original well still reposes beneath the floor of the present St. Lawrence Market) the water supply of the community was in a sorry state. Of this situation the editor of the *York Canadian Freeman* was to write: "It is really astonishing how the magistrates can allow the horrible nuisance which now appears on the face of this Bay. All the filth of the town—dead horses, cats, manure etc. heaped up together on the ice, to drop down, in a few days into the water which is used by almost all the inhabitants on the Bay shore.

"If they have no regard for the health of their fellow-beings, are they not afraid to poison the fish that supply their own tables? We hope that His Excellency will take cognizance of the state of the Bay from the Garrison down, and see the carrion-broth to which the worshipful magistracy are about to treat the inhabitants when the ice dissolves . . ."

Despite the fact that York's roads were seas of mud in the spring and fall, there were speeding and parking laws even at this early date. It was decreed that no person should "gallop, or ride or drive a horse or horses at an unreasonable rate in the streets of the Town or on the Bank or Beach in front of the Same." It was also illegal to leave a "Waggon, Cart, or Carriage of any description standing in the street for more than 24 hours."

The townspeople frequently called their community "the City of York" and were highly offended when outsiders referred to it as "Little York," an unflattering term often used by non-residents when they weren't insulting the capital with the name "Muddy York."

The incensed editor of the *Weekly Register* couldn't restrain his wrath when he received, from a correspondent in the United States, a letter addressed to him at Little York. "There is one hint," he testily wrote, "which we would like to give Mr. W. Patton, which is although there may be many '*Little*' Yorks in the United States, we know of no place called '*Little York*' in Canada; and beg that he will bear this *little* circumstances in his recollection when he again addresses us."

It was to such a dismal, touchy and somewhat despised little town that there arrived in the summer of 1820 a small and wiry Scot who was destined to liven up the community to an extent which has never since been equaled. Barely five feet six inches in height, he had a large head and a high brow and keen, restless, piercing blue eyes. He was twenty-five years of age, and, although his formal schooling in Scotland had been scant, he was an ardent reader with a wealth of "book learning."

William Lyon Mackenzie's first public introduction to York was as a partner in a book and drug business. But it was not until four years later, after moves to Dundas and Queenston and his emergence as the publisher of a newspaper called the *Colonial Advocate*, that he really got into his stride in the job of warming things up in York. Although he started his paper in Queenston, he moved his presses across the lake to York in 1824, setting them up in a small house overlooking Toronto Bay. From that moment, uneasy lay the heads belonging to those who represented the Crown in the capital of Upper Canada. Had he remained a businessman instead of venturing into the risky field of publishing a newspaper, he might have amassed a considerable fortune. But he was not satisfied with what he saw around him in his new land, and he had a passion to publicly comment on and have a hand in correcting that which he considered to be wrong.

And there was much in York and in Upper Canada generally which did not meet with the approval of Mackenzie. Firmly ensconced were the members of what he called the Family Compact, extremely jealous of the rights and privileges bestowed upon them by Lieutenant Governor Sir Peregrine Maitland, who, in those days, ruled with virtually complete power as the representative of the Crown. Archdeacon Strachan, who had caused the officers of the invading American forces to quail before his mighty will and anger, had risen to a position of influence which was scarcely less than that of the Lieutenant Governor himself.

Strachan's role as parson, schoolteacher, and legislator in the community at that time is described in Dr. Henry Scadding's *Toronto of Old*: "In the early days of Canada, a man of capacity was called upon . . . to play them all satisfactorily. In the case of Dr. Strachan the voice that would be heard in the pulpit, offering counsel and advice as to the application of sacred principles to life and conduct, in the presence of all the civic functioneries of the country, from Sir Peregrine Maitland to Mr. Chief Constable Higgins; from Chief Justice Powell to the usher of his court, Mr. Thomas Phipps; from Mr. Speaker Sherwood or McLean to Peter Shaver, Peter Perry and other popular representatives of the Commons in Parliament; the voice that today would be heard in the desk leading liturgically the devotions of the same mixed multitude, tomorrow was to be heard by portions, large and small, of the same audience, amidst very different surroundings, in other quarters; by some of them, for example, at the Executive Council Board, giving a lucid judgement on a point of governmental policy, or in the Chamber of the Legislative Assembly, delivering a studied oration on a matter touching the interests and well-being of the whole population of the country, or reading an elaborate original report on the same or some cognate question, to be put forth as the judgement of a committee; or, elsewhere, the same voice might be heard at a meeting for patriotic purposes; at the meeting of a Hospital, Educational, or other important secular trust; at an emergency meeting when sudden action was needed on the part of the charitable and benevolent.

"Without fail, that voice would be heard by a large portion of the juniors of the flock on the following day, amidst the busy commotion of School, apportioning tasks, correcting errors, deciding appeals, regulating discipline; at one time formally instructing, at another jocosely chaffing, the sons and nephews of nearly all the well-to-do people, gentle and simple, of York and Upper Canada."

Archdeacon Strachan indeed enjoyed the unusual privilege of simultaneously holding seats on both the Legislative and Executive Councils of the province. His magnificent home on Front Street was so impressive that it prompted his visiting brother, James, to gravely remark: "Jock, Jock, ye've a hoosie like a palace, an a wifie like a Queen. Eh mon, I hope it's a' come by honest."

In this period the best lands and the best jobs usually went to those who belonged to the best families, whereas the struggling small farmers and laborers of the area often faced both a present and a future which were bleak indeed.

Writing later about his decision to start a newspaper, Mackenzie said: "I had seen the country in the hands of a few shrewd, crafty covetous men under whose management one of the most lovely and desirable sections of America remained a comparative desert."

But perhaps a more lucid expression of Mackenzie's loathing for the situation he found in his adopted land of Upper Canada is contained in his *Sketches of Canada and the United States* which was later published in England (in 1833). He enumerated thirty of the prominent members of the Government party, giving the office or offices which they occupied, their salaries, pensions or emoluments and their family relationships, one to another.

"This family connection," he wrote, "rules Upper Canada according to its own good pleasure, and has no efficient check from this country [England] to guard the people against its acts of tyranny and oppression. It includes the whole of the Judges of the Supreme Court and criminal tribunal—active Tory politicians. It includes half of the Executive Council or provincial cabinet. It includes the Speaker and eight other members of the Legislative Council. It includes the persons who hold the control of the Canada Land Company's monopoly. It includes the President and solicitor of the Bank and about half the Bank directors . . . and it includes the list of the Crown lawyers until last March . . . This Family Compact surround the Lieutenant Governor and mould him like wax to their will; they fill every office with their relatives, dependents, and partisans; by them justices of the peace and officers of the militia are made and unmade; they have increased the number of the Legislative Council by recommending, through the Governor, half a dozen of nobodies and a few placemen, pensioners and individuals of well-known narrow and bigoted principles; the whole of the revenues of Upper Canada are in reality at their mercy; they are the paymasters, the receivers, auditors, King, Lords and Commons!"

Perhaps it should be briefly explained here how the pyramid of Government was constructed in Upper Canada's capital of York in these early colonial days. At the top stood the Lieutenant Governor, clothed in the dignity of being the King's personal representative but, in reality, little more than a minion of the British Colonial Office. His appointed advisers made up the Executive Council, which would roughly correspond to the Cabinet of today. Next came the Legislative Council. And at the bottom of this structure was the House of Assembly, elected by the people but actually possessing very little real power. (During the eight years of Sir Peregrine Maitland's administration, for instance, the Legislative Council rejected a total of 320 bills passed by the House of Assembly, an average of forty each year!)

Although, in the beginning, he was loyal to the King, Mackenzie did not extend these sentiments to those whom he considered to be mere opportunists growing fat in York under the sheltering authority of the Crown. "Not to gain the wealth of the Indies," he wrote in his newspaper, "would I cringe to the funguses that I have beheld in this country, who are more numerous and pestilential in the town of York than the marshes and quagmires with which it is surrounded."

For a while he grudgingly spared the Lieutenant Governor himself from the attacks of his acid pen, but soon found that he could restrain himself no longer. Commenting upon one of Sir Peregine Maitland's regular and stately moves from the vice-regal mansion at Niagara to Government House in York, the testy editor once described it in his newspaper as "the migration from the blue bed to the brown."

His feelings toward Sir Peregrine may have been influenced somewhat by an incident which occurred shortly after he had established the *Colonial Advocate* in Queenston. At the time, a monument was being erected in Queenston Heights to General Sir Isaac Brock, (hero of the War of 1812) and it was decided by a local group that it would be a fitting gesture if a copy of the first issue of the *Advocate* were placed in a bottle and enclosed in the cornerstone. When Sir Peregrine heard of this, he immediately ordered that 48 feet of recently erected masonry be torn out so the offending bottle containing the maiden issue of Mackenzie's newspaper could be removed.

In his determination to attack the Family Compact and its Tory ramifications in every possible way, Mackenzie was not above indulging in plain, ordinary muckraking and scandalmongering whenever he discovered what he thought to be an interesting skeleton in the closet of one of

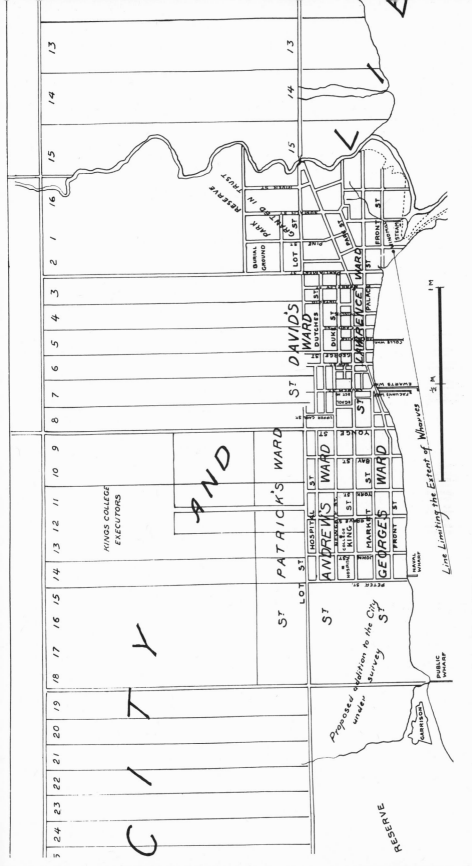

16. Toronto was incorporated as a city in 1834.

17. Sporting on Toronto Bay in 1835.

18. Colborne Lodge, the old home of John Howard in High Park, is still open to public in summer months.

19. King Street, 1836.

20. The Honorable Peter Russell.

21. Sir Francis Bond Head.

York's better families. It was after one such attack in the *Colonial Advocate* on June 8, 1826, that a group of York's hot-headed young aristocrats marched on Mackenzie's newspaper office and, forcing their way into the building, proceeded to wreck his presses and scatter his type. They even took some of this type and dumped it into Toronto Bay.

Mackenzie was across the lake on a visit to Queenston, but when he returned he lost no time in recovering, through the courts, damages for this brazen raid upon his premises. Because many of the young men who took part in the vandalism were well-known and had been observed during the destruction, even the Tory-dominated courts of York could not afford to ignore Mackenzie's plea and he was awarded damages amounting to the then considerable sum of £625.

The raid on his newspaper proved to be a blessing in disguise for Mackenzie. For one thing it aroused sympathetic discussion of himself and his newspaper all over Upper Canada. For another, the handsome cash settlement helped put the publishing enterprise back on its feet because, although the *Advocate* enjoyed a good deal of public support, the money for subscriptions was sometimes slow in coming in and Mackenzie had been experiencing financial difficulties.

In 1828 Mackenzie decided that the role of journalistic commentator in the affairs of York and Upper Canada was not enough for him. In the elections of that year he announced that he would run for office in the House of Assembly. He was elected with a large majority.

Continuing to operate his newspaper, Mackenzie was now also extremely busy in the House, helping to expose flaws in the administration wherever he found them. At one point he was chairman of five of the House's investigating committees. Although the House of Assembly might not be able directly to achieve correction of the government's faults, it could at least draw attention to them, and this Mackenzie and his committees did with great relish at every opportunity.

When Mackenzie stood for election the second time in 1831 after completing a hectic term in the House, he won handily.

But, by this time, the Family Compact, who looked upon him as a small package of poison, was determined to get rid of him. The Tory majority decided to lay against the fiery member a charge of libel, based on an item in the *Advocate* in which he described the House of Assembly as "a sycophantic office for registering the decrees of as mean and mercenary an Executive as was ever given as punishment for the sins of any part of North America in the nineteenth century." (Editorials of those days, especially in the *Advocate*, pulled no punches in their discussions of public affairs.)

Although his enemies might not have been able to make the libel charge stick, Mackenzie greatly helped their cause by not only standing up in the House of Assembly in defense of his statement, but doubling in spades everything he had said in his newspaper.

"Not one word do I retract!" he cried. "I offer no apology; for what you call libel, I believe to be the solemn truth, fit to be published from one end of the province to the other."

At the end of his harangue, he was expelled on a straight party vote for having libeled the character of the Assembly of Upper Canada, and a writ was issued for a by-election in York County. Back went William Lyon Mackenzie, with all banners flying, to take his case to the plain and hard-handed men in the hinterlands of his constituency. It was the kind of fight he enjoyed.

The electors of his riding did not disappoint him. In fact, they displayed their admiration for his courage by providing him with perhaps the most glorious moment of his whole turbulent life.

The election was held on the brisk and frosty day of January 2, 1832. From miles around, in their cutters and sleighs, the farmers gathered at the Red Lion Inn, a highly popular hostelry on Yonge Street, just north of the Bloor Street toll gate. One by one the voters mounted the hustings, an open platform beside the Red Lion, to announce their choice of candidate, because these were the days before the secret ballot had been introduced.

Mackenzie's opponent was a Tory named Mr. Street. By three o'clock that afternoon, Mackenzie had received 119 votes and Mr. Street but one. At this point Mr. Street conceded the election and the poll was closed. Mackenzie's jubilant supporters then escorted their champion to the Red Lion's ballroom, where a tremendous shout went up as the little pepperpot stepped forward to receive from his admirers a great gold medal and chain, made from melted sovereigns. Emblazoned upon the immense medal were the words KING AND REFORM and it long remained one of Mackenzie's most cherished possessions.

There he stood, his eyes burning with satisfaction, his large head crowned with the fiery red wig with which he covered the baldness that had been left in the wake of an attack of fever. (Although it is not recorded whether he resorted to such antics during his triumphant reception in the Red Lion's ballroom, it was said that in moments of great excitement or jubilation Mackenzie sometimes tore off this flaming wig and threw it to the floor.)

Now, the ceremonies in the Red Lion having been completed, there came the next phase of Mackenzie's great day. Mackenzie and the members of his committee climbed into a large, double-decker sleigh pulled by four teams of horses and proceeded to lead a parade down

Yonge Street to the skirl of the bagpipes on the frosty air. Sitting proudly in the place of honor, his great chain and medal draped around his shoulders, Mackenzie smiled happily as he surveyed one of the sleighs in the parade upon which a hand press had been mounted, with a fire burning beneath the ink pot to keep it from freezing. As the parade of 134 sleighs proceeded down Yonge Street, victory handbills were run off on the press and tossed to the onlookers at the side of the road. Flying bravely from a staff on the sleigh was a crimson flag bearing the motto: Freedom of the Press.

That evening, by torchlight, Mackenzie was carried bodily to the doorway of his home (located on the west side of York Street between Queen and Richmond Streets) by his well-wishers and deposited into his warm parlor filled with his family and friends. This time it is recorded he did take off his wig and throw it to the floor, after joyfully tossing to one of his daughters his gold medal and chain.

But, in these days of heavy-handed rule by the privileged few, public acclaim was not necessarily enough to keep a politician in power. On the day following his re-election Mackenzie ran in the *Advocate* another violent attack upon those who had called for his expulsion from the House. Once more he was charged with libel. Once more, this time proudly wearing his splendid new gold chain and medal, he rose in the House to defend himself in extremely blunt terms. And once more he was expelled by the Tory majority.

Back went Mackenzie to his constituents, addressing them with his compelling oratory from every available platform, including wagons and sleds. On one of his speaking tours, when he and his supporters were haranguing the populace from a wagon, it was seized by a group of youths who galloped off with it while the the speakers leaped to the ground under showers of rotten eggs.

During a visit to Hamilton he was seized by a trio of toughs, said to be in the pay of the Tories, and was kicked and beaten unmercifully until he was rescued by friends. William Kerr, Justice of the Peace, Member of the Assembly, and a prominent member of the Family Compact, was hailed before the court for his part in planning this attack and was let off with a small fine.

It would seem that in those days political activity in York could be an extremely strenuous pursuit, especially for such fiery campaigners as William Lyon Mackenzie.

On March 12, 1832, a Roman Catholic political meeting was held in the Union Hotel, attended by Bishop Alexander McDonell. A description of this hectic event was given by Francis Collins, editor of the *Canadian Freeman*, who was obviously not an admirer of his fellow journalist:

". . . Mackenzie and a contemptible mob took possession of the room, although notified not to attend, and refused to retire . . . Mackenzie and his faction have been turbulent, daring and insolent, hitherto, but we never saw them acting the part of the ruffian mob before this. The Bishop himself called upon them to retire—they clamorously refused, altho they were told that the room had been hired for the day by the Catholics. We looked around us to see if we could discover a man of common decency in the group, and the only men we could discover were Mr. Rutherford, the shopkeeper and John M'Intish, sailing master of a schooner . . . The rest seemed to us to be mere ragamuffins hired by Mackenzie to interrupt the proceedings.

". . . We never saw a set of men so deserving of a kicking in all our days—and had it not been for the presence of the Venerable Bishop, they would have met a lesson which would teach them never again to intrude upon a meeting of Irishmen.

"After the Bishop and his flock had repaired to another place of meeting, two manly Irishmen remained in the room, and little Mackenzie rose up on a bench to address his mob—when one of the Irishmen put his finger to the butt of Mackenzie's wig and pitched him, as a boy would a shuttlecock, from one end of the room to the other!—Little Mac fell, we hear, like a cat—all fours, and the wig went under a bench—the little man gathered himself up, picked up his wig, and ran for his life.

"As he arrived at the head of the stairs, the second boy met him, and gave him, we hear, a kick which landed him at the hall door, thus saving him the trouble of walking down stairs! Although about 50 of the mob were present, not one of them durst lift a hand . . . The report that Van Allan, the tailor, fainted when he saw Mackenzie knocked down, is not altogether correct, as we hear he recovered when he got out in the fresh air . . ."

In the spring of that year Mackenzie departed for England armed with a petition to the Colonial Secretary, said to have been signed by 25,000 citizens of Upper Canada who were complaining about their lot in the colony. In the fall he was back again, and when another by-election was called, he was once more returned to the House of Assembly by the electors of the County of York. Again he was expelled by the Tory majority of the House and promptly returned by the electors, in still another by-election in December of 1833.

This time, when he appeared in the House to be sworn in, he was accompanied by a large crowd of his supporters, who filled the galleries and the lobby. When the Speaker ordered the House cleared of these visitors, the sergeant-at-arms ordered Mackenzie to leave as well. When Mackenzie refused, he was seized by the neck and dragged toward the door. A brawny Highlander tried to block the way and the crowd surged at the entrance to help prevent Mackenzie's ejection. The members of Parliament rushed to hold and bolt the doors against both Mackenzie and his supporters. Considering such a scene, it seems small wonder that the flames of outright revolt were being fanned within the heart of the diligent reformer who was being repeatedly prevented from taking his seat in the House despite the overwhelming support of the people of his constituency.

In the House, Reform member Jesse Ketchum spoke a warning in words which were described as follows: "You have got Mr. Mackenzie very low down. Take care you do not end your proceedings by raising him higher and higher in the esteem of the province. The Canadians are a generous, friendly people. They do not like to see a man persecuted. They think, and I think, your conduct towards him unfair and unlawful. He makes some very great blunders but you cover them up by making still greater. Our persecution of him may end in placing him, Mr. Speaker, in the chair you now fill." (Great laughter.) "You may make him governor before the game is over." (Increased laughter.)

Finally, Sir John Colborne, who had by then succeeded Sir Peregrine Maitland as Lieutenant Governor, decided that if the Assembly would not permit Mackenzie to be sworn in, he would have the oath of allegiance administered by the clerk of the Executive Council. Incredible as it might seem to those who are familiar with the present procedures of Parliament, the sergeant-at-arms once more bore down upon Mackenzie when he attempted to take his seat, and ignoring the obvious approval which had been given the harried member by the Lieutenant Governor himself, pulled him from his seat and again ejected him from the House!

On March 6, 1834, the Town of York, which had so often been proudly called the City of York by its inhabitants, actually became the City of Toronto. Mackenzie promptly ran for civic office and within a month of being tossed bodily from the House of Assembly, was elected Toronto's first mayor. Once more the flaming red wig crowned a countenance flushed with triumph as His Worship Mayor William Lyon Mackenzie presided over the first municipal government of the first city in Upper Canada. It must have been a great day for the industrious righter of wrongs and a time of some frustration for the powerful and haughty enemies who had tried again and again to beat him down by every means at their disposal.

By this time Toronto had achieved, during a rapid growth of immigration, a population in excess of 9000 and boasted no less than forty taverns to dispense the cheer that could take the minds of the residents off their miserable roads, and their lack of street lights, drains, and sewers. One of the mayor's first moves was to design the coat of arms still displayed by the city today, bearing the words "*Industry, Intelligence, Integrity.*"

Shortly after Mackenzie became Toronto's first mayor, a strange tragedy occurred in the new city. The mayor and his council had called for an increase in taxation to pay for many much-needed civic improvements, including a new board sidewalk along King Street. A group of indignant citizens hotly objected to the proposed boost in their taxes and called a protest meeting in one of the galleries which ran around the walls of the recently completed brick building of the St. Lawrence Market. Beneath the gallery in which the meeting was being held were some butchers' stalls. The crowd grew noisier and angrier as the evening wore on and as the protesters were stamping their feet in ill-tempered response to some remarks by Sheriff William Jarvis, the gallery suddenly gave way, plunging most of the crowd to the floor below. Some of them were impaled upon the butchers' hooks which hung in the stalls beneath them. Eight persons were killed in this mishap and a dozen more were severely injured.

When the next provincial election took place in October of 1834, Mackenzie forsook city politics to return to his old battleground and run for a seat in the House of Assembly. He was again victorious at the polls and was soon once more playing one of his favorite roles, as Chairman of the Select Committee of the House of Assembly on Grievances. The committee called before it even such personages as the Receiver General of Upper Canada, the Inspector General of Public Accounts and the formidable Archdeacon Strachan, the powerful hand behind the Family Compact.

The report of this committee, when it reached the Colonial Secretary in London, had as one of its eventual effects the recall of Lieutenant Governor Colborne.

Colborne's successor, Sir Francis Bond Head, who had spent much of his life as a soldier and adventurer, was hardly an improvement on his predecessor. It has even been suggested that the King had had another man of the same name in mind when Head was mentioned and that his appointment was a mistake in more ways than one. At any rate, Sir Francis admitted, when he later wrote about his arrival in Toronto and his initial ceremonial ride to Government House, that he was "no more connected with human politics than the horses which were drawing me."

He took an immediate dislike to Mackenzie upon their first meeting. "Afraid to look me in the face, he sat, with his feet not reaching the ground and with his countenance averted from me, at an angle of seventy degrees; while, with the eccentricity, the volubility, and indeed the appearance of a madman, the tiny creature raved," wrote Sir Francis, in describing this initial encounter.

Fate, it seems, had managed to bring together two men of precisely the right temperaments to provide, in their conflict with each other, the clash of steel against flint required to strike the spark of revolution in Toronto and Upper Canada. Both had high opinions of themselves and the righteousness of their views. Both disliked each other intensely. Both were determined men and could be highly persuasive in their addresses to the public. In the art of hurling epithets at his opponents, Sir Francis had a certain colorful eloquence which sometimes almost matched that of Mackenzie himself. On one occasion when, to put it mildly, he was questioning the veracity of the energetic little editor, Sir Francis described him as follows:

"He lies out of every pore in his skin. Whether he be sleeping or waking, on foot or on horseback, talking with his neighbors or writing for a newspaper, a multitudinous swarm of lies, palpable and tangible, are buzzing and settling about him like flies around a horse in August."

Sir Francis had been in office only a few weeks when he set out to crush Mackenzie and the other Reformers, who at the time held a majority in the House of Assembly.

"Do you know why a little weasel kills a rat?" he asked in a letter to a friend in London. "I do not think you do, and therefore I will explain it to you. The rat is the strongest animal of the two, and his teeth are the longest, but he bites his enemy anywhere, whereas the weasel waits for the opportunity to fix his teeth in the rat's jugular vein, and when he has done so he never changes his plan until the rat is dead. Now, I have been following the weasel's plan . . ."

When the Reform-dominated House of Assembly tried to strike at Sir Francis by refusing to pass the supply bill (the first time the House had ever taken such drastic action) all lesser government salaries and pensions not covered by the civil list had to be suspended. Sir Francis promptly retaliated by refusing to sign the bills covering a fairly ambitious program for building roads and schools and carrying out other public works in the colony. This brought about a minor economic crisis, and many found themselves out of work.

Sir Francis then set out to fan the public's emotions and direct its wrath toward the Reform party by blaming it for the depression which now lay upon Upper Canada, although it had been created more by his own efforts than by those of the Reform party. At the same time he raised his persuasive voice on behalf of loyalty to the Crown and the British connection.

He also did not neglect to appeal to those who might not share such lofty and patriotic sentiments.

"Can you do as much for yourselves as I can do for you?" he demanded of the electors. "It is my opinion that you cannot! It is my opinion that if you choose to dispute with me, and live on bad terms with the mother country, you will, to use a homely phrase, 'only quarrel with your bread and butter.' If you like to try the experiment by electing members who will stop the supplies, do so, for I can have no objection whatever: on the other hand, if you choose fearlessly to embark your interests with my character, depend upon it I will take paternal care of them both."

Having created what he considered to be the right public mood, Sir Francis dissolved Parliament at the end of May 1836, and issued proclamations for a general election. Sir Francis was going for the jugular of the Reform party and it has been said that never before had there been such a successful pre-election campaign staged in Upper Canada. It has also been suggested that the election itself was perhaps one of the most crooked ever held in the colony, with the voting machinery manipulated in numerous and devious ways, even including the official bestowal of imaginary farms upon landless hired men who would not otherwise have had the right to cast a Tory vote.

When it was all over, the Reform majority in the House had been reduced to a fairly harmless minority and the Tory party held firm control of the Assembly. Among the victims of this rout of the Reformers was William Lyon Mackenzie.

His defeat at the polls shook to the foundations of his being the little man who for so long and so staunchly believed in the good sense and basic wisdom of the common people he had been proud to represent. Turning up at a small gathering of his supporters after the election results had been made known, Mackenzie bowed his red-wigged head and wept in uncontrollable grief.

While his steps along the unlighted Toronto streets that night led him toward his home, his mind and his resolve were carrying him along a darker and more fateful route, the road to outright revolution against the arrogant powers which that evening held York and the colony of Upper Canada so firmly in their grasp.

Chapter 12

1836–1837

THE PATHETIC REBELLION

The call for action. Plotting revolt. Liaison with Papineau. A declaration of independence. The rebels prepare. No heed to Colonel Fitzgibbon's warnings. The mustering at Montgomery's Tavern. The first bloodshed of the rebellion. The march down Yonge Street. The skirmish at College Street. Sir Francis Bond Head leads forth the soldiers of the Queen. The cannon shot that ended a rebellion. Mackenzie's flight to the United States and his years of exile.

The future leader of revolution in Upper Canada, in his characteristic way, lost no time in informing the public and the authorities of his intentions. In 1835 he had relinquished ownership of the *Colonial Advocate*. Now, on July 4, 1836, the sixtieth anniversary of the American Declaration of Independence, he launched a new publication called the *Constitution*, openly dedicated to the task of agitating an uprising against the powers of Upper Canada. He invited patriots to join him in this "bold, dangerous but delightful course" and in "preparing the public mind for nobler actions than our tyrants dream of."

Still directing a bitter attack upon the Family Compact and its recent political victory, he stormed, in one of the early issues of his new paper: "Tories! Pensioners! Placemen! Profligates! Orangemen! Churchmen! Brokers! Gamblers! Parasites! allow me to congratulate you. Your feet at last are on the public necks."

It might have been expected that Sir Francis Bond Head would have taken drastic action to throttle this new and much more clamorous voice of revolt being raised in the colony by the angry Mackenzie. But it seems that Sir Francis, after the great Tory triumph at the polls, was now content that he and his supporters were firmly established in the affection and admiration of the public and that all was well in Upper Canada. He could bide his time in the matter of Mackenzie and his strident call for revolution. Surely he could now be considered to be little more than a noisy nuisance.

Meanwhile, many of the small farmers and laborers in the colony were becoming disillusioned once more with their government, having had sufficient time to recover from the hypnotism exercised upon them by the shrewd tactics and convincing oratory of the Lieutenant Governor. Economic conditions had not improved and, as usual, the main burden of this situation fell upon the little man, such as the farmer who operated his holdings on an extremely narrow financial margin.

Down the St. Lawrence in Lower Canada at this time another man, who shared Mackenzie's convictions concerning the proper destinies of the colonies, was plotting his own revolution in that part of His Majesty's domain. Louis Joseph Papineau, leader of the "Patriots," was almost ready to launch his rebellion and he and Mackenzie kept in close touch with each other as the preparations progressed. On July 28, 1837, and again three days later, Mackenzie and a group of his followers met in John Doel's brewery at Bay and Adelaide Streets and drew up a document that was virtually a declaration of independence. With characteristic audacity, Mackenzie published it in the *Constitution.*

His harangues to the farmers as he moved about the country were even more outspoken than his diatribes in the *Constitution.* When he visited Lloydtown, a small settlement near Toronto, he was enthusiastically greeted by banners on the main street reading: *LIBERTY OR DEATH.* Still Sir Francis Bond Head refused to become disturbed by these activities and laughed them off as the work of a tiresome crank. Had he had a better sense of the public mood, he might have been more concerned, because times in Upper Canada were bad—discontent was growing and the desire for drastic change was increasing among the rural people to whom Mackenzie so often directed his pleas.

It was not long before pikes were being discreetly forged in the village blacksmith shops of the surrounding countryside and target practice was being held, disguised as turkey shoots and other contests, by men who had dusted off ancient muskets in their farm homes while considering with grim resolve their approaching struggle. Their trials were poignantly described by an Ontario farmer in a book he published only a few months before he died in a Patriot raid at Amherstburg:

"The author has been in Canada since he was a little boy, and he has not had the advantage of a classical education at the King's College, or the less advantages derived from a District School. The greater part of his time has been spent watching over and providing for an increasing and tender family. He had in most instances to make his own roads and bridges, clear his own farm, educate himself and his family. He had his bones broken by the fall of trees, his feet lacerated by the axe, and suffered almost everything except death. He waited year after year in hope of better days, expecting that the government would care less for themselves and more for the people. But every year he has been disappointed."

In spite of the fact that in some of the outlying areas the supporters of revolution were actually holding military drills, Sir Francis Bond Head appeared to be more interested in the activities of Mackenzie's fellow-revolutionary Papineau in Lower Canada than in events which were taking place right on his own doorstep.

So convinced was he of the basic tranquillity and loyalty of his Upper Canadian domain that he moved from Fort York and Fort Henry all of his troops and sent them to Lower Canada to augment the forces of Sir John Colborne, who was by now military commander-in-chief of British North America. When they moved to Lower Canada to help confront Papineau and his followers, the troops left behind them in York several thousand rifles and a goodly supply of ammunition. This alluring rebel-bait was stored by Sir Francis in the City Hall, guarded by only two lonely constables!

Here, then, stood the capital of Upper Canada, devoid of troops, its City Hall stacked with rifles and ammunition which were virtually there for the taking, and its Lieutenant Governor in a somnolent mood. Could there possibly have been a more ripe and available plum to be dangled before William Lyon Mackenzie and those who were prepared to follow him along the rash path of revolution? Even as Mackenzie was considering this attractive situation, an emissary from Papineau arrived from Quebec with word that the rebels were about to strike in Lower Canada. The leader of the Patriots urged that Mackenzie and his followers should make their move at the same time.

This momentous news arrived from Lower Canada on the morning of Monday, October 9, 1837. That very evening Mackenzie called a meeting of some of his followers and it was held once more in the brewery behind the home of John Doel. After a rather lengthy preamble, Mackenzie suddenly placed the following startling challenge directly before his companions: He was certain, he told them, that a comparative handful of bold men could take over the government of Upper Canada that very Monday night. Trustworthy scouts, said he, had informed him that both Fort York and Fort Henry, at Kingston, were virtually deserted. Sir Francis Bond Head himself was resting at Government House guarded by a solitary sentry. One quick move could make the Lieutenant Governor prisoner, occupy Fort York and obtain its artillery, and deliver into rebel hands the great store of muskets and ammunition now reposing in the City Hall.

There are those who maintain that this plan might have been successful and the history of Upper Canada drastically changed that October night had Mackenzie's companions, gathered with him in the candlelight in John Doel's brewery, possessed the fanatical zeal and audacity of the little rebel himself. Others have argued that the victory achieved in such a bold move would probably have lasted only until Sir John Colborne had time to march his forces into Toronto from Lower Canada. At any rate this golden hour, if such it was, was squandered when Mackenzie's friends demurred. They could not bring themselves to the idea of embarking upon such a perilous and fateful undertaking as outright revolution in such a sudden and impulsive manner. They made various excuses for their reluctance to take the great plunge right there and then on that October evening. Finally the meeting broke up with no decision made while the exasperated Mackenzie paced the floor in such acute frustration that he might well have been wishing he could attempt his revolution single-handed.

Throughout the rest of the week Mackenzie continued to discuss his plan for revolution with two of his most influential supporters, Dr. John Rolph and Dr. T. D. Morrison, a former mayor of Toronto. Both of these men were members of the Legislative Assembly and enjoyed a great deal of respect in Toronto. It was decided that if the revolution were carried out successfully, Dr. Rolph should become the provisional head of the new government, he being the solid kind of man who might command the necessary measure of public support in the critical days which would undoubtedly follow in the immediate wake of such a coup.

These deliberations and discussions used up the rest of October and finally, assured of the support of Rolph and Morrison, Mackenzie journeyed north up Yonge Street at the beginning of November for the purpose of sounding out radical opinion in the rural areas from which he expected to gain the most support for his planned revolution. But it soon became apparent to Rolph and Morrison that Mackenzie was doing more than merely testing public opinion in his travels among the farms and hamlets above Toronto. Word reached them that Mackenzie, with radical leaders Jesse Lloyd and Samuel Lount, had actually set a date for the beginning of the revolt. The uprising was to take place on Thursday, December 7, by which time 5000 men would be assembled at Montgomery's Tavern, situated on Yonge Street just above what is now Eglinton Avenue at a point that was then considered to be far to the north of the city. Lount and Captain Anthony Anderson were to take command of the troops. Anderson was a former soldier who had already been training volunteers for the revolution and Lount was a bighearted and greatly admired blacksmith who lived in Holland Landing.

Mackenzie confirmed these tidings when he returned to Toronto in mid-November. Although by this time rumors were coming to the ears of far more persons than Rolph and Morrison, the stories were still largely discounted by everyone in authority. One man, however, refused to dismiss them lightly. He was Colonel James Fitzgibbon of the militia, who had been a famed hero of the War of 1812. He was convinced that the capital was indeed in danger and tried in vain to arouse his superiors, including Sir Francis Bond Head, who still insisted that the rumors of imminent revolution were based merely on the babblings of a lunatic. Again and again Colonel Fitzgibbon was rebuffed by the colony's top authorities when he tried to alert them to what he considered to be Upper Canada's grave hour of peril. He begged Sir Francis to return at least a few regular soldiers to the city, for the effect they might have on the morale of the militia, if nothing else. But Sir Francis would have none of it.

"No," he said. "The doing of it would destroy the morale of my policy. If the militia cannot defend the Province, the sooner it is lost the better."

Colonel Fitzgibbon finally did, however, persuade the arrogant and complacent Sir Francis to move to Government House the rifles stored in the City Hall. Fitzgibbon also went about the task of compiling a list of those who might be dependable if called upon in an emergency, and made arrangements that, in case of attack, word should be sent at once to Upper Canada College, where the bell would be rung as a signal for those in other parts of the city to join in spreading the alarm. On his own initiative, he gathered up a band of militia and drilled them night and day. George Gurnett, then mayor of Toronto, would have nothing to do with Fitzgibbon and his urgently prepared plans when the Colonel asked him to help compile the list of reliable citizens. He considered him to be little more than a busybody. When Fitzgibbon sought the aid of Chief Justice John Beverley Robinson, this aristocratic gentleman and favorite of Archdeacon Strachan testily remarked: "I'm sorry to see you alarming the people in this way." Like many another old soldier before him and since, Colonel Fitzgibbon was finding that a military man received scant attention when peace appeared to reign. And those in charge of the safety of Upper Canada at this fateful moment obviously believed that all was serene, in spite of the rumors which were flying thick and fast. At a meeting on December 2, 1837, of the Executive Council, at which the possibility of revolution was discussed, Attorney General Christopher Hagerman declared that in all of Upper Canada not fifty men could be found who would be willing to take up arms against the Crown. He had hardly finished making this sweepingly confident statement when Colonel Fitzgibbon arrived with fresh news about the mustering of the rebels and the imminence of attack. The man who had brought the news to Fitzgibbon was ushered in and examined by the Attorney General.

"The statement made to us does not make half the impression upon one's mind as was made by Colonel Fitzgibbon's statement," said Hagerman, when he had finished questioning the man: "The information he brings is at third- or fourth-hand."

"What would you have, gentlemen?" asked William Allan, another member of the Council. "Do you expect the rebels will come and give information at firsthand?"

Finally, more as a tolerant gesture than anything else, Colonel Fitzgibbon was appointed Acting Adjutant General of the Militia and an order was given for the organization of two regiments. The rumor mill was now humming not only concerning the rebels' plans for attack but also regarding the government's plans for defense and Dr. Rolph, becoming alarmed at stories of these increasing preparations, sent word up to Mackenzie that the date of the attack should be advanced from the coming Thursday to Monday, four days earlier than called for in the original schedule. Even three hundred men, if they acted promptly, might achieve more than the several thousands who were expected to arrive later, suggested Dr. Rolph. Mackenzie could not be found and the message was left with Mrs. Lount. When Samuel Lount arrived home, he interpreted the message as a summons to march upon Toronto at once. He hastily sent for Captain Anthony Anderson, who lived nearby, and next morning they gathered as many of their forces as they could muster and proceeded down Yonge Street toward Montgomery's Tavern. As they marched along on this cold and blustery December day, the pitiful little army carried only a few rifles, the rest of their weapons being made up mainly of pitchforks, pikes, and clubs. While they moved south they picked up a few reinforcements and an occasional prisoner as a known Tory was encountered along the road.

Although Mackenzie, when he finally heard of the advanced date of the march, tried to have the attack delayed in accordance with the original plan, the countryside was now aroused and its men were on the move. Mackenzie accepted the new date and quickly had a guard placed on Yonge Street to prevent any one moving into the city. The rebellion was under way.

The situation which greeted the first weary marchers when they arrived around eight o'clock that evening at Montgomery's Tavern was far from encouraging. For one thing, their ally Montgomery had only a few days before turned his establishment over to a new proprietor named Lingfoot, who did not possess sufficient rebel zeal to relish the thought of feeding Mackenzie's men without seeing hard cash on the counter. He regarded the visitors glumly and his mood was by no means improved when the desperate Mackenzie angrily grabbed him by the collar and shook him when he refused to provide food. The hungry and bone-tired marchers also found, to their great chagrin, that there were no muskets waiting for them at the tavern as they had been led to expect. On top of all this they learned for the first time that the attempted uprising in Lower Canada had dismally failed. Some of the newly arrived volunteers lost their appetite for revolution then and there, and turned around to head back for their homes. For those who stayed, some food was finally obtained from farmhouses in the district whose occupants were more sympathetic to the rebel cause.

Mackenzie wanted to go ahead with the attack that night, but Lount and Anderson, pleading that their men were tired from their long trek, persuaded him to wait until the morning. It is possible that once more a golden opportunity was missed because at that moment the Governor, who had retired early that night, was blissfully sleeping in his bed and in other parts of the city scant preparations for its defense had been made. Only Colonel Fitzgibbon, still regarded as being a little touched in the head, roamed about restlessly, convinced that an attack might take place before the dawn. At ten o'clock that evening he went to Government House and, after considerable argument with the maids, managed to rouse Sir Francis and tell him of his fears. The highly irritated Governor, rubbing his eyes and clad in his dressing gown, listened impatiently to Fitzgibbon's warnings and then, grumpily dismissing him, returned to his bed. After leaving Government House, Fitzgibbon was hailed by an excited horseman who had just galloped into town with word that the rebels were at that very moment forming their ranks at Montgomery's Tavern and would soon embark upon their attack. By now it was getting quite late and even with his new information Fitzgibbon could arouse no reaction when he tried to warn Toronto's leading citizens of the approaching peril. The frustrated officer sent young John Cameron to Upper Canada College to ring the warning bell but the lad was pounced upon by the housemaster before the bell had sounded more than a few strokes.

Even as this bell was being abruptly silenced, an incident which was about to spill the first blood of Upper Canada's little revolution was taking place up Yonge Street near Montgomery's Tavern. Three horsemen, riding hard toward Toronto, came galloping over a rise in the road near Eglinton and aimed their sweating steeds directly at the guards who had been stationed to bar the way to the city. When the riders refused to halt, the rifles of the sentries cracked out in the night and Colonel Robert Moodie, a Tory from Richmond Hill, tumbled from his horse fatally wounded. A second member of the night-riding trio was captured but the third managed to continue his dash to the city.

Meanwhile, farther south, Mackenzie and five companions were carrying out a patrol to reconnoiter close to the city. While on this mission, they captured Alderman John Powell and a friend who had approached from the south with the same kind of scouting mission in mind. With his peculiar flair for the lofty gesture, Mackenzie refrained from searching the pair for weapons after they had given him their word "as men of honour" that they were unarmed. This noble concession was to have a high and tragic price. Accompanying Mackenzie on his patrol was Captain Anderson, a man in whom the rebel forces placed a great deal of confidence because of his previous military experience and other qualities. Upon taking Powell and his friends prisoners, the patrol split up, with Anderson escorting the captives back to Montgomery's and Mackenzie continuing south toward the city.

As they came near the end of their northward trip to the tavern, Alderman Powell, who had been made to ride before Anderson, suddenly swung his horse about and, aiming a pistol which he had kept concealed beneath his cloak, shot the rebel leader in the neck and killed him instantly.

Alderman Powell then dashed through the night down Yonge Street toward the city, encountering Mackenzie on the way. The rebel leader fired at Powell and missed. Powell then reined in his horse beside Mackenzie, pressed his pistol against his side and pulled the trigger, but Providence seemed, at that particular moment, to be watching over the little rebel, because the weapon misfired. Powell hastily continued his flight to Toronto, where he at once made his way to Government House.

At first Sir Francis Bond Head was in a towering rage when he was dragged once more from his warm bed, but one look at Powell and he sensed that this time he was being rudely aroused from his slumbers by no false alarm of revolution. Having at last shed his apathy and his nightshirt, Sir Francis quickly dressed and set out for the City Hall, now all aquiver with the high drama and excitement of the hour.

"I walked along King Street . . ." he wrote, when later he recorded his reactions. "The stars were shining bright as diamonds in the black canopy over my head. The air was intensely cold, and the snow-covered planks that formed the footpaths of the city creaked as I trod upon them. The principal bell of the town was in an agony of fear, and her shrill irregular monotonous little voice, strangely breaking the serene silence of the night, was exclaiming to the utmost of its strength—*Murder! Murder! Murder! and much worse!*"

But the attack did not come that night. It was not until the next morning, at about eleven o'clock, that Mackenzie, who had decided to take charge of the attack himself, mustered his men outside Montgomery's Tavern. Mounted on a white pony and with several greatcoats bundled layer upon layer about his slight body, he addressed his entire company, which by then was about eight hundred strong. His eyes blazed so wildly that some of his followers later said that they had several times had occasion to doubt his sanity. Whisps of hair from his red wig straggled below his hat and the outer of his many greatcoats was buttoned up to his chin. Thus, burning with mighty and righteous wrath, did William Lyon Mackenzie ride off down Yonge Street in his great hour of destiny, followed by his rather bewildered little army with their strange array of weapons. Those who were fortunate enough to possess rifles marched at the head of the parade, the others following with their pikes, pitchforks and clubs.

Down in the city, largely due to the disdain in which Sir Francis Bond Head had held the rumors of revolt, the loyal subjects of the Crown were still virtually unprepared for an attack. In the market place about two hundred men bravely awaited the onslaught from a force they believed to number five thousand or more. The Governor had moved his family to a ship anchored in the Bay. Under the leadership of Alderman Powell, time was taken out from defense preparations to make another attack on Mackenzie's newspaper office, where the destruction was this time more complete than that which resulted from the raid of the young hotbloods a few years before.

Late that afternoon, as dusk began to fall, the rebels had reached a point—still in the open country north of the city—where Yonge Street now crosses College Street. Here, hidden behind the rail fence of a farm belonging to William Sharpe lay an advance picket organized on his own initiative by Sheriff Jarvis. They had spent most of the afternoon in this position and now, as the rebels appeared, they nervously tensed their trigger-fingers and waited for the Sheriff's command. From openings in the rail fence twenty-seven muskets poked their muzzles. When the vanguard of the rebels had approached well within range, Sheriff Jarvis shouted the order to fire and the muskets roared out with a flash of flame that seared the gathering dusk. For a moment there was a stunned pause in the rebel ranks and then confusion broke out among both attackers and defenders. After firing their first volley, Sheriff Jarvis' men dropped their muskets and ran for their lives. The front rank of rebel riflemen fired toward the rail fence and then dropped to the ground to allow the next rank behind them a clear field for shooting. Hearing the rifle fire and seeing their comrades at the front of their column appearing to collapse, the rebels at the rear of the march mistakenly believed that they were falling from the bullets of the enemy. Seized with sudden panic, they broke ranks and ran back up Yonge Street as fast as their long farmers' legs could carry them. In this one quick skirmish—a hit-and-run affair on both sides—the back of Mackenzie's great revolution was broken.

The rebels who didn't keep right on running until they reached their homes remustered at Montgomery's Tavern. There they waited and tended several of their comrades who had been wounded in the skirmish with the men of Sheriff Jarvis. Two of these died from loss of blood. Throughout Wednesday, Mackenzie went about the regrouping of his forces, hoping that by Thursday at the latest old Colonel Anthony Van Egmond, who had fought at Waterloo, would be arriving with the men he was bringing to join the revolt from the Huron tract to the west. Wednesday passed without any movement up Yonge Street by the Loyalist forces.

But, by Thursday, Toronto's defenders, who had by now been reinforced by militia from out of town, including a group of sixty from the area around Hamilton and led by Colonel Alan MacNab, were ready to march. It was a brave column that moved off up Yonge Street bent upon defending Queen and Country. It was accompanied by two bands and was led by Colonel MacNab and Colonel Fitzgibbon. Riding along with the city's defenders in his black robes, was Archdeacon Strachan. In the middle of the advancing column, astride his big charger, rode Sir Francis Bond Head himself, graciously acknowledging the cheers of the bystanders. With the troops were trundled two cannon under the command of Major Thomas Carfrae, an ex-artillery officer who had come out of retirement to take part in the great undertaking.

Flags were flying from the top windows of the houses along Yonge Street and it has been reported that so heroically splendid was the scene on that early December day that even some of the radicals in the city forgot themselves and cheered lustily as Queen Victoria's troops marched by. Up at Montgomery's Tavern the rebels also had cause for elation, because Colonel Van Egmond and his men, whose arrival had been so anxiously awaited, had finally appeared. But Van Egmond had scarcely had time to hold a meeting with Mackenzie and Lount before a scout arrived with word that the Governor's troops were already marching up Gallows Hill, the slope which runs up Yonge Street toward what is now St. Clair Avenue.

Mackenzie rushed 150 of his men to a point about half a mile down Yonge Street, where they scattered into the woods on either side of the road. When the militia approached, the rebels opened fire, but Major Carfrae turned his guns on them and sent his grapeshot whistling through the woods. Although they held their ground for a while, the rebels finally scattered and retreated back to Montgomery's Tavern when a unit of the militia circled through the woods and suddenly came in upon their right flank.

The soldiers then continued their advance until they reached Montgomery's Tavern which was crowded with rebel troops. It was here that one of Major Carfrae's pair of cannon struck a second and mighty blow for Queen and Country. Taking careful aim, the major pointed one of his guns at the tavern and put a cannon ball right through its dining-room window and out the other wall. That did it. From Montgomery's Tavern there spewed two hundred unarmed rebels who went racing off in all directions with the bullets of the militia singing after them like a horde of angry hornets. Mackenzie and his lieutenants leaped to their horses and sped off to avoid capture. Such was the ignoble end of the rather sad little revolution of 1837.

Mackenzie, after a series of narrow escapes, finally made his way to the Niagara frontier and crossed the river to the haven of the United States. Colonel Van Egmond was captured and died after a short stay in Toronto's damp and drafty jail. Two other close associates of the rebel leader, Samuel Lount and Captain Peter Matthews, were captured, tried before Chief Justice Robinson for treason and hanged in front of Toronto's jail before a great crowd of the citizens who gathered to observe the grisly affair. Dr. Rolph, who was to have headed the provisional government had the rebellion been successful, escaped to the United States and Dr. Morrison was arrested and jailed for his part in the uprising.

A general roundup of all suspected radicals took place after the crushing of the revolt and some of the desperate men who had turned to revolution to better their hard lot in Upper Canada found themselves sentenced to transportation to the far-off British penal colony in Van Diemen's Land on the other side of the world. A few of the prisoners who had received this harsh sentence, including old John Montgomery, the former owner of the tavern which had been a focal point for the revolution, escaped from prison at Kingston, while en route to the penal colony, and reached the United States. Montgomery lived to return to Toronto, in the amnesty granted the rebels in 1849, and start another pub.

Mackenzie also came back to Toronto after a twelve-year exile in the United States. He was again elected to the Legislature in 1851, but resigned in 1858. He died, in 1861, in the house on Bond Street which had been purchased for him, upon his return to Canada, by a group of friends. This house, which in later years became just another ramshackle dwelling occupied by various families in poor circumstances, has now been restored as nearly as possible to its original appearance and has been preserved as a historical monument in the present great city over which William Lyon Mackenzie presided as the first mayor.

Chapter 13

1830–1848

THE RISING CITY

The new steamships. The paper makers. The big pigeon hunt. The terrible year of the cholera. A ferry to the Island. The first taxicab. Bustling St. Lawrence Market. The public whippings. The theater. The crowds at the hangings. Arrival of the gas light era. Charles Dickens comes to town. The Orange Order. The first telegraph. Toronto's first strike.

While the hectic events leading up to the rout of William Lyon Mackenzie's pathetic little army at Montgomery's Tavern were under way, there was more than rebellion and talk of rebellion taking place in York and later Toronto. It was announced in the *Gazette* of August 12, 1826, for instance, that the new steamboat *Canada*, a vessel of 250 tons under the command and ownership of Captain Hugh Richardson, had completed her maiden voyage to Niagara in the spectacular time of "four hours and some minutes." The *Gazette* marveled at the rapid improvement of transportation on Lake Ontario, which was still the colony's most important route for the movement of passengers and freight during the months when navigation was possible.

"In noticing the first trip of *another* Steam Boat, we cannot help contrasting the present means of conveyance with those ten years ago," remarked the *Gazette*. "At that time only a few schooners navigated the Lake, and the passage was attended with many delays and much inconvenience. Now there are five Steam Boats, all affording excellent accommodation, and the means of expeditious travelling. The routes of each are so arranged that almost every day of the week the traveller may find opportunities of being conveyed from one extreme of the Lake to the other in a few hours."

In this same year a paper plant had been established by John Eastwood and his brother-in-law, Colin Skinner, on the Don River three miles from York. It was a great boon to the community, reported Simon E. Washburn, Clerk of the Home District, in the comments which accompanied his list of new industries in York.

"Prior to the establishment of the mill in this District and the only other one in the Province, in Gore, the publishers of newspapers and shopkeepers, for their wrapping and coarse paper particularly, were solely dependent on the United States for their supplies . . ." wrote Mr. Washburn. "A very considerable quantity of a good common writing paper is also made and sold at a moderate price which answers every good purpose for common use in offices and such places . . . Vast quantities are, however, even yet imported, or rather in four cases out of five, smuggled, from the opposite coast."

Down on the waterfront, at the foot of Yonge Street, stood the busy soap and candle factory of Peter Freeland. So abundant were the wild ducks in Toronto Bay that Mr. Freeland occasionally took down his fowling piece and bagged a brace or two from his office window.

A nimrod named Richard Tinning one day spooked a flock of ducks from the water near Mr. Freeland's factory and blazed away at them as they swung by the building, missing the ducks but sending a charge of shot through one of Mr. Freeland's windows. Evidently thinking that Mackenzie's rebellion had already started, Mr. Freeland rushed out with a group of his employees to repel the invasion.

Although firearms were not supposed to be discharged within the town, the abundance of game in the area at that time sometimes made it difficult to obey the law. In the summer of 1830 a huge flock of passenger pigeons blackened the skies over York.

"For three or four days the town resounded with one continued roll of firing," wrote Dr. William (Tiger) Dunlop, in describing the event, "as if a skirmish were going on in the streets—every gun, pistol, musket, blunderbuss and firearm of whatever description was put in requisition. The constable and police magistrates were on the alert, and offenders without number were pulled up—amongst whom were honorable members of the executive and legislative councils, crown lawyers, respectable staid citizens, and last of all the sheriff of the county; till at last it was found that pigeons flying within easy shot, were a temptation too strong for human virtue to withstand; and so the contest was given up, and a sporting jubilee proclaimed for all and sundry."

Up at Bloor and Yonge Streets, near the toll gate where the farmers had to pay a fee before continuing down the rough road to the town itself (which, at that time, scarcely extended up to what was then Lot Street and is now Queen Street) stood the separate little community of Yorkville. Bloor Street had been named after Joseph Bloor, an Englishman who in 1830 established a brewery in a ravine just north of this road. He had previously operated the Farmers' Arms Inn, down near the market place in an area then known as the Devil's Half Acre. Mr. Bloor and Sheriff Jarvis had played a prominent part in the establishment of Yorkville.

At the northwest corner of Bloor Street and Avenue Road, on the ground now occupied by the luxurious Park Plaza Hotel, stood a notorious roadhouse called the Tecumseh Wigwam. It was a low one-story log cabin with a veranda and was one of the favorite tippling spots for the young blades of Toronto.

At the northwest corner of Yonge and Bloor Streets was the Red Lion Inn, one of the district's most noted hotels. (As mentioned previously, it was here that William Lyon Mackenzie was given his great ovation and presented with his gold medal and chain after being successful in a by-election which returned him to the House of Assembly.)

As well as being a favorite stopover place for farmers coming into Toronto on market day, the Red Lion also later served as a meeting place for the village council of Yorkville. A shield of arms, sculptured in stone, reposed for some years over a circular window in the front gable of the inn. It bore a beer barrel, with an S below; a brick-mold with an A below; an anvil, with a W below; and a jackplane with a D below. In the center of this shield was a sheep's head, with an H below. The symbols commemorated the first five councilors of Yorkville and their trades or callings; the initials being those, respectively, of the surnames of John Severn, a brewer, Thomas Atkinson, a brickmaker, James Wallis, a blacksmith, James Dobson, a carpenter, and Peter Hutter, a butcher. Over the shield, as a crest, was the Canadian beaver.

Upper Canada College was established in 1830. (The town had already acquired its first bank, the Bank of Upper Canada, back in 1822.)

By 1832 the fine new Parliament Buildings were rising on a six-acre plot facing Front Street near Simcoe Street. Constructed of brick in handsome Georgian style, the main building was 133 feet long and 90 feet wide, with two wings each 90 feet long and 55 feet wide. It was in this year also, that William Gooderham and James Worts established the Gooderham & Worts flour mill on Trinity Street. Like most millers of the day, they accepted grain in payment from the farmers for grinding their flour, instead of money. Soon they had more grain than they knew what to do with, so they began turning it into whiskey. The firm is still in the whiskey business today, as part of the world's second largest distilling complex.

It was in this year that York was hit by a terrible epidemic of cholera. It was a disease characterized by violent diarrhea, vomiting, and cramps, followed by a comatose stage in which the victim often died within a few hours of falling ill. One resident of the city at the time described his meeting of a distraught widow who had just that morning come into town with her husband from their nearby farm. Evidently healthy when he drove in that morning along the dusty road, the man lay dead before nightfall. The disease, carried from Asia by ships' crews, reached England in 1831. By the opening of navigation in the spring of 1832 it had reached Canada and the fearful residents of York watched helplessly as it steadily moved up the St. Lawrence toward them in the wake of the arrival of immigrants from Great Britain. Although there are no accurate reports of the ravages of the disease in Toronto during that awful year, it was estimated by Archdeacon Strachan that one person in every five of the town's 6000 people contracted it and that at least one out of every three of these died from it.

". . . Three *cases of cholera* announced by the Physicians to be *in the Hospital in Town*," wrote druggist James Lesslie in his diary on June 19, 1832. "Emigrants by the late steamers. A Public Meeting called to take such measures into consideration as may tend to mitigate its destructive power and Committee appointed to the various wards in Town to see that the greatest cleanliness is observed . . .

". . . two new cases of Cholera reported in Town to-day" reads an entry for June 22. ". . . the wife of the person who died two days ago it is said was seized with Cholera and died shortly after being taken to the Hospital . . ."

Although worried about the rapid spread of the dread disease, Mr. Lesslie could not help but note in his diary the effect the epidemic was having on his business.

"The Cholera increasing in Town," reads an entry made on June 23. ". . . a Mr. Stevens, a portrait Painter, took ill last night at midnight and is now no more—4 new cases reported since yesterday. —The Communication between Montreal and Prescott is stopped—Camphor and opium have risen very much—the former 70 cts. 2 months ago is now $3 to $3.50!

". . . This morning," reads an entry for June 25, "when up at the Collectors and passing that part of the town *Henrietta Street* where some of the worst cases have appeared, I saw a poor man carried out and put in the covered car to be conveyed to the Hospital—and he is now dead— Heedless to the danger to which Intemperance peculiarly exposes them at the present period, he had been laying on one of the wharves in a State of Intoxication all night!

". . . nine new cases of Cholera and six deaths since yesterday!" wrote Mr. Lesslie on June 29. "—the alarm excited by it very great so that few persons are found coming in from the country but many leaving and going to a distance—The most active measures adopted by the Magistracy to prevent its spreading—*all drunkards* found on the Streets taken and put either in Jail or in the Stocks—Houses occupied by poor persons cleaned and washed in Lime—drains making from undrained parts of the Town—The dusty streets watered every day by means of carts fitted for the purpose—The burning of Tar, pitch—Sulphur recommended and adopted by many and the use of 'Chloride of Lime' as an anti-contagion. Hand Bills circulated to persuade people not to use Brandy—opium etc as *preventatives . . .*"

In subsequent entries in his diary Mr. Lesslie gives other glimpses of the spread of York's horrible plague. ". . . The various Christian denominations have appointed special Prayer Meetings to implore the mercy of God in His awful visitation upon our Land . . . all intercourse with the United States and the Canadas now closed . . . Rumoured today that a Pensioner and 4 or 5 of his Associates were carousing and became all intoxicated (about '*Stuart's Block*')—that he died *there* in the Cholera unknown to his Companions and that every one of them were afterwards seized by it and are now in their Graves! O what a solemn and affecting warning to man and particularly to the Intemperate! . . . No less than ten cases of Cholera since yesterday and five deaths—seven persons taken ill in one house and three have died! The house is situated on the north corner opposite the Kirk (in Newgate Street) . . . This day Seely the Jailor dies of Cholera—took ill this morning at 6 and was a corpse in the afternoon!—a rapid and solemn transition! . . .

"This day the mortality of Cholera truly alarming," wrote Mr. Lesslie on August 6. "—there being now forty new cases—report says from fourteen to twenty-four deaths!—Mr. Bell, the Chandler, cut off in two or three hours—Mr. Bell the Tavern Keeper also among its victims . . ."

Not until the end of September did the fearful epidemic subside. During its height William Lyon Mackenzie could often be seen bravely helping to man the cholera carts which traveled from house to house collecting the dead and moving the sick. He finally contracted the disease himself, but recovered a few days later. In fairness to Mackenzie's hated enemy and leader of the Family Compact, Archdeacon Strachan also frequently drove the cholera carts and busily moved about the city performing other missions of mercy to the sick and the dying.

". . . as the deaths were principally adults and more men than women we have about 90 widows and about 60 orphans and nearly four hundred Fatherless Children," wrote Dr. Strachan to Richard Whatley, Archbishop of Dublin, after the plague. "What adds to the calamity they are nearly all strangers and have recently emigrated—the greater number this year and are without relatives friends or protection but what the remain-

22. William Lyon Mackenzie.

23. The house on Bond Street where William Lyon Mackenzie spent his last years has become a prominent Toronto landmark.

24. The shooting of Colonel Robert Moodie, first casualty of the Mackenzie Rebellion. Montgomery's Tavern is seen in background.

25. The execution of Lount and Matthews for their part in the Rebellion.

26. The Queen's Rangers proclaim Victoria's coronation at Fort York.

27. The *Globe* office on King Street West (1854) on site of present Canadian Imperial Bank of Commerce Building.

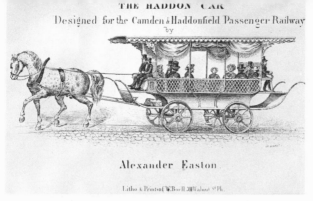

THE HADDON CAR
Designed for the Camden & Haddonfield Passenger Railway
by

Alexander Easton.

Litho & Print of W. Bor H. 3H Walnut St Ph.

28. John Easton's first horse-car line, between Toronto and Yorkville, provided fancy transportation around 1858.

29. Toronto's first Union Station, 1859.

30. The first Crystal Palace, in 1858.

der of the population gives them. My people especially have come forward with great spirit and I am incessantly employed in arranging and providing for them. This terrible dispensation came among us like a thunder bolt and brought with it increased and heart rending duties upon our Clergy. Often I have been in the Cholera Hospital with six and even eight persons expiring around me but blessed be God I felt no apprehension and by my example arrested much of the alarm, which was fast spreading and threatening to destroy the charities of our nature . . ."

During the height of the plague even the prisoners in Toronto's jail received special consideration from the authorities when they submitted a petition for release. The plea, signed by the inmates, read as follows:

> The appearance of the Cholera amongst the Debtors in airy, well ventilated apartments in the prison of the Home District, has caused great alarm amongst the prisoners more closely confined in the cells, and although every precaution has been tried to avoid contagion, yet when persons are closely confined and without the means of preventing a contact with persons of filthy habits, the danger is considered great. Your memorialists the undersigned persons confined under sentence humbly implore Your Excellency to Exercise the Royal Prerogative of remitting the remainder of the respective terms of imprisonment. They trust that Your Excellency's clemency on this occasion will be by them properly appreciated and tend to impress upon their minds the necessity of abstaining from crime in the future.

All of the prisoners, except two under sentence of death, were released. Even this unfortunate pair had reason to be thankful, because as a result of the petition, their sentences were reduced to banishment from the province for seven years.

"Their crime was not very heinous, though sentence of death was necessarily passed," remarked Chief Justice John Beverley Robinson, in his order reducing their sentences.

Although little in the way of organized charity existed in Toronto at the time the cholera epidemic struck, a Society for the Relief of the Orphans, Widows and Fatherless was formed, under the guiding hand of the energetic and public-spirited Dr. Strachan and arrangements were made in many cases to take the destitute women and children into various private homes in and around the city.

Some idea of the dismal fears which gripped the little community in the wake of the cholera epidemic is contained in a grisly editorial which appeared in the *Freeman* the following spring:

> The most dangerous nuisance in York, in our opinion, is the burying ground of the English Church. It is situated, in the first instance, where no cemetery ought to be, in the very centre of the town (Church and

King Streets) and so crowded already, that they had to bury last year the cholera sufferers in a swampy corner where it is revolting to see remains of human beings deposited in mud and dirty water! such low, wet soil, it will crack open in summer to a considerable depth, and who can say but pestilence and death may be exhaled from such chinks?—Besides during the existence of the late malady, bodies were interred at twi-light, sometimes by aid of lanterns, sometimes clandestinely in the dark, and so carelessly that in walking across the cemetery, when the frost left the ground this spring, we saw some of the graves, which had sunk a foot or more in places, and the grounds seemed to open at the sides down to the coffins lid . . . Is it not notorious that the late pestilence raged most in the neighbourhood of the cemetery in question in this town? And who can tell but the opening of one grave in it this summer may spread pestilence and death in York? . . . in the meantime, the cholera-swamp in the north-east corner ought to be covered six inches deep with lime . . .

But, as the long warm days of summer arrived that year without a revisitation of the cholera, the life of the town began to return to normal. The present Toronto Island, which was at that time still a peninsula (it wasn't until 1858 that a severe storm made it an actual island by opening the eastern gap), was starting to become the summer mecca into which it grew in the following years. In the 1830s it could be reached only by rowboat or by traveling overland, crossing the Don, and then following the peninsula out from the mainland. But in 1833 an entrepreneur named Michael O'Connor inserted an advertisement in the *Almanac* announcing some sensational new facilities for island visitors:

"Horse boat to the Island. A boat propelled by four horses runs every day from the Steamboat Wharves to the Starch Factory on the peninsula or island across the Bay—her trips regulated to suit public convenience. Fare to and from the island, 7½d. A hotel has been opened on the island to accommodate sportsmen, parties of pleasure, etc."

The horses walked upon a treadmill which propelled the paddlewheels on either side of the craft and its progress must have been slow. The impressive name of this first island ferry was the *Sir John of the Peninsula*. Mr. O'Connor, it seems, was an old soldier who had in mind the Spanish Peninsular War and General Sir John Moore when he applied this rather grandiose name to his horse boat.

On the lake at the foot of Frederick Street, lay John Cull's Royal Floating Baths, 110 feet long and 21 feet wide, with ten warm and ten cold baths, an 80-foot promenade deck, a drawing room, a reading room and refreshment room. Mr. Cull's establishment did a brisk business because, in those days, few of the town's residences boasted much in the way of bathing facilities.

In October of 1833 a visiting reporter from the *Canadian Courant*, of

Montreal, noted in his newspaper that in the previous year nearly three hundred buildings had been erected in York "and this year four hundred have been built, are building or contracted for within town and suburbs; and a good portion of them are substantial and commodious brick buildings."

The building business was booming and it was perhaps only natural that the skilled workers engaged in it should start putting some extra pressure upon their employers. It seems that the Carpenters and Joiners Society was formed at this time and an editorial supporting this move had been printed in the York *Patriot*. This news was followed by a highly indignant letter to the *Patriot* from a correspondent who signed himself "A Master Builder."

"Observing an article in your paper of June 12 [1833] from a body of the Carpenters and Joiners of this town, who have formed themselves into a Society, under pretense of assisting any of their members who may sustain loss by fire or robbery, or other accidental causes, I beg to inform the public that this body have organized themselves for the sole purpose of supressing their employers; by calling upon them to comply with rules and regulations laid down by the body of Journeymen Carpenters; and to which the latter have all signed their names—sending a copy of same to all their different employers in town; giving notice that after a certain date, they would not go to their work, unless their demands were complied with. The principal of these demands is; that five dollars must be paid them every week on account, and the balance cleared up every month. Ridiculous demands! For under the present system in which money circulates, how is it possible that five dollars per week can be collected every Saturday night for twenty or thirty men, when money is scarce and consequently long credit is expected?

"The Carpenters and Joiners in this town have less reason to complain than any other mechanic in it. Their wages are 6s. 3d. per day; of which they receive from three to five dollars per week, at an average; and a settlement when the employer gets his money, or obtains instalments upon his contracts, when the Journeymen are often paid from $5 to $20 of arrears. But the fact is, that the Journeymen Carpenters of this town, in consequence of being well employed, and better paid this summer than any summer previous, have resolved to become their own masters . . ."

As has been mentioned previously, Muddy York proudly blossomed forth as the City of Toronto in 1834. It was divided into five wards bearing the kind of loyal and God-fearing names which fitted the mood of the day in the new city: St. Andrews, St. David, St. George, St. Patrick and St. Lawrence for Canada. Even the names of some of the community's more important streets reflected the staunch devotion of the townspeople to the

Royal Family and the British connection—King Street, George Street, Duke Street, Duchess Street, and Frederick Street, to mention only a few.

It was around this time that Toronto obtained its first taxicab, a gleaming red and yellow vehicle drawn by one horse. It was called the *City* and held four passengers, who entered it from the rear. The driver sat on the box in front. This first cab business was conducted by Thornton Blackburn, a Negro, who enjoyed a monopoly for only a short time, because it was not long before others got into the remunerative trade.

Some of the new conveyances, though smaller than the *City*, bore much more magnificent names. A gentleman engaging a cab on King Street might be picked up by the *Chief Justice Robinson*, the *Queen* or the *Princess Royal*.

The cabs soon became so numerous that the city fathers had to draw up a lengthy list of regulations governing their operations. Among these was the stipulation that no driver might "wantonly snap or flourish his whip" nor use any "abusive, obscene or impertinent language of any kind whatever" while in charge of his vehicle. During night travel, "unless it be moonlight" each cab was required to have "two well-lighted lamps with glass fronts and sides."

The market was a bustling and exciting place in those days and, because Toronto was still small, most of the characters who moved about the area on market days were well known to the residents. If public punishment was being carried out in the market place upon some unfortunate wrongdoer who had been sentenced to the lash—as often happened—the man who applied it would probably be a large and muscular Negro known to most Torontonians only as Black Joe. When Black Joe was not carrying out these unpleasant duties for the sheriff, he was making a living as a porter and a groom in the livery stables.

Strolling along King Street in the vicinity of the market, you might also encounter two of Toronto's best-known, if not most-gifted poets. Spencer Lydstone could be recognized from afar by his dazzling scarlet vest. He specialized in printed broadsides containing poems dealing mainly with the faults and virtues of various Toronto citizens—much after the manner of the West Indian calypso singer—and it was said that how you were treated in these odes depended largely upon how you responded when Mr. Lydstone approached you for a contribution toward the furtherance of the arts.

The other notorious poet of the day was a man claiming the title of Sir John Smythe, who sometimes got his works published in the local papers. Sir John's great passion, other than poetry, was the promotion of his idea for a railway to the Pacific coast. He even brought out a lithographed map, with a straight line drawn across it from Fort William to the mouth of the Columbia River. His detailed tract on the proposed railway, which he distributed to one and all, was signed "*Sir John Smythe, Baronet and Royal Engineer, Canadian Poet, LL.D., and Moral Philosopher.*"

"The concourse of traffickers and idlers in the open space before the old Market Place were free of tongue," writes Dr. Henry Scadding, in *Toronto of Old*. "They sometimes talked, in no subdued tone, of their fellow-townsfolk of all ranks. In a small community every one was more or less acquainted with every one, with his dealings and appurtenances, with his man-servant and maid-servant, his horse, his dog, his wagon, cart or barrow.

"Those of the primitive residentiaries, to whom the commonalty had taken kindly, were honored in ordinary speech with their militia titles of Colonel, Major, Captain or the civilian prefix of Mister, Honorable Mister, Squire, or Judge, as the case might be; whilst others, not held to have achieved any special claims to deference, were named, even in mature years, by their plain, baptismal names, John, Andrew, Duncan, George and so on.

"And then, there was a third marking-off of a few, against whom, for some vague reason or another, there had grown up in the popular mind a certain degree of prejudice. These, by a curtailment or national corruption of their proper prenomen, would be ordinarily styled Sandy this, Jock that. In some instances the epithet 'old' would irreverently precede, and persons of considerable eminence might be heard spoken of as old Tom so-and-so, old Sam such-a-one."

Although Dr. Scadding may have had a warm and affectionate view of such homely familiarity among the residents, newcomers continued to sniff rather haughtily at what they considered to be Toronto's hick town atmosphere.

"The arguments of friends to induce us to settle in Toronto were drawn more from the absence of rudeness and inconvenience before we were born, or the wonderful future that lay before the city, than from any attractive features the present afforded," wrote Conyngham C. Taylor, who had come over from Dublin. ". . . The young friends with whom we became acquainted, and whose ideas were circumscribed by the visible horizon, would not admit of the superiority of any other place in any respect. If you spoke of London, Dublin, or New York as great places, you were immediately met with the question 'Was not Toronto also a city?' And the statement that she had one street forty miles long extinguished all your arguments and left them masters of the situation."

(This "longest street" boast, incidentally, is still proudly used upon visitors when Torontonians are describing the glories of Yonge Street, although they now add a few more hundred miles of Highway 11 to the claim when they want to really impress a stranger.)

Mr. Taylor was somewhat bored with the quality of the conversation he encountered in Toronto:

"The extent to which regard for local boundaries, customs, and everyday chit chat is sometimes carried, can only be realized in a small town," he complained. "At home, in this nook, all life is lived under minute inspection of neighbours, and perhaps the unavoidable supervision of parson or squire.

"The fierce light that beats upon the throne is not clearer than that which exhibits the young man 'sowing his wild oats.' He sins under a microscope, and the professional gossip finds rich material for the next social or tea-party by placing him under the instrument for the general entertainment of the company, and so the engagement of lovers is discussed as earnestly as if each person were personally or directly interested in the result of every matrimonial arrangement . . . Every birth, marriage and death furnished material for discussion in every family circle, and very much as it is on board ship, out at sea, the most trivial matters were invested with exaggerated importance . . ."

At the corner of Market Lane stood Frank's Hotel, the ballroom of which often served as a theater for the companies of actors who arrived in Toronto from time to time. Music for these productions was usually provided by a Mr. Maxwell, a small man who wore an eyepatch as he ground out appropriate melodies on his violin. In the improvised theater of Frank's Hotel were presented such exciting dramas as *Barbarossa or the Siege of Algiers*, *Ali Baba and the Forty Thieves*, *The Lady of the Lake*, and *The Miller and His Men*.

By 1834 a full-time theater had been established on King Street in a converted chapel located on the site where the head office of the Canadian Imperial Bank of Commerce now stands. It was called the Theatre Royal and though it was well patronized, some of its offerings were harshly panned by the critics. The editor of the *British Colonist* was particularly rough on one show put on by "a party of strolling players from Yankee-land." He reported that "the performance commenced with what was styled in the bills 'The much-admired farce of *Nature and Philosophy*.' . . . Both the farce and the actors of it are altogether too contemptible for criticism . . ."

After a Scottish song had been "brutally murdered" by a Mrs. Lennox, wrote the reviewer, there followed "an attempt to act the opera of *The Maid of Cashmere*, and it was but an attempt. Miss Ince danced tolerably well, and that is all that can be said in favour of the performance. By this time our patience was quite exhausted; we left, and immediately set to write this notice, lest by delay we might so far forget what we had witnessed as to do injustice afterwards to any of the company by detracting from their just merits as players . . . There is no reason why such a miserable catchpenny as that at present in operation should be tolerated. The municipal authorities should interfere and abate the nuisance."

For those whose tastes in entertainment were less critical than those of the editor of the *Colonist*, the October 13, 1835, issue of *The Courier of Upper Canada* had an interesting theatrical notice:

"The extraordinary Exhibition of the Industrious Fleas from England has just arrived in this city and will be open for exhibition at the Steamboat Hotel on Thursday next . . ."

The proprietor of this hostelry must surely have been an extremely courageous patron of the arts to run the risk of leaving in the minds of his customers the lurking suspicion that some of the performers in this exhibition might linger on as permanent guests in his establishment.

But the shows which invariably drew the largest crowds in those days were the public hangings. A great deal of preparation was made for these ceremonies, the gallows being attractively painted and decorated for the occasion. For the purpose of improving their minds, the school children were excused from classes to allow them to attend these events.

During one of these spectacles, when two men were being hanged at the same time, it was reported that 10,000 persons from Toronto and points out of town gathered to witness it.

Perhaps the most famous of these early executions were those of Samuel Lount and Peter Matthews, the two Mackenzie lieutenants who were captured during the rebellion. An eyewitness account of this event was written by Charles Durand, who was an inmate of the jail at the time.

"The hours of April 12, 1838, were the saddest we ever spent," he wrote. "None of us could sleep and we were all early astir. It was a fine spring morning. Looking through the window of our room we saw the scaffold. It was built by the late Mr. Storm. His foreman was Matthew Sheard, then a fine young Yorkshireman, afterwards Mayor of the city. He was expected to share in the work of building the scaffold. 'I'll not put a hand to it,' said he. 'Lount and Matthews have done nothing that I might not have done myself, and I'll never help to build a gallows to hang them.'

"So, without the foreman's assistance, the gallows was erected near the spot where the police court building now stands. Around the gallows the Orange militia stood in large numbers with their muskets. The authorities dreaded a rescue. While we were watching and talking we heard steps on the stairs and then the clank of chains. It was poor Lount coming up, guarded by his jailors, to say good-bye to us. He stopped at the door. We could not see him, but there were sad hearts in that room as we heard Samuel Lount's voice, without a quiver in it, give us his last greeting: 'Be of good courage, boys, I'm not ashamed of anything I've done. I trust in God and I'm going to die like a man.' We answered him as well as we could, and sorrowfully listened until the sound of his sturdy tramp and clanking chains died away.

"I don't know why Peter Matthews didn't come up with Lount, but I saw him as they were led through the Jail yard to the scaffold where two nooses were swinging. They never faltered. I saw them walk up the steps to the floor of the scaffold as firmly as if they were on the pavement. Again Bishop Richardson, who attended Lount, and another clergyman who attended Matthews, prayed. Deputy Sheriff Robert Beard officiated. Lount and Matthews shook hands with the clergymen, and when we looked again they were both dangling in the air. Matthews struggled hard but Lount died instantly. When the bodies had been exposed for a short time they were cut down and quietly buried in Potter's Field, near where the Yorkville Avenue fire hall now stands."

In 1843 two admirers of the rebels removed their bodies from Potter's Field (a non-denominational cemetery situated near what is now the northwest corner of Bloor and Yonge) and transferred them to the Necropolis, where they were reburied under a marble slab bearing the simple inscription: *"Samuel Lount, Peter Matthews, 1838."* Later on a granite column was erected to mark the spot.

On December 28, 1841, King Street and a few of the other downtown thoroughfares took on a new luster as the first gas lights were turned on. The initial illumination of this kind was provided by a hundred lamps of only about ten candlepower each, but it was considered to be a dazzling display by the residents who came down on that crisp winter evening to marvel at the new glory of the city.

Gas was still expensive, and was out of reach of most of Toronto's homeowners, who still used tallow candles. It was the custom to celebrate such occasions as Royal marriages and births (which were learned of only many weeks or even months after the events) with special "illuminations" which were achieved by placing candles in the windows of the residences and other buildings of the little city.

Charles Dickens was greatly impressed by the new street lighting and other features of Toronto when he visited it in 1842. He wrote:

"The country around this town being very flat is bare of scenic interest, but the town itself is full of life and motion, bustle, business and improvement. The streets are well-paved and lighted with gas; the houses are large and good; the shops excellent. Many of them have a display of goods in their windows such as may be seen in thriving country towns of England,

and there are some which would do no discredit to the metropolis itself. There is a good stone prison here; and there are, besides, a handsome church, a court house, public offices, many commodious private residences, and a Government Observatory for noting and recording the magnetic variations. In the College of Upper Canada, which is one of the public establishments of the city, a sound education in every department of polite learning can be had at very moderate expense, the annual charge for the instruction of each pupil not exceeding nine pounds sterling."

During Mr. Dickens' visit, he stayed in what was then one of the finest hostelries in town. The American House was situated at the corner of Yonge and Front Streets. Although it may not have been expanded to its full glory at the time of Mr. Dickens' visit, it did, during its most flourishing days, boast 90 rooms and a dining room 60 by 30 feet in which two hundred persons could be seated. Board was $2 a day.

The Ontario House was another prominent inn that stood on the northwest corner of Wellington and Church Streets and was enjoying its heyday before the American House was built. It was proud of its facilities and in the 1830s its proprietor advertised in the *Patriot* that "the parlours are spacious and elegantly furnished with bedrooms attached, airy and pleasant. The beds are large and double, well suited for summer and winter, and it may not be amiss to state that they are warranted free from vermin or insects of any kind and will be kept so . . . A splendid pianaforte with a choice selection of music for the use of ladies and gentlemen . . . For the accomodation of the country gentry wishing to dine before leaving town the dinner hour through the summer season will be at 2 pm."

It is recorded that in 1836, when Toronto had a population of only 9652, there were 79 inns and taverns of various kinds in and around the city.

The English writer Captain Frederick Marryat, after a visit to Toronto, compared it to similar communities in the United States. Writing in his *Diary in America 1839*, he said: ". . . you are at once struck with the difference between the English and the American population, system and ideas. On the other side of the lake, you have much more apparent property, but much less real solidarity and security. The houses and stores of Toronto are not to be compared with those of the American towns opposite. But the Englishman has built according to his means—the American according to his expectations.

"The hotels and inns of Toronto are very bad; at Buffalo they are splendid; for the Englishman travels little; the American is ever on the move. The private houses of Toronto are built, according to the English taste and desire of exclusiveness, away from the road and are embowered in trees; the American, let his house be ever so large, or his plot of ground however extensive, builds within a few feet of the road that he may see and know what is going on. You do not perceive the bustle, the energy and activity at Toronto that you do at Buffalo, nor the profusion of articles in stores . . . If an American has money sufficient to build a two-storey house he will raise it up to four storeys on speculation . . . whilst at Toronto they proceed more carefully."

It was around this time that the Orange Lodge, destined to exert a great influence upon Toronto's affairs and, indeed upon the very character of the city itself, was becoming more powerful. Many of its original members were Northern Irishmen who had come to the country with British regiments on garrison duty. They were rabidly anti-Catholic and staunchly loyal to the Crown. Displayed upon their banners was the heroically mounted figure of King William of Orange, victor of the Battle of the Boyne, in which the soldiers of Northern Ireland triumphed in the cause of Protestantism. For years they paraded every July 12 in huge numbers. Although these "Orange walks" are still held on what is still called "the Glorious Twelfth," both the parades and the Orange influence in Toronto have greatly waned in recent years.

"For nearly a century the Orange Lodge has been so strong in Toronto," wrote historian Edwin C. Guillet, in 1934, "that the greater part of almost every city Council have been those appearing on the Orange slate; in fact, with the exception of but a few each year, the aldermen have commonly been members of the order."

In an election of 1841 the Orangemen figured in one of the most violent disorders of an era in which such events were often quite hectic as passions ran high between the supporters of the various candidates. The secret ballot had not yet been introduced and a man who let it be known he was voting for a candidate who did not have Orange support might find himself confronted by toughs armed with clubs.

On this election day, J. H. Dunn and Isaac Buchanan, who were members of the Reform party, defeated in a close contest Henry Sherwood and J. Munro, who were Tories and had the enthusiastic support of the city's Orangemen.

The events of the celebration which followed this victory are described by historian J. E. Middleton: "At 1 o'clock in the afternoon the successful candidates, escorted by so many citizens that the parade was over a mile long, set out from the Ontario House on the Market Square, proceeded by way of Market Street to Yonge, along King Street to Simcoe, up Simcoe to Lot (now Queen Street) eastward to Yonge, then south to King and east past the City Hall and the market. All along the route there were indications that supporters of the other party meditated some measure of violence. Too many bully-boys with knobby sticks were on the streets, and particularly in the grounds of St. James Church. Mayor Munro was warned that police protection might be necessary, but he is reported to have said they might go to the Devil for protection. Since His Worship was one of the defeated candidates, his testimony might be understood.

"East of the market, on King Street, stood the North of Ireland Coleraine Inn, where an Orange flag was displayed. The Reform hangers-on had a menacing attitude. They drummed on the doors and on the outside of the building with their sticks, and a woman threw a stone of protest against the Orange order. The persons in the house appeared at the upper windows, and one of them fired a pistol at the crowd. A man named James Dunn, of course an innocent bystander, recently arrived from overseas as an immigrant, fell dead. Several other shots followed. Four or five other persons were wounded . . .

"The mob would have torn the house to pieces if it had not been for the appeals of Dunn and Buchanan, the Members, but while their angry followers halted between two opinions a company of British Regulars came upon the double, pressed back the mob, and brought seven or eight persons out of the house, conveying them safely to the jail. These seven or eight were said by the *Examiner* to be 'as bloodthirsty-looking men as ever disgraced human form.'

"Neither party had a monopoly of hard words and extreme statements, for the atmosphere was electrical. It was said by Francis Hincks [the Inspector General] that during the polling in the two provinces, from ten to twenty persons had been murdered and hundreds had been beaten and mauled. In Toronto during the week about fifty followers of Dunn and Buchanan had their heads laid open. The *Examiner* considerately neglected to mention how many Tories received similar treatment."

In the 1840s, $500 a year was considered to be an extremely good salary. Bricklayers were paid $1 to $1.25 a day and carpenters at about the same rate. Ordinary laborers were paid only about 75¢ a day. But in those times such modest incomes had considerable buying power. A fairly good house could be rented for from $100 to $125 a year. Some other typical prices of the period were as follows: Beef 5¢ to 7¢ a pound; butter 10¢ a pound; eggs 10¢ a dozen; apples $1 to $1.50 a barrel; chickens 25¢ a pair and turkeys 50¢ each; wood $2.25 to $2.50 a cord; and whiskey 25¢ a gallon!

On St. George's Day in 1842 the Governor General, Sir Charles Bagot, laid the cornerstone of King's College, Toronto's first institution of higher learning. The college was situated close to the present site of the Legislative Buildings in Queen's Park and from it would grow the great University of Toronto. It was a proud day of pageantry which included a vast parade, said to be a mile long, which formed on the grounds of Upper Canada College on Front Street and marched up Graves (now Simcoe)

Street and along Lot (now Queen) Street to University Avenue. In the
procession were not only the academics in their solemn robes but also representatives of many other sections of the city's life, such as municipal and
provincial officials, members of the military and even of the Fire Department.

Although numerous newspapers came and went during the early days
of York and Toronto, there was still work for a town crier or bell-ringer,
whose principal job was to go about the streets shouting out descriptions
of lost children or animals. The newspapers of the day were often extremely casual in their approach to their coverage of events which are now
treated with great urgency. A newspaper called the *Examiner,* for instance,
ran an item which read as follows: "Word came to the city that a murder
was committed in Weston one day last week. No further information has
been received." Much more prominence was given in the same issue to a
lengthy letter attacking the principle of the church Establishment. Even
so, the news coverage offered by the papers of the 1840s was still a great
improvement over that contained in such earlier publications as the *Upper
Canada Gazette,* York's first newspaper, which had announced the great
news of Nelson's victory at the Battle of the Nile *five months* after it had
happened.

In 1844 a young Scot named George Brown founded a weekly newspaper called the *Globe* which was to show a great deal of enterprise.
When it increased the frequency of its publication to three times a week,
it helped attract new readers by carrying out the then spectacular circulation stunt of running a serialization of Charles Dickens' latest novel,
Dombey and Son. But in many other respects, the *Globe* was an extremely
sedate journal. It carried no advertising for theatrical performances, and
horse races and other sporting events were ignored in its news pages. A
measure of the *Globe*'s respect for the Sabbath was provided by the fact
that, when it became a daily in 1853, it ceased all typesetting activities
promptly at midnight Saturday and resumed them at 12:01 the following
Monday morning. George Brown and his God-fearing publication were
destined to become powerful voices in Canada.

On December 19, 1846, a marvelous new means of communication was
officially inaugurated in Toronto when the first commercial telegram ever
to be transmitted in Canada was sent from the City Hall on Front Street
(the building which is now incorporated into the southern section of the
St. Lawrence Market). With various city dignitaries gathered to observe
the event, Mayor W. H. Boulton sent greetings to the mayors of Hamilton, St. Catherines and Niagara-on-the-Lake over the recently completed
89 miles of telegraph line erected by the Toronto, Hamilton, Niagara and
St. Catherines Electro-Magnetic Telegraph Company.

By 1847 the population of Toronto had grown to 21,050. Its post office, in a small building on Wellington Street, was operated by Postmaster Charles Berczy and three assistants. One lone letter carrier named John McCloskey delivered mail to customers who chose to indulge in this luxury, at a charge of one "copper" for each piece. The rest of the populace picked up its mail from boxes at the post office or from the general delivery wicket. There were no postage stamps, at this time. Charges on paid letters were simply marked on the envelope in red and those upon which postage had to be collected had the charges marked in black. Mail from England arrived once a fortnight and usually brought a stampede to the post office.

Although postal service was fairly regular, it was extremely slow and very expensive. Torontonians who now pay 12 cents for a postage stamp and fret if their jet-propelled letters don't arrive in Vancouver on the very next day, might consider some of the postal rates which applied during the 1840s: Halifax mail, 2s. 9d.; Quebec, 1s. 6d.; Montreal, 1s. 2d.; Kingston, 9d.; Windsor, 10½d.

King Street, for many years Toronto's main thoroughfare, had by this time become more than two miles long and a goodly section of it boasted not only board sidewalks, but also a macadamized roadway. A writer of that day marveled at the improvement:

"Few who now stroll down the well-boarded sidewalks of King Street reflect upon the inconvenience attending this recreaction to their sires and grandsires and granddames, who were compelled to tuck up their garments and pick their way from tuft to tuft and from stone to stone," said he. "It was no unusual sight to behold the heavy lumber waggon sticking fast in the mud, up to the axle, in the very middle of King Street . . . The partygoing portion of the citizens were content either to trudge it, or be taken in a car drawn by two sturdy oxen. The fashionable cry then was 'Mr. McTavish's cart is here.' and the 'gee up' resounded as clearly among the pines as the glib 'all right' of the modern footman along the gas-lit street."

During King Street's more muddy period, there was a standard joke making the rounds which was often dragged out to taunt a visiting Torontonian whenever he traveled to another town or city. According to this humiliating Toronto legend, a gentleman walking down King Street saw an interesting-looking hat lying in the roadway. When he stopped to pick it up, he discovered beneath it the head of its owner, who was almost submerged in the mud. The deeply mired citizen called desperately for help, not only for himself, but for his horse, stuck in the mud beneath him!

In 1847 Toronto had its first strike. Like some of the labor disputes of today, it was brought on by the introduction of automation and, in this case, the workers won their point after a brief battle. A tailoring firm named Walker & Hutchinson had just acquired Toronto's first sewing machine. The employees, citing the fact that the good old, hand-wielded needle had been in use since sewing began, promptly walked off the job. Fortunately for the cause of the workers, their employers found, after a few days, that the newfangled sewing contrivance was more bother than it was worth and not only called back its tailors, but handed the balky machine over to them to do with what they liked. The triumphant workmen hauled it along King Street in the center of a victory parade, after which it was shipped back to its manufacturers in New York. So happy were Mr. Walker and Mr. Hutchinson at the end of the dispute and the good riddance of their bothersome sewing machine that on the evening following the parade they held a banquet for their workers to celebrate the return to their establishment of blessed serenity.

Chapter 14

1849–1857

TRIAL BY FIRE

Destruction of St. James's. Death at the Patriot office. The rebuilding of the city. St. Lawrence Hall. The new Normal School. Railway to the North. P. T. Barnum shows Toronto his circus. Grand Trunk Railway opens between Toronto and Montreal. Toronto's first V.C. The flood of booze. Building of Osgoode Hall.

Shortly after 1:30 on the morning of Saturday, April 7, 1849, the door of St. James's Cathedral was hastily unlocked by a man who rushed up the steps after obtaining the key to the church at the police station in the nearby West Market Place, where it was kept for emergencies. Once inside the building, he hastily seized the ropes hanging from the belfry and proceeded to toll the bells in the wild and urgent clanging which heralded the outbreak of fire in Toronto. St. James's was still the official point for the ringing of such alarms and upon hearing them, the good citizens were supposed to take up their chorus with shouts of "fire!" to alert as many as possible of their fellow townsmen.

In the center of the block bounded by Duke, George, King, and Nelson (now Jarvis) Streets, in some stables at the rear of Post's and Covey's taverns, a fire, believed to have been started either by an overturned lantern or a careless smoker, was licking through the straw and dry pine boards of the rickety outbuildings. This blaze, located in the middle of one of the most heavily built-up sections of the city, was to be the kindling fire for the great Toronto conflagration of 1849, the biggest disaster of its kind to hit the community since the Americans put the torch to York's public buildings in the invasion of 1813.

While the fire rapidly spread, there galloped to the scene the horses drawing Toronto's rather meager collection of fire-fighting equipment, which included four engines and two hook-and-ladder companies, all manned by volunteers. From other directions came the water-carters, who sped to the blaze as soon as they could harness their horses, because the first four to arrive at a fire were given bonuses of four, three, two, and one dollar each and many of them, at the end of the day, kept their carts full of water at home in case they should get an emergency call during the night.

There was a small system of hydrants in the town at this time, but their water pressure was woefully feeble and had often been criticized by Toronto's hard-pressed volunteer firemen. This system was owned by the Toronto Gas & Water Company and it was not unusual for Albert Furness, one of its proprietors, to turn up at the height of a fire and announce testily to the citizens that they were getting all the hydrant service the city was willing to pay for. He seemed dissatisfied with an arrangement with the city under which his firm received $250 a year for the use of his hydrants or fire plugs as they were sometimes called.

Of the pumpers which sped to the fire, three were of the "goose neck" type, a name gained from the fact that the hose was attached to a pipe which rose about three feet above the deck of the engine and was curved like a goose's neck. These engines were not very powerful. Each had a water tank attached to its rear and its pump was operated by seven or eight men working bars on each side of the engine. All citizens between the ages of sixteen and sixty were subject to call for the job of working the pumping bars or handling other chores if they were ordered to do so by those in charge of the fire-fighting. Section X of the Fire Act clearly stated: "The Mayor and Alderman of the city, who are recognized as bearing a wand with a gilded flame at the top, have the authority to command the assistance of others at such fires. Persons refusing liable to be sent to jail." The volunteer firemen often complained bitterly, however, that most of the citizenry was content to just stand there and gawk rather than help in the dirty job of fighting fire.

The fourth of the engines which responded to the early morning alarm was the British America, a fairly powerful machine which required twelve to fifteen men on each pumping bar. It had been presented to the city in 1837 by the insurance company whose name it bore, a practice that was not uncommon among such firms at that period, some of which were plunged into bankruptcy when a particularly large fire swept through a community.

Rapidly engulfing the center of the block, the fire began to burn in all directions. At this point there was not much wind, but as the great blaze began to spread it created a minor gale of its own, carrying sparks and blazing brands across the rooftops of the city. Proof that the fire did indeed furnish its own treacherous wind was the fact that, while the official

Weather Office in the university grounds recorded for that night only a mild northeast breeze of six to nine miles an hour, embers from the fire downtown were found by the editor of the *Christian Guardian* in his yard a half mile away and Bishop Strachan reported that some of them were carried two miles.

The fire quickly spread north up to Duke Street, destroying some dwellings on the south side, and on the east the fire enveloped the Bank of the Home District on George Street and other buildings. Burning south through Covey's Tavern to King Street, the fire rapidly spread both east and west along that thoroughfare.

At the southwest corner of what is now Jarvis and Duke Streets, Richard Watson, who had been the publisher of the recently discontinued *Upper Canada Gazette*, joined some others in an attempt to rescue some type from the top floor of the *Patriot* office. As the building began to fill with smoke and flame, Watson tried to make his way down the stairs but his companions were rescued through a window against which the ladder was placed a few moments after Watson had left. In the confusion he wasn't missed, but when he failed to return to his home a search of the ruins of the *Patriot* building later that morning disclosed his body.

By three o'clock in the morning most of the large stores along King Street, from Francis to George Streets, were ablaze. An hour later troops from the garrison were fighting side by side with the volunteer firemen but there was little mere men could do to halt the roaring march of flames. At the height of the great fire, six blocks in the heart of the city were burning furiously, and it was later reported that the flames could be seen across the lake at St. Catharines.

One of the most important landmarks to fall was St. James's Cathedral itself, the bell of which had signaled the beginning of the disaster. What is considered to be the best eyewitness report of the burning of the historic edifice that stood on the site of Toronto's first church was provided by Dr. Henry Scadding:

"The energies of the local fire brigade of the day had never been so taxed as they were on that memorable occasion," he wrote. "Aid from steam-power was then undreamt-of. Simultaneous outbursts of flame from numerous widely-separated spots had utterly disheartened everyone, and had caused a general abandonment of effort to quell the conflagration. Then it was that the open space about St. James's Church saved much of the town from destruction.

"To the west the whole sky was, as it were, a vast canopy of meteors streaming from the east. The church itself was consumed, but the flames advanced no further. A burning shingle was seen to become entangled in the luffer-boards of the belfry, and slowly to ignite the woodwork there:

from a very minute start at that point, a stream of fire soon began to rise —soon began to twine itself about the upper stages of the tower, and to climb nimbly up the steep slope of the spire, from the summit of which it then shot aloft into the air, speedily enveloping and overtoppling the golden cross that was there.

"At the same time the flames made their way downwards within the tower, till the internal timbers of the roofing over the main body of the building were reached. There, in the natural order of things, the fire readily spread; and the whole interior of the church in the course of an hour, was transformed, before the eyes of a bewildered multitude looking powerlessly on, first into a vast 'burning fiery furnace,' and then, as the roof collapsed and fell, into a confused chaos of raging flame.

"The heavily gilt cross at the apex of the spire came down with a crash and planted itself on the pavement of the principal entrance, below, where the steps, as well as the inner walls of the base of the tower, were bespattered far and wide with the molten metal of the great bell.

"While the work of destruction was going fiercely and irrepressibly on, the Public Clock in the belfry, Mr. Draper's gift to the town, was heard to strike the hour as usual, and the quarters thrice, exercising its functions and having its appointed say amidst the sympathies, not loud but deep, of those who watched its doom; bearing its testimony, like a martyr at the stake, in calm and unimpassioned strain, up to the very moment when the deadly element touched its vitals."

There were other eyewitnesses who complained after the great fire that St. James's could have been saved had a little more presence of mind been shown by the onlookers.

"One of the cakes of fire, with which the air was loaded for a great distance, fell into the wooden window of the spire of the cathedral," wrote a reporter in the *Examiner*. "It was a long time before it burst into flame. Spectators indulged in speculations as to whether sparks would ignite the wood, some expressing one opinion and some another; while if they had acted instead of idly speculating and talking, the cathedral might have been saved. At length the spark burst into flame and it was not long before some persons were inside wasting pails of water of the flames which a single pail would have prevented when the fire was confined to a mere spark."

At any rate there was enough time to rescue virtually everything which could be moved from the cathedral, including the library, the organ, and the hymn books in the pews.

When the fire was over, about fifteen acres of the main business district of the city had been laid waste. Yet, times were good in this period and before the end of the year a great part of this section had been rebuilt.

Among the buildings destroyed was the market and the new structure on this site included the St. Lawrence Hall, which was for years to be one of the main social and entertainment centers of the city and which still stands on King Street today.

During the twenty years which followed its completion many memorable events took place in the St. Lawrence Hall. It was capable of holding a thousand people and from its walls echoed the oratory of Sir John A. Macdonald and George Brown and Horace Greeley as well as the lilting voices of Jenny Lind, the Swedish Nightingale, and Adelina Patti, the great coloratura soprano, not to mention the more deep-throated strains of the first Toronto performance of the *Messiah* in 1857. The historic auditorium, which was for many years allowed to grow dilapidated and served for a time in recent years as a flophouse for the members of Toronto's Skid Row, has been handsomely refurbished and returned to some of its former glory as part of the city's Centennial project. The building's ancient and mellow beauty, with its façade based on a temple of Jupiter Stator and its circular bell cupola with Corinthian columns, complements the streamlined and ultramodern St. Lawrence Center for the Arts.

The rebuilding of St. James's Cathedral, the fourth (and present) church to stand on this site, was not completed until 1875, largely because of delays in raising the necessary funds and disputes concerning what form the new building should take. In the meantime, members of its congregation worshiped in other churches.

Many other fine new buildings, both residential and commercial, sprung up in the city in the wake of the great fire. Even a visitor from Montreal, Toronto's traditional rival, couldn't help being impressed by the city's widespread building boom.

"Upon King Street," wrote a correspondent of the Montreal *Herald*, "we noticed the builders at work in five or six places, besides observing several new and handsome brick houses, where a year ago wooden ones stood. Our readers who are acquainted with Toronto will remember the corner of Bay and King Streets, which used to be disfigured by some wooden shanties; these have been completely swept away, to make room for elegant brick houses."

By 1852 the population of Toronto had grown to 30,763. There was a great spirit of optimism in the new community which was arising from the ruins of the fire. A Mr. Robertson advised the populace in an advertisement that he was ready to offer, in his premises at 64 King Street West, an introduction to "the highly admired new dances, the Esmeralda Gallopade and the Zinquarella Mazurka."

The tracks were being laid for the Ontario, Simcoe & Huron Union Railroad from Toronto to Bradford, bringing new importance and usefulness to the general route of the ancient Toronto Carrying-Place. From the footpath of the Indians along the Humber had grown Yonge Street, a few miles east, and now it was becoming a trail for the newfangled iron horse.

A deft but guarded salute to the modern trends was given by that aristocratic pillar of the Family Compact, Chief Justice John Beverley Robinson, when he spoke at the opening ceremonies of the new Normal School.

"It would be wise to reject the use of railways because an occasional train runs off the track," said he, "as to hesitate to give education to the multitude for fear it might in some instances, as no doubt it will, be perverted to bad purposes."

The first sod of the Ontario, Simcoe & Huron Union Railroad was turned on October 15, 1851, by Lady Elgin, wife of the Governor General. It must have been a great day for F. C. Capreol, who had managed to raise the money for the railway in England after the project had been the subject of a great deal of ridicule in Toronto.

"No longer laughed at and spoken of as 'Mad Capreol,' as the writer has often heard him called, he had shown great method in his madness," remarked C. C. Taylor in his book *Toronto Called Back*. By the time the rails had extended for only about fifteen miles northward the officials of the company were anxious to try out their new locomotive, the *Lady Elgin*, and a great crowd turned out at a spot on the waterfront near the Queen's Wharf to witness the tests as the engine snorted back and forth along the tracks on trial runs, with the sparks flying from her big smokestack. It was not long after this that the first locomotive to be built in Upper Canada was completed at the Toronto Locomotive Works. It was proudly named the *Toronto*.

"The *Toronto* is certainly no beauty," admitted the *Canadian Journal* when it ran a lithograph of the locomotive after its completion in 1853, "nor is she distinguished for any peculiarity in construction, but she affords a very striking illustration of our progress in the mechanical arts, and of the growing wants of the country."

Down at a place called the Fair Green, near the Don, traveling circuses and other shows were coming to town. The greatest of them all, of course, was P. T. Barnum's Grand Colossal Museum and Menagerie, which offered, among its numerous attractions, "A team of 10 Elephants" drawing "a Great Car or Juggernaut" and a "Baby Elephant" which "will carry upon his back, around the interior of the immense Pavilion, the Lilliputian General Tom Thumb."

Toronto had come a long way since Ely Playter and his friends had paid a shilling admission to see the "Saigou Brown" orangutan at Hinds Hotel.

By 1855 the loyal city of Toronto was following anxiously the course of the Crimean War and on October 5 of that year a public holiday was declared to celebrate the fall of Sebastopol. The Yonge Street music firm of A & S Nordheimer advertised some of the latest popular sheet music: "Mother, Is the Battle Over?," "The Ratcatcher's Daughter," "Sebastopol Is Ours," "Sebastopol Is Won," and "Barnum's Baby Show Polka."

It was in this same year that the Rossin House (later to become the Prince George Hotel) was opened with great fanfare at the corner of York and King Streets and was proudly heralded as the best-appointed hotel west of New York City.

In the *Colonist* there appeared a small item that signaled the end of the candlelit era in Toronto households and other homes of the continent which were not already illuminated by the more expensive gas:

"A new light produced from an oily liquid extracted from bituminous coal or native bitumen, rock oil or naphtha, has been tested lately in New York and is said to afford a light exceeding the best gas in brilliancy and whiteness. It is called kerosene and is very cheap in its manufacture."

An 1856 census disclosed that Toronto had reached a population of 41,760 persons and that its number of dwellings had risen to 6205. The national origins of its people at this time were listed as "natural born, 12,554; Irish, 14,015; English, 6855; and Scots, 3085." No mention was made of residents of other descents.

It was in this same year of rapid growth and high hopes in Toronto that the Grand Trunk Railway was completed between the city and Montreal and, on the opening run, a train composed of ten cars of Toronto guests was hauled by two engines on a gay journey that took fifteen hours to complete. The *Toronto Globe* remarked darkly about the $485 expense account of the city's official delegates in the party, suggesting that the taxpayers' money had been spent "mostly on oysters and champagne."

In the autumn of 1856 a great ball was held in the St. Lawrence Hall to welcome home a native son of Toronto who had been one of the few survivors of the historic charge of the Light Brigade at Balaklava, two years earlier. Lieutenant Alexander R. Dunn V.C., a dashing young giant who stood six-feet-three-inches tall, was the son of Honorable James Dunn, Receiver General of Upper Canada. When, after the famed charge, the Victoria Cross was placed at the disposal of the 11th Hussars, they unanimously awarded it to Lieutenant Dunn, so shining was his record of heroism during the feat of the "noble six hundred." Balaklava Dunn, as he later came to be known in his native city, was killed in a hunting accident in far-off Abyssinia eight years later while accompanying General Sir Robert Napier in a campaign against King Theodore of Abyssinia.

But all was not light and progress and glory during this seemingly upbeat phase of Toronto's history. For one thing, the city was looking as though it might become engulfed by the tidal wave of alcohol which was pouring from its hundreds of drinking places and whiskey stores. In 1857, 4996 persons, including 1025 women, were arrested on various charges connected with drinking or the selling of booze. This figure amounted to about one-ninth of Toronto's entire population.

The city had developed its slums and they were miserable ones. A writer of this period described them as follows:

"You enter a house from the front door and find yourself in a room twelve by fourteen feet, in which are huddled together, as if they are frightened to look at their fellow-creatures, a man, five women, three boys and a couple of young specimens of the *genus homo* in arms. The stove is almost reddened with heat, the room is fumigated with the fumes of the mid-day meal which is in the course of preparation, the walls are so black that one would think sable was their original color, and, on the back door being opened to admit one to the yard, the stench of the pig-pen within three feet of the back door is so foul that you could cut it with a knife. In another yard we have a pig-pen four feet six inches square, with a floor a couple of feet thick with offal, filth, dung and manure, and no less than five pigs lying snorting and snoring within it.

"Going further down the same street the visitor sees in every yard and closet the same accumulations. Near Nelson Street, on the south side of Stanley Street, we have a house the rear room of which is occupied by a brigade of pigs. The next room, (with a doorway between the two), a few feet from this nest of filth, the residents of the house use as a cooking, eating and sleeping room. Just fancy the sickening odor of a pig-pen curling through the cracks of the door and winding around the kitchen stove and dinner table!"

Another contemporary writer mentions the "sink of death and disease" at a place called Bethune's Lane or Fish Alley, near the corner of George and Duchess Streets:

". . . in a former year, during the heavy rage of cholera, every resident was affected and the dead-cart a daily visitant. This lane contains nine apologies for houses and is inhabited by about fifty souls. There are no back yards to these miserable hovels, and slops, filth and dirt are thrown out in front of the doors. At one end of the lane the necessary is in fearful state, and it is credibly believed that a well, situated a short distance from it, received the sewage, and that it was to residents drinking this water in 1854 the severe attack of cholera in that quarter was attributed."

Yet, in other parts of the city, Toronto was taking on certain prospects of grandeur. Numerous church steeples towered above the skyline. The third and present version of Osgoode Hall had been completed on Queen

Street, surrounded by its ornate iron fence with special gates to keep out the cattle. The fine City Hall stood on the present site of the south St. Lawrence Market, where it has now been incorporated into the building.

But perhaps the most impressive building of all in this Toronto of the late 1850s was the Mental Asylum which still stands at 999 Queen Street West. It looks huge enough now, but in those days, even before its additions, it must have seemed an overpoweringly mammoth building when viewed from Queen Street or even from the more distant vantage point of Lake Ontario as the traveler sailed by on his way to Toronto's busy harbor in the Bay.

Chapter 15

1858–1885

AN ERA OF PROGRESS

The "Island" finally breaks away from the mainland. The first Crystal Palace. The first Queen's Plate horse race. The first visit of Royalty. Horse-drawn cars come to Yonge Street. The big snow battle between the merchants and the street railway. Celebration of Confederation. The glory of King Street. Timothy Eaton opens a store. Robert Simpson starts business across the road two years later. John Howard gives the city High Park. Toronto acquires a full-time fire-fighting force. Ned Hanlan brings fame to his town. Toronto introduces May 24 holiday. Canadian National Exhibition is born. Sandford Fleming describes his standard time proposal. Hart Massey starts an agricultural implement plant. Electric lights are demonstrated at the CNE. An electric railway is unveiled at the "Ex."

In April of 1858 the winds howled and the Lake Ontario breakers crashed and battered with unusual fury against the peninsula which had for so long protected Toronto's bay from the often heavy seas of the open waters. When the storm had subsided the narrow sandbar which formed the most tenuous link with the mainland had disappeared, along with the nearby Quinn's Hotel, which had been a popular watering (and wining) place for Torontonians. Unruly nature had formed the Eastern Gap, and the five-mile arm of land which had for years been erroneously called the Island now actually became one. A year later the steamship *Bowmanville* sailed through this new entrance to Toronto Harbor and other large vessels soon followed this route when it was more convenient to do so.

The lake steamers, which were rapidly replacing the sailing vessels, were plying a brisk trade in and out of Toronto's harbor. Moonlight excursions were all the rage and often had a lively climax when Orangemen came

*The first delivery wagon of T. Eaton & Co.—
drawn by the pony "Maggie"*

31. Maggie pulling first T. Eaton delivery wagon past first store on Yonge Street, 1869.

32. The Queen's Hotel, famed Toronto hostelry (shown here in the 1870s), stood near the present Royal York.

33. The old City Hall on Front Street.

34. Waterfront immediately behind City Hall and St. Lawrence Market in 1870. Scene indicates how much land has been reclaimed since then.

35. Flogging of prisoners in Toronto jail in 1871.

36. Early rendering of Osgoode Hall, showing cow gate.

37. Sandford Fleming outlines his plan for universal Standard Time to members of Canadian Institute in Toronto, February 8, 1879.

38. The mighty Ned Hanlan, winner of World's Rowing Championship at Henley in 1880, and 150 other major sculling contests at home and abroad.

down to the docks to stone a returning Catholic party (or sometimes the other way around, if an Orange-sponsored outing were under way).

Although various provincial fall fairs had been held in Toronto, the one in 1858 was particularly noteworthy because it was held in a permanent building called the Palace of Industry, or the Crystal Palace. Enclosing an area of 44,000 square feet, it was made of cast iron and glass and was 256 feet long and 96 feet wide. The building was completed in less than three months. Among the displays listed in the Exhibition's *Descriptive Catalogue* was that of Parson Brothers, whose coal oil lamps were considered by the makers to be much superior to those of British and American design and W. H. Rice's "ingenious rat-trap, well calculated to deceive the most wary of those very troublesome customers."

The *Descriptive Catalogue* also suggested amusements for visitors who wanted to enjoy themselves in Toronto after they had seen the Exhibition. Two of the better saloons listed were the Terrapin and the Apollo, on King Street. Although they weren't very fancy, Toronto's night spots of those days did allow the visitor a little fling at much more reasonable prices than those charged by today's swanky establishments. At the Apollo, for instance, you could have "a smoke or a drink" and watch the floor show (featuring Negro minstrels) for 12½ cents.

On June 27, 1860, Torontonians trudged or drove along the dusty Dundas Road to the village of Carleton, about four miles west of the city, to watch the first running of the Queen's Plate horse race, an event that was to become Canada's leading turf classic. About 4000 people gathered on this sunny day at a course which was situated near the spot where Keele Street now intersects Dundas Street. A speedy mount named Don Juan won the Queen's 50 guineas in this great event.

In the autumn of that heady year another mark of Queen Victoria's esteem assured Toronto's 42,000 inhabitants that their city was indeed taking on considerable stature. On this great day, the young city received its first visit of Royalty when the Prince of Wales arrived aboard the steamer *Kingston* during his Canadian tour. He was accompanied by the Duke of Newcastle, who had issued a firm warning along the way that His Royal Highness would countenance no special demonstrations by members of the Orange Order who, although they were in official disfavor in London, were eagerly anxious to display their loyalty to the Crown. This determination to discourage the Orangemen—whose members were so numerous in Toronto—had already been impressively displayed by the Prince at Kingston. The Orangemen of this community had been warned that unless they canceled their planned demonstration, the Prince would not come ashore. The Orangemen ignored this warning and stood ready to offer their greetings. The Prince then proceeded to completely spurn Kingston by sailing away to Cobourg after his steamer had lain off the town for several hours while the Royal party awaited the withdrawal of the determined Orange welcomers.

In Toronto the Orangemen had erected a fine archway along the route to be followed by the Prince and his party. It had been decorated with Orange symbols of various kinds, including a picture of King William crossing the Boyne. The city fathers ordered the Orangemen to remove the symbols, although the arch could remain. Somehow the ardent members of the order managed to flout these instructions and the symbols weren't discovered by the Duke of Newcastle, who was riding with his back to the horses, until the carriage had passed under the arch. That evening the mayor received a thorough dressing down from the indignant Duke, but Toronto's determined Orangemen had succeeded in offering their unwelcome pledge of loyalty to the Crown.

A presumably unbiased account of Toronto's first Royal visit was given by the correspondent of *The Times* of London, who had been following the Prince's tour since his arrival in Canada.

"The decorations of Toronto were exceedingly beautiful," he wrote. "At the landing place a pavilion had been erected, surrounded by a wide amphitheatre of seats, with a magnificent lofty arch in the center. The main street [King Street], too, was a perfect arcade of arches, having in the centre where four streets meet, a trophy which deserves special mention. It was in shape like the old Market Cross at Salisbury, or the peculiar vaulted arch which supports the spire of Salisbury Cathedral. It was composed entirely of pine covered with rough pine bark. Where the four ribs of the arch met in the centre, over King Street, was a magnificent crown almost large enough to accommodate a dinner party inside it. All the ribs of the arch were covered with sheaves of ripe corn. At the corners, whence the arches sprang, were tall waving plants of Indian corn, with large openwork baskets filled full of melons, apples, peaches, grapes, and other fruit and vegetable products of the Colony which are now in full season. Altogether the whole idea as a kind of autumnal harvest home welcome was admirable . . ."

The Times correspondent reported that as the Prince came to the landing place, the upper tiers of the amphitheater were filled with ladies and gentlemen, the lower seats being occupied by 3000 children dressed in white.

"As His Royal Highness stepped on shore all these infant voices broke out with the National Anthem, and the effect of the whole scene—the dark, gloomy sunset over Lake Ontario, the cheering of the crowd outside, just heard over the strong, solemn chorus of the children, the flags of the arches and the dim illumination of the city in the distance, along the streets of which the crowds were running with a great rush by the thousands—all made it one of those pictorial and poetical displays which no description however vivid can recall."

By the time the civic dignitaries were well into their addresses of welcome it had become difficult for them to read their speeches, because night was falling over the city.

"The greatest blaze of light which was shed on the subsequent procession," wrote *The Times* reporter, "was at the Rossin House, the principal hotel in Canada, where many of the Royal Suite were to stay and which was illuminated from top to bottom as if it were on fire."

Another visiting writer in 1861 made some comparisons between the streets of Toronto and those of Montreal and Quebec City. Wrote Anthony Trollope: "The streets in Toronto are paved with wood, or rather planked as are those of Montreal and Quebec; but they are kept in better order. I should say the planks are first used in Toronto, then sent down the lake to Montreal, and when all but rotted out they are again floated off by the St. Lawrence, to be used in the thoroughfare of the old French capital."

Next year, Toronto proudly entered the era of the street railway. Alexander Easton announced that his new service would provide horse-drawn cars at intervals of not more than thirty minutes. In summer they would operate sixteen hours a day and in winter fourteen hours a day. These schedules would be effective only on week days (it would not be until more than thirty-five years later that Toronto could bring itself to allow Sunday streetcars, and only then after a hot and bitter argument that lasted five years).

The routes of the first streetcars were to extend up Yonge Street from King Street to Bloor Street, along Queen Street from Yonge Street to the Mental Asylum and along King Street from the Don River to Bathurst Street. The Yonge Street section of the new system was opened with much fanfare on September 10, 1861. The ceremonies began with a dinner at Yorkville (then still a separate village at Bloor and Yonge). The first car was hitched to the horses at four o'clock in the afternoon and started down Yonge Street crowded with civic dignitaries and with the Artillery Band sitting on the roof blaring out jaunty airs. Twice, on the way down Yonge Street, the car ran off the rails but was quickly restored to its tracks by the crowds of excited youngsters who ran along beside it during its triumphant progress. The start of the horse-car service had been scheduled for one o'clock in the afternoon but had been delayed until four o'clock,

while the large crowds who had gone to Yorkville to witness the great
event waited patiently. Onlookers filled the windows in the houses
overlooking Yonge Street and the village was gay with banners and flags.

"Seldom," said a press report, "has the quiet village seen such a bustle
and excitement and when the first car came out of the depot and was
placed on the track a grand cheer arose from the assembled multitude."

When the first car from Yorkville arrived in downtown Toronto at St.
Lawrence Hall, the crowd sang the National Anthem and shouted three
cheers for the Queen. The great day in the history of Toronto and of
Yorkville was capped that evening with a gala concert party in the Yorkville Town Hall.

Following the concert there was a supper and then a ball, during which
the gallant red-jacketed members of the 30th Regiment were the envy of
the civilian blades as they whirled into waltzes with the local belles. The
ball didn't get under way until midnight and lasted until the small hours
of the morning.

In their runs between downtown Toronto and Yorkville, the cars of the
new street railway didn't need any elaborate turntables or other devices to
reverse their directions. The horses were merely unhitched from one end
and brought around to the other end of the car. In the winter the open
cars were bitterly cold because they were not equipped with stoves. The
driver, who sat out on a platform completely exposed to the weather, managed to keep his feet warm in a box of pea straw. Straw was also spread
upon the floor of the cars to give the passengers a little something into
which to snuggle their feet. At first there were no fare boxes or even
tickets. The passengers could embark or alight from either the front or the
back of the car, paying their fares in cash to the driver if they were honest.
Most of them were, because in those days the driver knew the majority of
his passengers and sometimes halted in front of their houses instead of
continuing to the proper stop, or even waited for a few moments while
one bolted down the last of his breakfast before dashing out to catch the
car.

During the winter months there was often a good deal of dispute between the storekeepers, particularly those along Yonge Street, and the employees of the street railway. After heavy falls of snow, the railway plowed
the strip occupied by its tracks, piling up banks on either side so high and
in such a narrow path that the streets were sometimes made impassable to
other vehicles. On one occasion shop hands from all of the Yonge Street
stores turned out with shovels and energetically tore down the snow-
banks and pushed them back out on the railway tracks again. The railway
lost the battle and ended up with at least eight of its cars piled up and
helpless at one point. The grinning shopkeepers and clerks went back to

their stores with a cheer as a large section of Toronto's public transportation system ground to an ignoble halt.

On June 30, 1867, at the stroke of midnight, the bells of St. James's Cathedral rang out joyously to herald the birth of the new Dominion of Canada.

"The day was observed by the greatest rejoicings in the city," wrote historian C. C. Taylor, who witnessed the event. "What with bonfires, fireworks and illuminations, excursions, military displays and musical and other entertainments, the citizens and the thousands who crowded the streets did not want for amusement. Since the visit of the Prince of Wales no such day had been witnessed in Toronto."

To celebrate the event a banquet was held in the Music Hall over the Mechanic's Institute at which the Honorable John A. Macdonald and the Honorable George Brown, two of the leading architects of the new Confederation, were the principal speakers. Brown and Macdonald had long been bitter political opponents. But on this great night their animosities were put aside.

"Their mutal interchange of compliments," wryly remarks Mr. Taylor, ". . . when each spoke of the other as respectively the greatest statesman and patriot Canada had ever produced, was a striking feature on this memorable and festive occasion."

King Street had become the pride and joy of Toronto's citizens. It was along this thoroughfare that most of the important mercantile establishments were located, but the street had become a social as well as a business center. The sentiments of the young city toward its main street were glowingly expressed in the words of an enthusiastic writer of the day who rather grandly described King Street in the *Canadian Illustrated News*:

"Between the two principal streets of the Western Capital is a great gulf, made by the inflexible laws of society and fashion—a gulf as great as separates the Bowery from Broadway, the Rue de Rivoli from Rue Montparnasse, or Regent Street and Rotten Row from the humble thoroughfares of Pentonville and the City Road.

"The buildings on King Street are greater and grander than their neighbours on Yonge; the shops are larger and dearer; and last but not least King Street is honoured by the daily presence of the aristocracy while Yonge Street is given over to the business man, the middle-class and the beggar. Amid the upper classes there is a performance that goes on daily that is known among the *habitues* as 'doing King.' It consists principally of marching up and down a certain part of the street at a certain hour, performing, as it were, *ko-tou* to the goddess of Fashion, and sacrificing to her sister divinity of Society.

"At three o'clock in the afternoon the first stragglers appear on the scene, which extends perhaps a quarter of a mile. These consist principally of young ladies, whose proper place should be at school, and young men attired in the height of fashion. By the time these ardent devotees have paraded a few times, the regular *habitues* make their appearance, and till six o'clock in the evening one side—for one side only is patronized—is crowded to excess.

"It is rather considered 'the thing' to patrol King Street in this manner; and of a fine evening every one who belongs to the *elite*, as well as many who do not, may be seen perseveringly trudging up and down, no doubt to their great comfort and to the immense discomfiture and dismay of others less smiled upon by nature or less favoured by their tailors or dressmakers. King Street is in a way a great social 'Change, where everybody meets everybody and his wife; where the latest fashions are exhibited, and the latest quotations of the matrimonial market are exchanged.

"Would you see the newest style in hats or panniers? They are to be seen on King Street. And would you know how many young swells are doing nothing for a living? You are sure to find them on King Street. Would you wish to hear the latest imprudence of young Harum Scarum, or the progress of Miss Slowcome's engagement? You may be sure before you take a half-a-dozen turns some conversant, intelligent busybody of your acquaintance will have whispered the facts of the case in your ear, all of which he has 'On the best authority, sir.' It is on King Street that Clelius makes his appointment with Clelia for their afternoon walk; that Thersites, jealousy-stricken, scowls at Adonis; and that Pomponia depreciates the value of her dear friend Amaltheus' new silk and trimmings. There Cornelia, the careful mother, brings out her treasures and exhibits to the public gaze those desirable lots of which she is anxious to dispose on advantageous terms. While far above all, Diogenes, in his garret, little more roomy or commodious than the ancient 'tub,' looks down upon the motley throng, notices their petty follies and foibles, and thanks his lucky stars that he is not as other men."

There was one young newcomer among Toronto's merchants, however, who refused to be impressed by King Street's reputation as the haunt of the carriage trade and decided to launch his business in modest 24-foot-wide premises on Yonge Street at the southwest corner of Queen. Timothy Eaton had purchased the store and stock of the Britannia House for $6500 and it was here in 1869 that the immigrant boy from County Antrim in Ireland founded the firm that was to become one of the world's greatest mercantile empires. The original stake which permitted him to buy the Britannia House had come from the proceeds of the dissolved partnership in a general store he had opened, with his brother James, in St. Marys, Ontario, nine years earlier.

He unlocked his new drygoods store, with a staff of two clerks and a boy, on December 8, a cold day on which the Bay had frozen from shore to shore and the good people of Toronto were beginning to have thoughts of the coming Christmas. At first the public was amused at his then novel policy of selling goods only for cash and at one low but inflexible price. It was the custom in those days to do a considerable amount of haggling, even at the better stores. And, of course, "putting it on the bill" was a standard method of doing business in a town which had once had "debtors' posts" for those allowed out for a stroll after being imprisoned when they couldn't pay up.

When Mr. Eaton advertised his offer of "goods satisfactory or money refunded" his fellow Toronto merchants concluded that their new colleague from Ireland must certainly be a little touched in the head. But young Timothy knew what he was doing. His special "door dressing" of large baskets heaped with such bargains as thread at one cent a spool or neckties at five cents began to catch the public eye. The customers soon became resigned to the fact that the prices marked plainly on the tags meant exactly what they said, because along with his refusal to dicker, Mr. Eaton had injected an impressive and rigid policy of absolute honesty into his dealings with the public. It has been recorded that, when one of his clerks agreed with a woman shopper who commented that some material she was examining looked like pure wool, Mr. Eaton stepped in and firmly remarked: "No, madam, it is half cotton." A Methodist of stern convictions, Mr. Eaton refused to sell either playing cards or tobacco in his store.

It was only two years later that a thirty-eight-year-old Scot named Robert Simpson opened a small drygoods store in Toronto. He also spurned fashionable King Street, opening his store on the northwest corner of Yonge and Queen Streets and from humble beginnings his business also flourished to become one of the two towering giants of the Canadian retail trade. Curiously enough, Eaton's and Simpson's later swapped locations by moving across Queen Street from each other to the sites their stores occupy today.

By 1872 Toronto had achieved a population of more than 56,000. It had jumped by 7000 in the brief span of two years and by 1874 it would soar to 69,000.

It was in June of 1873 that John G. Howard, architect, surveyor and Toronto's first City Engineer, made a generous offer to his city which would provide benefits for many generations of residents to come. He was willing to present to the city his beautiful 165-acre farm, High Park, as a playground for the people of Toronto. The offer, however, carried certain conditions. One was that no intoxicating liquor should ever be served in the park. Another was that the land must be forever held as a public park for the free use and enjoyment of Torontonians. Mr. Howard also requested, in the terms of his offer, that his residence, Colborne House, along with 45 acres of the farm, should be retained by himself and his wife during their lifetimes and that after their deaths, they should be buried there, with their graves properly maintained by the city. Another condition was that he and his wife should receive from the city an annuity of $1200 and that in addition, Mr. Howard should receive a salary of $1 a year as honorary Forest Warden of the park. (The name High Park came from its lofty location overlooking the lake and Colborne Lodge, which still stands, was so named in tribute to Sir John Colborne.)

The value of the land and buildings when Mr. Howard made his offer was about $24,000 and the city authorities, considering the fact that Mr. Howard was then seventy years of age, decided the offer was an attractive one that should be accepted. However, although Mrs. Howard died in 1877, Mr. Howard lived on for seventeen more years after making his arrangement with the city, collecting a total of $20,400 in annuities and $17 as honorary Warden. Those who stroll the wooded pathways of this spacious park today will agree that the city obtained a very fine bargain, just the same. In the ensuing years since taking over the Howard farm, the city has acquired additional bordering tracts of land, including the area which encompasses Grenadier Pond—said to have received its name from the legend that a soldier stationed in Toronto during the War of 1812 fell through the ice and was drowned.

In 1874 Toronto acquired its first full-time fire-fighting force of thirty-six men, which was maintained at a cost to the taxpayers of $12,000 a year. It was also noted during this year that the city now possessed no fewer than 610 taverns, shops and wholesale houses selling liquor. Application was made in 1876 on behalf of the Clipper Baseball Club for permission to practice in Queen's Park and a brawny young oarsman named Ned Hanlan became champion sculler of Ontario. Before long Ned Hanlan would gain wide renown for his rowing triumphs at home and abroad. So proud were his fellow citizens of the mighty Ned, when he became champion sculler of the world, that they built him a fine home on the Island. A statue of the great athlete now stands in Exhibition Park.

In these times May 24 was one of the most important holidays of the year. Indeed, the special day celebrating the birth of good Queen Victoria is said to have been introduced to Canada in the intensely loyal city of Toronto.

Historian J. E. Middleton wrote the following description of the peculiar mood with which Toronto observed the great holiday:

"Loyalty to the British Crown had been a main principle of action with the founders of Upper Canada and of Toronto. With their successors it was something more than a mere principle; it was a passion. The colors of chivalry and romance were woven into the fabric of loyalty for, after all, the Queen was a lonely and pathetic figure as well as a regal one. Those who imagine that political science is scientific, even in the slightest measure, will not appreciate to the full the magic of Victoria's name in a city 5000 miles from Windsor.

"It was sentiment that made the Queen's birthday a festival almost delirious in its enthusiasm, while the national holiday known as Dominion Day was celebrated with polite languor. Ulstermen and Southern Irish, however they might differ during their private days of rejoicing, were united on the 24th of May. Stern non-conformists, for all their distaste of frivolity, bought firecrackers for the children on this day, for was not the Queen the first moralist of the Kingdom?"

In 1878 the *Globe* reported a May 24 sidelight which must surely have caused the Warden of High Park to raise an eyebrow in disapproval: All during the day the Great Western Railway had been running excursion trains from downtown Toronto to the park.

"Towards night," sniffed the *Globe*, "the scene became more disgraceful and more riotous. Several anxious women were seen endeavouring to persuade their male companions to abandon altercations with imaginary enemies and to take short siestas on the grass to sleep away their drunken stupor."

It was in 1878 that there occurred what might be called the forerunner of the present huge Canadian National Exhibition, largest annual event of its kind in the world. In that year the Toronto Industrial Exhibition was held in permanent buildings constructed on land within the present site of the CNE. Among these buildings, which had been erected at the cost of $150,000, was a new Crystal Palace, utilizing the upper part of the old palace that had been built in 1858. There was also a machinery hall and agricultural, horticultural, dairy and poultry buildings. The Exhibition was opened by Lord Dufferin, Governor General of Canada and, during the ceremonies, the choir of the Toronto Philharmonic Society sang "The Heavens Are Telling" and "The Hallelujah Chorus." Visitors to the Exhibition were carried to the grounds by hourly excursion trains of the Great Western Railway and aboard special steamers which loaded up at the docks at the foot of Yonge Street. Among the points of interest proudly suggested to visitors touring Toronto during the Exhibition were the four corners of King and Simcoe Streets, which then contained Government House, Upper Canada College, St. Andrew's Church and a saloon. These corners had been respectively dubbed, by Toronto residents, Legislation, Education, Salvation and Damnation.

Entrance to the Exhibition Grounds cost twenty-five cents and visitors were warned in newspaper ads to have the proper amount ready because no change would be given at the gates. As Toronto's Exhibition grew, it began to lose some of the wholesome characteristics of a fall fair which had marked most of the earlier events of this nature. A kind of Midway had developed and visitors from the country were given warning of the pitfalls which might lurk there. Remarked one writer of the day:

"In the immediate vicinity of the main gates, booths and tents are being put up with amazing rapidity in order that no opportunity may be lost in turning an honest penny—and, it is to be feared many dishonest pennies also. In this booth will be sold intoxicating liquors, and in that jugglers and thimbleriggers will doubtless ply their nefarious trades. In fact 'wide-awakes' who infest every city during exhibition times may be expected in large numbers on the present occasion also. Thieves, pickpockets, gamblers, swindlers and vagabonds generally, may be expected to hold forth in the neighbourhood of the main gate, and consequently it is to be hoped that a large number of detectives will be kept in that quarter to look after them and protect the unwary citizen or credulous countryman from being fleeced by those who live by picking and stealing."

The *Globe* sternly disapproved of the sale of liquor within the grounds, but it went merrily on for some years.

In 1879 a Canadian engineer named Sandford Fleming addressed a meeting of the Canadian Institute in Toronto to describe his idea for a system of time zones extending from the Greenwich Meridian around the world. Although it was not until five years later that standard time was adopted on a world-wide basis, there is probably a great deal of merit to the suggestion that it was born in Toronto at the meeting in which the man who later became Sir Sandford Fleming first publicly revealed his plan.

In this year also Hart Massey, who had taken over his father's tiny agricultural implement firm in Newcastle, Ontario, moved it to Toronto where, as Massey-Harris and later Massey-Ferguson, it became the world's largest manufacturer of farm tractors.

In 1882 a startling innovation was introduced to the Exhibition, providing a sight that was described with awe throughout Upper Canada by those who witnessed it during their trip to the fair. Electric lights were installed in the grounds by the Fuller Electric Light Company of New York and the Ball Company of England. With the buildings and grounds bathed in the spectacular glow of the arc lamps, it was now possible to visit the Exhibition at night, as well as in the daytime and many were the exclamations of startled wonder from those who witnessed the miracle of electric lighting for the first time.

Next year an even more sensational invention was unveiled during the Exhibition. The first electric railway in Canada was demonstrated and, although it wasn't a spectacular success, it did cause a great deal of excitement in Toronto. The first demonstration of the new conveyance was scheduled for September 12, 1883, but it had to be delayed for a day. On September 14, the press reported that "the locomotive and track having been completed yesterday, the trial trip of the electric railway was made. The wheels and bearings of the different parts of the locomotive were stiff, having never been in use before, and it was thought that some difficulty would be experienced in making this first trip. When the engine that generates the electricity was started and the lightning caught up by the little locomotive it started away at a good speed and ran from the little station near the ring to the terminus of the track at the road leading to the ferry wharf. The locomotive ran over the track several times, and once drew the car over it. The car is a neat little platform arrangement for about sixteen persons. It was thought by some that the electric railway would be a failure and its ultimate success was not expected to come up to anticipations. The success of the railway, its promoters, say, may now be looked upon as certain, and the silent steed will be ready to do service for an admiring crowd of passengers today."

Three days later, however, it was announced in the *Globe* that all of the bugs had not yet been eliminated from the fantastic new transportation system. It seems that the promoters of the train had merely gone down to Chicago, where it was already in use, and then returned to Toronto to attempt to copy the device in a do-it-yourself fashion. Although the special dynamo located at the Exhibition Grounds developed enough power to propel the locomotive, it could not provide sufficient current to haul the passenger car as well and Torontonians had to be content to merely watch the engine going up and down the tracks, instead of actually taking a ride on the newfangled train.

The *Globe*, never a journal to be stampeded into wild enthusiasm over every new thing that came along, was reserved in its editorial comment concerning the demonstration of the curious electric conveyance:

> The electric railway was not so great a success as the people expected. Enough was shown to demonstrate that electricity can be used for traction purposes, but those who witnessed the performance of the model must have left the grounds fearing that it would be their grand-children's time before electric railways would be of practical use. It is understood that

while attending the Exhibition of Railway Appliances in Chicago some of the members of the Association saw the electric railway at work. They did not want to pay the large sum demanded for the use of this railway, so they came home and made one "out of their heads." The confidence in their own ability thus exhibited was a manifestation of the very qualities which have made the Exhibition a success, but the failure of the Exhibition should not be imperilled by the use of "attractions" which are partial failures.

Next year the *Globe* had to eat its words of criticism about the marvelous new electric railway. This time the Exhibition authorities brought to Toronto Charles J. Van Depoele from Chicago to take charge of the project. Although, on its first run the car did not go far because "the belt attached to the engine running the dynamo flew off," on September 6, 1884, the electric train was acknowledged as a complete success. The *Globe* admiringly reported that on one run the train of cars speeded along at fifteen miles an hour on the curves!

"The electricity, which is generated by two large-size generators in Machinery Hall, is conveyed into two copper bars which run the whole length of the railway track between the rails. The bars are partly covered over, for protection against shock and from the rain. Attached to the motor are two pieces of metal which run along the copper bars, and the electricity is thus carried to the dynamo on the car, which, when in motion, drives the car wheels by means of a system of pulleys and belting.

"The electrician on the car has full control of the movements of this motor, just as if he were running a marine engine or locomotive. By means of a handle he immediately reverses the motion of the dynamo on the car. He controls the speed of the cars by means of a governor, just as the amount of electricity given to a man from a galvanic battery is controlled. To stop the car he simply breaks the current of electricity through the car, and the motor stops . . . The thought of a motor run by an invisible force and drawing a car with fifty people aboard seems almost an impossibility, but it is even so."

The line through the Exhibition to the ferry wharf road (near Dufferin Street) was one mile long and was at that time the longest electric railway on the continent. By 1885 it was making use of an overhead wire and trolley instead of the copper bars between the rails and sometimes carried as many as 250 passengers in a single trip. During that year's Exhibition it carried 50,000 people. Yet it would for years be considered little more than a visionary novelty, in much the same fashion as the monorail trains at a world's fair are regarded today.

Chapter 16
1886–1939
THE DREAMER

Young Henry Mill Pellatt sees the possibilities of electricity. A champion runner. A stake in the opening of the West. Founding of the Toronto Electric Light Company. Harnessing Niagara. The first electric automobile in Toronto. Lieutenant Colonel Pellatt leads Canada's Coronation Contingent at crowning of Edward VII. Knighthood. Sir Henry takes his Queen's Own to Aldershot. The building of Casa Loma. The many roles of Toronto's famed castle. The death of a colorful Torontonian.

It was only about two years after the successful demonstration of the electric railway at the Toronto Industrial Exhibition that young Henry Mill Pellatt, gazing out of the window of his father's brokerage office on King Street, watched a horse-drawn car rumble slowly by.

"Do you know, Father," said he, "some day those streetcars won't need horses. They'll all be driven by electricity."

The demonstrations of the electric train at the Exhibition were still considered to be merely a stunt, and the elder Henry Pellatt laid down his quill pen and studied his son.

"Sometimes," he said, "I think you're crazy."

Because young Henry Pellatt did indeed have a great deal to do with the eventual electrification of Toronto's street railway and also contributed to his city one of its most romantic legends and monuments to a dreamer, it would perhaps be permissible to stray here for a while from the chronological course of Toronto's story to dwell upon some of the highlights of the career of one of its most colorful citizens.

Henry Mill Pellatt, who joined his father's brokerage firm at the age of seventeen, had been born in Kingston, Ontario, and had moved to Toronto with his family at the age of two. His father had come to Canada from England and proudly traced his genealogy back to A.D. 1230. In his youth Henry was a distinguished athlete and pistol shot and his most cherished souvenir was said to be a yellowed clipping from a New York newspaper of 1879 describing how he had won by two feet the one-mile running championship of North America.

Just before the turn of the century, when the Canada Northwest Land Company was formed to help develop the seemingly boundless expanses of the West, stock in the enterprise could be picked up at $10 to $12 a share. Young Pellatt, who had toured the area after traveling there on the recently completed Canadian Pacific Railway, was highly enthusiastic about its prospects and never lost a chance to acquire as much Northwest Land Company stock as he could afford to buy. When settlement of the West began in earnest a few years later, Henry Pellatt's holdings in the land company began to pay rich dividends and it was upon this first stake that he founded what was to become one of Canada's greatest fortunes. He was only in his early twenties when he established the Toronto Electric Light Company, with an initial modest contract for thirty-two arc lamps in the downtown area. Meanwhile, he had noted that at Niagara the Americans were proceeding to harness the power of the great falls. He decided to develop his own power on the Canadian side of the cataract and bring it by transmission lines into Toronto. He thus became chairman of the Electrical Development Company, financed by money raised by young Pellatt in Canada and Britain. The project marked the birth of the great power network which was to become, after being turned over to public ownership some years later, the Hydro-Electric Power Commission of Ontario.

It was only fitting that a man who had shown so much interest in electricity as a source of power should acquire the first electric automobile to be seen on the streets of Toronto. But it was not to be the last time that Henry Pellatt would startle his fellow citizens. He branched out into shipping lines and mining and even extended his interests to the Pacific coast when, with a number of associates, he formed the British Columbia Packers' Association.

But it was the availability of large amounts of electricity in Toronto from Henry Pellatt's Electrical Development Company at Niagara that made Toronto's electric railways a reality in 1892. However, it was not his financial and organizational abilities which made Henry Pellatt a noteworthy citizen of Toronto so much as the flamboyant ways in which he used the great wealth which had been provided by his ingenuity. At the age of seventeen he had joined the Queen's Own Rifles of Canada as a private and it was upon his beloved regiment that Henry Pellatt lavished his money in such spectacular fashion that his name was soon familiar in many parts of what was then the British Empire. His only active service with the regiment occurred when it was called out on New Year's Night of 1877 to deal with a riot in Belleville. But his association with it extended over half a century, during which time he was to rise from private to the rank of Major General Sir Henry Pellatt.

By 1902, after Queen Victoria had died and the Throne passed to King Edward VII, Henry Pellatt had become a lieutenant colonel and was appointed to command a composite unit, the Canadian Coronation Contingent of six hundred men sent to take part in the Coronation ceremonies. Overjoyed at receiving this great honor, Lieutenant Colonel Pellatt indulged in one of the first of the grand gestures which were to repeatedly amaze his fellow Toronto residents.

He decided to take with him to London, at his own expense, an entire military band. With Lieutenant Colonel Pellatt riding at its head, attired in the splendid uniform of an officer of the Queen's Own Rifles, Canada's contribution to the Coronation ceremonies was the talk of London. By 1910 Henry Pellatt had not only become a full colonel of the Queen's Own but had also been elevated to knighthood. In that year the British Army was holding autumn maneuvers at Aldershot. Sir Henry resolved to perform a gesture which had never been matched by a private individual in any of His Majesty's far-flung colonies and dominions. He led 670 members of his regiment over to England to take part in the military exercises, paying entirely out of his own pocket for their transportation to and from the Old Country and the heavy expenses of maintaining them there for several weeks. Toronto was awed. Imperialists were delighted. Britain was thrilled by this great gesture of Canadian loyalty at a time when the shadows of the coming First World War were already lengthening across Europe. The new King George V invited Sir Henry to Balmoral Castle and there made him a Commander of the Victorian Order. The Queen's Own was made an affiliate of the famous British line regiment, The Buffs. It was a proud day for Canada and a proud day for Sir Henry Mill Pellatt. Many of the Queen's Own who returned to Canada in all of their glory in their elaborate peacetime uniforms were to return four years later in drab khaki to lay down their lives in the War that was to End All Wars.

But Sir Henry Pellatt had not performed his last grand gesture in the city where he had won his great wealth. After his return from the memorable events in England, he acquired several hundred acres of what was then farmland on the northern outskirts of the city in an area known as Wells Hill. It was his original plan to subdivide this land as a real estate venture, but then he conceived a much more romantic project which, if accomplished, would certainly add to the value of the lots he intended to offer to the early suburbanites. Sir Henry had often dreamed of someday entertaining Royalty in his own home when some such personage as the Prince of Wales should make a visit to Toronto. With this thought in mind, he decided to build the most magnificent residence that could possibly be found in all of North America.

In 1911 he began to build, on the prominence of Wells Hill, his fabulous Casa Loma. It took three years to erect, although Sir Henry and Lady Pellatt moved in in 1913 before their sumptuous dwelling was completed. There they lived in splendor, surrounded by treasures brought from all over the world. The great, baronial halls of Casa Loma were filled with priceless tapestries, gorgeous rugs, and fine pictures and furnishings created by the most accomplished artists and craftsmen.

"All my life," said Sir Henry, "I have been a student of architecture and I have traveled extensively, particularly in England, Scotland, Ireland, Germany, Austria, and Italy. I had an opportunity to observe and carefully examine many ancient fortresses and castles. Casa Loma is a result of my observations and travels."

One architectural critic, however, has described Casa Loma as "a mixture of 17th century Scotch baronial and 20th Century-Fox." Among other things, Casa Loma had 98 rooms, three bowling alleys, 30 bathrooms (some with gold-plated fixtures); 25 fireplaces, its own telephone system, a $75,000 pipe organ, a huge fountain, a palm room, a marble swimming pool, a kitchen range large enough to cook a whole ox, 5000 electric lights, a special tunnel to the spacious stables, a shooting gallery and a huge wine cellar filled with the finest vintages procurable.

It was not unusual for Sir Henry and Lady Pellatt to entertain 3000 guests at some grand soiree. Sometimes Sir Henry would have his men of the Queen's Own Rifles up for a weekend visit, on which occasion up to a thousand troops would be quartered in Casa Loma's basement.

In building this fantastic and tremendously expensive residence, Sir Henry was the shrewd businessman as well as the romantic dreamer. It is said that so much prestige did Casa Loma—which never did house Royalty—give to the new real estate development that Sir Henry realized a profit that was at least $1,000,000 in excess of the amount it had cost him to build the strange castle on the hill.

In the 1920s, with the increasing taxes of the growing city weighing more and more heavily on the huge dwelling in which he was spending less and less time, Sir Henry finally turned the property over to the municipality, which then had a hard time deciding what to do with it. In 1929 a New York syndicate leased the place and spent $200,000 on it in an attempt to convert it into a luxury hotel. It is said that the establishment's $10,000-a-year chef arrived at the place each day wearing a top hat while being carried to work in a chauffeur-driven limousine. However, the latest

Casa Loma project never did get off the ground and was finally given up when the arrival of the depression severely cut down the number of prospective clients who could pay hefty amounts for the privilege of living in a castle.

After that, while the city fathers scratched their heads over the problem of the castle no one wanted, it gradually fell into disrepair.

Finally it was about to be torn down when, fortunately for Toronto, a service club acquired it and, after refurbishing it, raised money for various causes by conducting guided tours of the strange, somehow sad castle which stands on a hill that is now surrounded by the great city. Regular dances are still held in what is now one of Toronto's prime tourist attractions and one of the groups which provided music for the early patrons of the castle spread its fame throughout the United States, where it became known far and wide, as Glen Gray's Casa Loma Orchestra, one of the most renowned dance bands on the continent.

Sir Henry died in 1939, two months after having been the guest of honor at a great testimonial banquet given by his old comrades and friends to mark his eightieth birthday. The grand surprise of the evening was when a handful of aged survivors of the Queen's Own Rifles Bugle Band, which had accompanied Sir Henry to Edward VII's Coronation thirty-seven years earlier, marched by the head table. Those who were there that night saw the old man's eyes fill with tears as the remnants of his band tottered by, bravely blowing on their bugles. The military funeral of Major General Sir Henry Mill Pellatt, on the raw afternoon of Saturday, March 11, 1939, was one of the most impressive ever witnessed in Toronto.

Chapter 17
1886–1900
THE GAY NINETIES

The lacrosse games. The winter sports. The Sunday drives. Electric lights spell end of gas light era. The steam-powered Belt Line Railway. The electric streetcar appears. A new City Hall. The zoo at York and Front Streets. Toronto gets its first look at movies. Jake Gaudar wins world sculling championship. Toronto eyes the North. Mary Pickford, Lord Thomson, Raymond Massey, Walter Huston, Beatrice Lillie, and Garfield Weston are born in Toronto. John Ross Robertson dedicates himself to Hospital for Sick Children. The Toronto newspapers.

In the Toronto of 1885 life moved with a certain placid kind of dignity. It was a time when the red plush photograph album with brass clasps occupied a place of honor on the drawing-room table. This room itself, sometimes called the "parlor," was a severe sort of place normally reserved for the reception of guests. When the family itself gathered it was usually in the dining room or the kitchen. Gloomy colors and huge patterns were the vogue in wallpaper and the favorite gray and tan carpet bore enormous floral designs in red, green, and brown. There were no telephones, of course, and the butcher and the grocer called for their orders each morning at the kitchen door. Central heating was just coming into vogue, but in most cases dwellings were still kept warm in winter with open fireplaces and stoves. Croquet and archery were the fashionable games for women and lacrosse was the game for men. Some of the most exciting lacrosse games were those played between Toronto teams and those from the Indian reservations, because the Red Men were said to have invented the game and were still extremely skillful at it. Pressing autumn leaves was a diversion to which many young women were addicted. Making wool cross-stitch slippers for their men was another popular pastime.

Uncle Tom's Cabin was still a popular play. On the winter evenings the streets of Toronto resounded to the jingle of harness bells. Sometimes the jam of sleighs and cutters on King Street would become so great it was only with difficulty and danger that the pedestrian dared to cross the thoroughfare. Owners of spirited horses liked to show them off in the traffic and complaints about "furious driving" were quite common. One equipage vied with another in the smartness of its fur robes. Bearskins were the favorites, the finest being mounted on bright colored felt of red, orange, green or blue. Some idea of the variety of winter vehicles available at the time may be gained from the following advertisement of the period:

CUTTERS AND SLEIGHS OF THE LATEST AND MOST
APPROVED STYLES

Handsome three-seated family styles.
New Style Phaeton Sleighs, with servant's seat.
Latest style Piano-box Cutters.
Portland Jumpers.
Democrat Sleighs, double and single.
Albany Swell-side cutters.
Ontario Two-seat Family Sleighs

Among the prime sights of the winter season was the turnout of the Garrison Driving Club on Wednesday and Saturday afternoons. The procession of sleighs which dashed gaily through the principal streets was sometimes half a mile long. The officers of the 13th Hussars made a particularly gala show with their four-in-hands, tandems, and pairs. The ladies, wrapped handsomely in furs, were provided with foot muffs and hot water tins. At the end of the afternoon, the procession would break into smaller groups of sleighs which, heading off in different directions, would pull up in front of certain hospitable houses from whence would be brought out muffins, cakes, and hot drinks of various kinds. Often some Mrs. Grundy looked out upon this gay scene and questioned whether it was proper for a young lady to drive about in such public fashion with a young man to whom she was not engaged.

"The winter enjoyments consist of skating, curling, tobogganing, and iceboating, and for all of these the facilities are unlimited," wrote historian C. C. Taylor. "The bay in front of the city, with its thousands of skaters, with numerous rinks in all parts of the city . . . might well excite the envy of skaters who, for want of better, hasten to the 'Serpentine' in London when ice has formed, and continue to use it long after it has lost its native purity, and when it would not tempt any small boy in Toronto to skim its dark surface. Canada is indeed beautiful in her winter aspect.

"One cannot imagine how animated and brilliant is Toronto when she puts on her snowshoes and gets herself up on runners and fills all the air with the chimes of sleighbells. There is an endless variety in design, pattern, and colour of sleigh, and robe, and bell, and plume, and the streets look like Christmas as long as the snow lasts. Even the street cars feel the infection, and mount themselves on bobs [short runners] and jingle the loudest bells, and take the best half of the street."

A visitor from south of the border was also captivated by what he saw at this time of Toronto in its winter garb. Wrote Robert J. Burdette:

"Who are these in blanket suits? It is pleasant to tarry among people whose girls wade through snow. Our fair Canadian cousins have no dread of discomfort. The snow has no terrors for them. They dress prettily; and if there is a prettier figure on the North American continent than a daughter of Canada apparelled for the ice or the toboggan-slide, herself a part of the snow-drifted landscape, a picture of health and comfort that fairly softens the piercing wind into a sense of warmth, I have not seen it. She dresses in perfect harmony with the winter landscape. She has a complexion clear as the ice of Ontario, and her warm blood shines through it rich as the flashes of the Aurora, graceful and free in every movement."

The lamplighter still made his rounds on many streets as early winter dusk descended upon the young Toronto. At one period, during an economy wave, the city decided to completely extinguish about half of the street lights and darken the remainder during times when there was considered to be sufficient moonlight.

The Toronto Electric Light Company had been granted permission to install poles on some of the downtown streets. The Consumers' Gas Company gamely tried to fight back, as is indicated in the following item which appeared that year in the *Globe*:

"Last evening the Consumers' Gas Company gave an exhibition on King Street between Yonge and York Streets of 14 improved street lamps and burners known as the Whitehall and Lambeth lanterns, manufactured by William Sugg, the well-known inventor of London, England. These lamps, which are of 100-candle effective lighting power, are similar to the lamps erected by Mr. Sugg on Charing Cross, Whitehall Place and Trafalgar Square in London, England. The Gas Company have erected them with a view of meeting the requirements of the city for high candle-power lamps, being ten times that of the street lamps now in use in Toronto. The management of the Company say they feel satisfied that they can supply a larger amount of effective lighting for a less sum than can be obtained by the electric light. These lamps, they affirm, have superseded the electric light in the city of London."

But the gas light era was coming to a close in Toronto, and soon the sputtering electric arc lamps were appearing on an increasing number of its main streets. Some gas lights did survive for many years, however, the last one not being removed until 1911. But the ones which stayed on were largely in back streets and lanes. The electric arc lamps, in turn, began to give way to Thomas Edison's newfangled invention, the incandescent bulb, but long after the bulb was being used for illumination on the important thoroughfares some of the old arc lamps continued to throw their eerie blue light over many of the back streets of the city.

In 1891, while horse-drawn streetcars still hauled most of the Toronto populace to and fro, a daring innovation appeared in the form of the Toronto Belt Line Railway. Its sixteen-mile Yonge Street Loop followed the Don Valley up to a point near Mount Pleasant Cemetery, where it crossed Yonge Street and continued westward to the Humber Valley, where it then proceeded southward to the waterfront and thence eastward to complete its circle. There was a second circuit of about 14 miles called the Humber Loop, which followed the main line of the Grand Trunk Railway for seven miles and then diverged to the southward, striking the Humber Valley at Lambton and running down the east side of the valley to Swansea, where connection was made with the southern line of the Grand Trunk for the return to the city.

The steam-driven Belt Lines were opened with the high hopes of their promoters that a building boom would begin in the open country which then surrounded much of the length of the two routes. In an enthusiastic booklet describing their plan, the proprietors of the Belt Lines wrote:

"The most important accession to the residential property of the city will be the immediate result of the Belt Line Railway. Those who have not witnessed the revolution in residential areas as resulting from rapid transit can scarcely imagine the effect. It will be a new era. It will lift toiling men and women for at least a little while each day out of the grime and scent and smoke of the city. A cheap fare, a comfortable seat, a well-heated, well-lighted and well ventilated car, a quick ride, and here, on the Highlands, away from the hustle of the throng, and beyond the clatter of the street—here the balmy air and restful surroundings will win back bloom to the cheek and courage to the heart."

It all sounded like the sales pitch of a modern real estate developer and the Belt Line promoters certainly had a good idea, except that they evidently had it too soon, because the expected rush to the suburbs didn't then materialize. The trains ran for a few years through open country in which few people lived and the line finally folded in 1894 from an acute lack of passengers and revenue.

The electric streetcar finally came to Toronto in 1892. The first ceremonial run was held on Civic Holiday, August 15. The *Mail* reported the great event next day:

"It was nearly 3.30 p.m. before the first electric car left in front of the

City Hall on its way to the terminus of the Church Street route, at the upper end of North Sherbourne Street. Among the party on board were several aldermen and ex-aldermen and some prominent citizens in addition to several city officials. The progress of the car was watched by crowds at several intersecting points, and twelve minutes after the start had been made it reached the bridge at Sherbourne Street. The trip was made without a stop, the car slowing up occasionally at the crossings, and no incident of note occurred during the journey. After arriving at the terminus the party adjourned to a large marquee where they were welcomed by officers of the company, which had provided solid and liquid refreshments."

The *Globe* carried the humorous "Impressions of Uncle Thomas" concerning the new wonder which had come to Toronto. He noted that the term "your trolley is off" had already become part of the slang of the day and went on to say:

"The new cars are wider than the old horse cars, and a man of ordinary dimensions can sit reasonably cross-legged in them without his boot on the shin of his travelling companion on the opposite side. They have a fresh, store-like appearance and are as bright inside and out as the new paint on the City Hall door. The springs and padding in the cushions are in perfect order, and long rows of commodious and upholstered straps hang invitingly from the roof for the suspension of standing passengers. Everything connected with the trip was auspicious, even the weather, and when the motorman, whose title has recently enriched the language, clanged his bell in front of the City Hall, the rows of distinguished personages that festooned the front steps foregathered in the cars. The binder-poles on top were fastened in their places with ropes, and as the motorman turned on the taps the cars started."

Although the first part of the inaugural streetcar run was done at a fairly staid pace, Uncle Thomas records that upon passing Queen Street the car suddenly became quite frisky!

". . . the trolley overhead struck up *Scots Wha Hae*, and I held my breath and the straps waiting for what tragic writers call the final plunge," wrote Uncle Thomas. Dogs barked, children screamed, and telegraph poles looked like rungs of a ladder as the car flew past. Groups of smiling ladies were out of sight before one could smile back, he complained.

Probably the first man to be hit by a Toronto streetcar was a startled American visitor from Rochester, New York, named Charles Z. Zwick, whose curiosity got the better of him when, while riding in a horse-drawn car, he saw one of the new electric conveyances approaching and craned his neck to get a better look at it.

". . . he stretched over too far, lost his balance and fell in front of the electric car, which struck him on the shoulder and inflicted an ugly scalp wound," reported the *Mail* on the very day after the first electric car had gone into service. Dr. [Alton Huyck] Garratt was called in, and the injured man was removed to St. Michael's Hospital, where he was reported to be doing as well as could be expected."

Friends of the horse looked with gloom and foreboding upon the introduction of the clanking new electric cars.

"What will be the result of the trolley's application to King, Queen and Yonge Street?" asked a skeptic in one of the Toronto newspapers. "The trolley will drive carriages off these streets, decrease the value of the property, and increase the danger to life . . . It is a mistake to accept it, and it will be a curse when it does come."

In the same year that Toronto was set agog by its first electric streetcar, another exciting event took place. On an admirable site where Bay Street ran into Queen Street, the cornerstone was laid for Toronto's new City Hall. In order to obtain the finest possible design for such an important building, an international contest was held in which fifty architects submitted drawings. Modern Torontonians familiar with the many arguments which went on about the present City Hall and the various designs for it submitted in an international contest, may be interested to know that there was also a great deal of heated discussion concerning the shape which would be taken by the City Hall which would for many years look down upon Bay Street.

The long controversy, which finally ended with the appointment of a local architect to carry out the job, resulted in the plans submitted from around the world being discarded. Edward J. Lennox was the man who got the commission and before drawing up final plans for the new City Hall, he traveled to such places as Pittsburgh, Washington, Baltimore, Philadelphia, New York, Boston, Albany, Rochester, and Buffalo, to make a thorough study of public buildings in those cities. The City Hall was constructed from red sandstone removed from a quarry near the forks of the Credit River.

Perhaps it was because it was raining on the day when the cornerstone was put in place for the City Hall, but there's still some doubt as to exactly where it is. There are those who claim it is the third stone from the ground in the southwest corner of the tower. Others, however, maintain that it is the second one from the ground. At any rate, a collection of items of the day, including a crisp new $4 bill, was placed in the cornerstone, so it will probably be identified eventually if the wreckers go to work on the old building.

While the new City Hall was under construction, what was then called the "old" City Hall still continued to function on Front Street as it had since 1844. Part of it still forlornly stands today, although you'd have to look hard to make it out. Thousands probably pass through the front doors of the south building of the St. Lawrence Market every Saturday without realizing they are entering the portals of Toronto's "old old" City Hall. The original front of the City Hall has been incorporated into the market structure itself, which seems to have enfolded and engulfed it. Yet, if you study the front of the market building carefully, you will see a square section containing the arched doorways and two rows of windows which were part of the face of the old City Hall for more than half a century. In 1926 the Historical Sites and Monuments Board of Canada gave at least a small amount of recognition to the shabby old place by placing on its front wall a plaque commemorating the fact that it was from this building that Canada's first commercial electric telegrams were sent in 1846.

The building which now stands behind the face of Toronto's old City Hall houses meat, fish, and vegetable stalls and on Saturdays is a clamorous and hectic spot as the merchants loudly hawk their wares. Sometimes the original gilt of the old City Hall windows shows through as the coatings of whitewash on the sashes flake off and fall to the dirty floor.

While the construction of the new City Hall dragged on and on and on for eight long years, the city fathers grew more and more restive as they carried out their deliberations within the rickety old building on Front Street. Finally John Shaw, who then occupied the mayor's chair, decided that his patience could bear no more. According to the story that has since been told, his Worship suddenly arose at a Council meeting, picked up his chair and ceremoniously carried it up to the uncompleted City Hall on Queen Street. Marching past the startled carpenters, he plunked his chair down in the unfinished Council Chamber. It seems the delighted aldermen followed him. So Mayor Shaw called the group to order, there among the tools and pieces of timber, and proceeded to hold the first Council meeting in the new City Hall.

But in September of 1899, the impatient Mayor Shaw was able to officially open the splendid new City Hall, which had at last been completed at a cost of $2,500,000. On the opening day, the Mayor and Council were borne from the old hall to the new one in two streetcars, each drawn by twelve gray horses. His Worship formally opened the front door with a golden key. It had been arranged for bands to play from noon until ten that evening but afternoon showers drove them to shelter and rained out the concert. That evening the new building was packed with excited citizens eager to see the new civic wonder in all of its marble and mahogany opulence.

At one time, the tower of the old City Hall was a favorite lofty vantage

f Toronto and there was even an elevator to take sight-
    ut higher buildings began to spring up around it, and
        levator broke down, so the traditional look-out just beneath
the great face of the clock was abandoned. While it existed, those who
made the ascent to its heady heights sometimes came back down with
their ears still vibrating if they happened to be there when Toronto's version of Big Ben mightily struck the hour.

Architect Edward Lennox saw to it that a full measure of healthy civic
pride was incorporated into the new building. Every doorknob bore the
city's arms, although someone slipped up in decorating the City Clerk's
office with a crest in which the lions were facing the wrong way. Mr. Lennox also saw to it that the building's architect received due recognition, by
stealthily placing one letter of his name on each of several of the stone
brackets under the eaves. Its front was decorated with many strange stars
and suns and other mysterious symbols which might have led a stranger to
believe it was the headquarters of some secret order rather than a center
for administering the city's affairs.

While the City Hall was under construction, another famed Toronto
landmark was also taking shape. Massey Hall, considered by experts to be
worthy of inclusion among the auditoriums with the best acoustics in the
world, was built in 1894. It was donated to the city by agricultural implement manufacturer Hart Almerin Massey, in memory of his son Charles.
It was among the many contributions to Toronto and to Canada which
would be made by the Massey family over the years.

About this time, at the corner of York and Front Streets, where the
Royal York now stands, was Harry Piper's Wild Animal Zoo, located next
door to the Queen's Hotel. Guests at the famed old hostelry needed only
to walk a few feet to see the whale, the elephant, the beaver, waterfowl,
and numerous other interesting birds and animals.

On the whole, the city was beginning to make a much more favorable
impression upon its visitors than was the case during the first half century
of its existence.

In describing a voyage on the Great Lakes, G. Mercer Adam had this to
say about a stop in Toronto during the 1880s: "The reign of solitude on
the Great Lakes has nowhere been more pleasantly broken by the life and
movement which indicate the approaches to a great city than in the case
of Toronto . . . To the traveller whose brain has been stunned by the
sights and sounds of Niagara, and to whom the restful passage of the Lake
has brought relief, the view of the 'Queen City of the West' with its array
of dome and turret, arch and spire, and the varied movements of its water
frontage, is one that cannot fail to evoke pleasure and create surprise . . .
Coaches and cabs are flying to and from the hotels. The street cars glide

past, diverging, a short way on, towards various points . . . Massive ware-
houses and piles of buildings block in the traffic, though the vista of
crowded streets opens everywhere to view.

"The city, which covers an area of ten square miles, is built on a low-
lying plain with a rising inclination to the upper or northern end, where a
ridge bounds it, which was probably the ancient margin of the lake.
Within this area are close upon 120 miles of streets, laid out after a rigid,
chessboard pattern, though monotony is avoided by the prevalence of
boulevards and ornamental shade trees in the streets and avenues not
given up to commerce.

"What the city lacks in picturesqueness of situation is atoned for in its
beautiful harbour, in the development of an aesthetic taste among the
people . . . We have now less flimsy sheet-iron ornament and more deco-
rative work in stone . . . On the whole there is a creditable display of architectural taste and skill . . . The Custom House, with its adjoining Examining warehouse, is perhaps one of the most striking instances of the
new architectural *regime* . . . The American Hotel . . . the Queen's . . .
the Bank of British North America . . . the Ontario, Imperial, Toronto,
Standard and Federal Banks . . . the head office of the Bank of Commerce . . . Toronto street, the upper end of which is terminated by the
Post Office, an imposing building in Italian style of architecture . . . The
County Court Buildings and the headquarters of the Police Department
and Fire Brigade . . ."

In 1896 the first movie program was offered to Torontonians at Robinson's Musée, on Yonge Street near King Street. For just the one admission
price the customers were allowed to gape not only at Edison's Wonderful
Vitascope, but also Professor Roentgen's Great X ray.

It was during this same year that still another Toronto oarsman added
luster to the fame already brought to the city by the sculling deeds of the
great Ned Hanlan. Jake Gaudar won the world's professional sculling
championship. Perhaps it was Toronto's lakeside location and its proxim-
ity to the quiet waters of the Island's lagoons, but the city was to turn out
many world-renowned figures over the years in the field of aquatic sports.

It was in 1898 that Toronto, feeling its muscles as a lusty city, began to
eye the North and the treasure house on that wild frontier which would
eventually pour a stream of pure gold into the city's economy and make it
a center where more mining stock was exchanged each day than in any
other spot on earth. Mayor Shaw urged his fellow members of Toronto's
Council to consider the establishment of a Toronto-Hudson Bay Railway
Commission to explore the possibilities of building a line from the city to
James Bay.

Nothing ever came of the proposal, although Mayor Shaw himself journeyed to the North to personally look the situation over. Upon his return, it is recorded, he received a bill, addressed to "the Lord Mayor of Toronto" from the proprietor of the Matabani Hotel in Haileybury. It was for $10.30 and covered "29 meals and a flask of rye." Someday the railway to James Bay would indeed be built, but not by Toronto. Toronto, however, would be the terminus to which much of the wealth of this vast area would flow.

As the century neared its close, Timothy Eaton's little store on Yonge Street had expanded to a hefty mercantile firm employing 2500 workers which now had its own factories and a thriving mail order business which earned for Mr. Eaton the title "merchandiser to the whole nation." About this time one of Mr. Eaton's boldest rivals, for a brief period, was none other than his own nephew, John Weldon Eaton. Young John opened a store on Yonge Street only two blocks below *the* Eaton's, and named the firm *The J. Eaton Co.* This piece of impertinence finally aroused the ire of Uncle Timothy, who promptly hauled his nephew into court and won the case, after which the new store was to be known as *The John Eaton Co.* instead of its former name, which was a little too close to *The T. Eaton Co.* for the taste of Uncle Timothy. But shortly thereafter, the building housing the John Eaton store was burned to the ground, three hundred employees were thrown out of work and John Weldon Eaton moved away to New York where he died three years later.

Evidently never having heard of Mark Twain's classic essay on the tremendous stupidity of ants, Timothy Eaton used to end his remarks at the annual meeting of the board of directors by intoning the words: "Go to the ant, thou sluggard, consider her ways and be wise." Business, he declared, would improve if each man present would take the earliest opportunity to "study what goes on at an ant hill." Although he had for years insisted upon writing all of his own advertising (his first small ad, one column wide and only six inches deep, had appeared in the *Globe* in 1869) he had to pass this chore on to others when the growth of the business made heavier demands on his time. To those who would now speak to the public for Eaton's, he sent a stern note, written in his vigorous, sprawling handwriting:

"Tell your story to the public—what you have and what you propose to sell. Promise them not only bargains but that every article will be found just what it is guaranteed to be. Whether you sell a first rate or a third rate article, the customers will get what they bargain for . . . Use no deception in the smallest degree—nothing you cannot defend before God and Man."

If such advice sounds corny and square today, let it not be forgotten that it was one of the guiding principles of the Irish immigrant who founded and oversaw a good deal of the growth of what is now one of the largest establishments of its kind in the world. Using similar methods of doing business, Eaton's closest rival, the Robert Simpson Company, also continued to flourish and grow into the giant firm it is today.

Perhaps the struggle of the little city from a despised settlement beside the swamps of the Don to a community of some standing in the country created a mysterious quality of tenacity which rubbed off on some of its people. At any rate, during the closing years of the nineteenth century there were born in Toronto at least six children who would someday become figures of world-wide renown. Five were of relatively humble birth and the sixth was born into one of the first families of Canada. In 1893 Gladys Mary Smith was born. She would become Mary Pickford, "America's Sweetheart" and the undisputed queen of the silent movies. In 1894, in a little house on Monteith Street, barber Herb Thomson and his wife, who had been a hotel maid, had born to them a son named Roy Herbert. Roy H. Thomson would become Lord Thomson of Fleet, the greatest press baron the world had ever seen and a man who included in his vast newspaper, television, and radio empire even *The Times* of London and *The Scotsman* of Edinburgh.

Raymond Massey, who was born in Toronto in 1896, was a member of the socially prominent family who had built up a fortune in the manufacture of agricultural implements and were the donors of Massey Hall and Hart House at the University of Toronto. He would become renowned as an actor on the London and New York stages and later in Hollywood films and in television. His elder brother, Vincent, would in 1952 become Canada's first native-born Governor General.

Walter Huston was born on Major Street in 1884 and it was here that he gave his first public performance by walking down the road on a pair of stilts. He made his first actual stage appearance at Massey Hall when he took part in a minstrel show presented by St. Simon's Church.

Also destined to shine brightly as a theatrical star on stages all over the world was Beatrice Lillie, who was born on Sherbourne Street in 1898. Her father, John Lillie, was a former officer of the British Army who had served in India. In Toronto he worked as a civil servant. As a gangling youngster in her early teens, Beatrice Lillie got her early training in the theater by appearing in some of the summer amateur shows over at the Island. Of her, after she had become Lady Peel, her good friend Noël Coward was to say:

"Beatrice Lillie has frequently been described as the funniest woman in the world. We have, of course, no absolute proof of this statement. There may be, for all we and the critics know, Dyak matrons in the forests of

Borneo, hilarious female Pygmies lurking in the jungles of the Congo, or jolly veiled priestesses in the vastness of Tibet who might reduce you to helpless laughter. But I think we can state with reasonable assurance that Beatie has been for years and still is the funniest woman of our civilization . . ."

Occasionally Lady Peel gets back for a visit to the city she left at the age of sixteen when she went to England with her mother.

It was also in 1898, in a flat over his father's bake shop, that Garfield Weston was born. It was he who would become one of the world's greatest grocery tycoons, with holdings all over the United States and Canada as well as in Great Britain, South Africa, and Australia. If Lord Thomson was to acquire *The Times* as the jewel of his press crown, Garfield Weston was to do something similar for his grocery empire by eventually bringing into it the famed Piccadilly institution of Fortnum and Mason. Londoners were aghast when an entrepreneur from a country still vaguely associated in some minds with the colonies bought the great city's swankiest specialty food shop, where the clerks still wear black tailcoats.

Back in 1875, Mrs. F. S. McMaster and some of her women friends had decided to open a small hospital, containing about half a dozen cots, which would be used only for the treatment of children. When, a few years later, John Ross Robertson, the founder of the *Telegram*, discovered the project which had been so humbly launched by the group of Toronto ladies, he became highly enthusiastic about it, and, largely through the publisher's efforts, it grew into what is now known as the Hospital for Sick Children on University Avenue, one of the finest institutions of its kind in the world.

Mr. Robertson, a young man who was so keen on journalism that he started a newspaper while he was still attending Upper Canada College, had in 1876 realized his boyhood dream by founding the *Telegram*, with which he set out to challenge the *Mail, Leader, Sun* and *Globe* which at that time served Toronto readers. (Many newspapers had come and gone since the *Upper Canada Gazette or American Oracle* had made its appearance in 1798 as York's first newspaper. The Toronto Public Library lists no less than eighty-two different newspapers which were published in Toronto before 1867.) It was not until 1892 that the newspaper which would for many years shine brightly in the afternoon field arrived on the Toronto scene. In that year the printers of the *News* went on strike and set out to publish their own newspaper which they called the *Star*. In 1899 Joseph E. Atkinson, who had been editor of the Montreal *Herald*, took the little paper over and thus launched what was to become Canada's larg-

est afternoon newspaper, a journal renowned all over North America for
its razzle-dazzle enterprise and a collection of brilliant staff by-lines which
includes such names as Gregory Clark, Frederick Griffin, Pierre van Paas-
sen, Gordon Sinclair, Matthew Halton, and even Ernest Hemingway.

Chapter 18
1900–1914
LAST OF THE TRANQUIL YEARS

The South African War. Toronto soldier wins Victoria Cross. Population tops 200,000. Death of the Queen. Visit of the Duke and Duchess of York. The silver discoveries at Cobalt. The automobile challenges the horse on Toronto's streets. The great fire of 1904. The rebuilding of the downtown area. The first Toronto parking tags. A new Grandstand at the CNE. The triumph of Tom Longboat. The great flying exhibition at Scarborough Beach. Gold rush to Kirkland Lake. Controller Horatio Hocken stumps for a subway. Toronto switches on the Hydro.

The twentieth century was ushered into Toronto by the sonorous gongs of the clock high up in the tower of the spanking new City Hall as it rang out the hour of midnight on December 31, 1899. Over in Britain, good Queen Victoria, so deeply revered by the people of Toronto, was about to begin the final year of her long and comparatively serene reign over the Commonwealth and Empire upon which the sun still never sets.

Up in Ottawa, Sir Wilfrid Laurier, the great French-Canadian statesman who had predicted in stirring tones that the twentieth century would belong to Canada, presided over Her Majesty's Canadian Government. The only cloud on the horizon was the Boer War in South Africa. Canadian soldiers, including many from Toronto, had recently marched aboard the troop transport *Sardinian* at Quebec City to the tune of "The Girl I Left Behind Me" and were soon to go into action on a front far from home. Dispatches from the South African Campaign filled most of the front pages of the Toronto newspapers and the *Globe* announced the creation of a Patriotic Fund to help alleviate the distress of wives and families of Toronto soldiers who had volunteered for service. It seems a grateful government had provided these women with an allowance of sixteen cents a day while the breadwinners were serving for Queen and Country against the Boers.

In November of that year Toronto proudly received the great news that one of its native sons, twenty-three-year-old Lieutenant Hampden Zane Churchill Cockburn, had won the Victoria Cross in the South African Campaign. The citation accompanying the Empire's highest award for valor read: "*Lt. Cockburn, with a handful of men, at a most critical moment, held off the Boers to allow the guns to get away: to do so he had to sacrifice himself and his party, all of whom were killed, wounded or taken prisoners, he himself being slightly wounded.*"

Toronto's population had at last topped the 200,000 mark and as a result of the annexation of such neighboring villages as Yorkville, Riverside (just east of the Don) and Brockton, High Park and Parkdale in the west, its boundaries now embraced twenty-four square miles.

Responding to the new burst of patriotic fervor aroused by the dispatches from the South African War, the *Globe* offered the complete works of Rudyard Kipling for $16, a little down and a little a week. Women's chemises were being featured in Simpson's January white sale for 25 cents each and dress goods for 15 cents a yard.

After frequent balloting in which the proposal had always previously been defeated, Toronto's good citizens finally ended years of controversy by voting by a narrow margin to allow the operation of trolleys in the city streets on the Sabbath. When the measure was passed, many residents of the bustling city shook their heads sadly and remarked that growth was ruining Toronto and sending its people straight down the road to Hell.

Modern Torontonians may recognize a familiar note in the statement of the new mayor, E. A. McDonald, when he made his inaugural address shortly after his election to office on New Year's Day, 1900. His Worship, who had formerly been an alderman, was not favorably impressed by Toronto's new City Hall. Said he:

"We have a great municipal building. I am glad to say I opposed its construction at every stage. Had we expended a couple of years' interest on the vast sums of capital [$2,500,000] that we have spent in the building, we could have erected plain, simple, commodious apartments without neglecting the sanitary conditions of our city."

On January 22, 1901, a heavy cloud of gloom fell upon the city which proudly claimed it had introduced Victoria Day, the great May 24 holiday. News arrived that the Queen, who had been Sovereign for more than sixty-three years, had died and been succeeded by the Prince of Wales, now to become King Edward VII. Nowhere in her Canadian realm had she been more respected than in the loyal city of Toronto, which had always been fiercely devoted to the Crown and particularly to the stately woman who had worn it longer than any other British ruler. Wrote Toronto historian J. E. Middleton, looking back on the event from 1923: "No one under thirty years of age can understand the effect of Queen Victoria's death on the mental processes of the leaders in civic life and of the public in general. Almost none could remember a time when a man was on the Throne, and in consequence the emotion of loyalty was commingled with a sense of chivalry, with a curious sentimentality, that we now regard as the hallmark of the Victorian Era. The oldest buildings for government uses bore V.R. God Save the Queen seemed a settled song, a verse coeval with Deuteronomy and the Psalms. 'Q.C.,' the distinguishing mark of the eminent lawyer, seemed as old as Coke or Blackstone. The militia regiments were Soldiers of the Queen, and drilled with a strange exultation . . . To root up the word 'Queen' from our vocabulary and substitute for it the less interesting, less lovely and less gracious word 'King,' seemed difficult, if not impossible."

When it was announced a short time after the sad news of Victoria's death that the Duke and Duchess of York would visit Toronto in October of that year, enthusiastic plans were made to give them a rousing welcome. The Duke, during his Toronto visit, thanked the citizens for the brave way in which its soldiers had responded to the Empire's call in the Boer War.

Romantic descriptions of the search for gold in the Klondike were still being avidly read by the people of Toronto in 1902 when a workman employed in the construction of a railway through the Ontario wilderness 300 miles north of the city threw his ax at a fox. Fred Larose missed the fox but bounced his ax off a projection of rock, chipping a piece from it that revealed a rich vein of silver ore. Thus, according to the legend, was discovered the great silver deposits at Cobalt and so began the development of a mining industry in northern Ontario that would pour vast wealth into Toronto and make it one of the most important mining capitals in the world. Many fortunes from the depths of northern Ontario's rocky face have been made and lost in Toronto since Fred Larose threw his ax.

It was also in 1902 that another significant thing took place which aroused little interest at the time but signaled the beginning of a tremendous change in the living habits of Toronto's people. The city in that year amended its traffic by-laws to make them apply to motor-driven vehicles as well as those hauled by horses. The era of the automobile had begun, and life in Toronto would never again be quite the same.

But perhaps the most sensational event to occur in Toronto in the years immediately after the turn of the century was the great fire of 1904 . . . At 8:04 on the evening of April 19 someone noticed a tiny wisp of smoke issuing from the building of the E. & S. Currie neckwear company on the

north side of Wellington Street between Yonge and Bay Streets, but by
the time the quickly responding fire reels had arrived, the flames were
leaping from the top of the elevator shaft of the Currie building. Fire
Chief John Thompson led his men, with their horses, up to the third story
of the adjoining warehouse of A. Ainsley & Co., from where he hoped to
pour water into the upper section of the burning building. But they had
hardly more than turned their hoses on the Currie building when they discovered that the fire had somehow worked its way into the lower floors of
the building in which they were standing. When they found they were
trapped and unable to return by the stairways, they used their hoses for
escape ropes and slid down to the ground. All made it without mishap except Chief Thompson, who slipped on his way down and fell to the pavement, fracturing his ankle and putting himself out of action at the very
moment when he and his firefighters were about to face the greatest challenge of their lives.

While Chief Thompson lay in the hospital being treated for his injury,
the fire, whipped by a brisk north wind, quickly leaped to the five story
warehouse of Pugsley, Dingman & Co., and it soon became apparent that
little within human power could halt the march of the flames which were
racing through the very heart of the city's commercial district. Calls for
aid were sent to Hamilton, Buffalo, London, and Peterborough and
firemen from these centers were soon racing toward Toronto in special
trains. As flames leaped for more than a hundred feet into the air, thousands of sightseers came downtown to watch the conflagration. The
firemen were hampered by a feeble water supply and in spite of the efforts
of the city's five steam fire engines and two hundred firemen, the huge
blaze continued to devour building after building, until the flames had
devastated a section of the city 500 feet wide and more than a quarter of a
mile long running in an east-west direction from Bay Street.

J. William Gerred, then a Toronto streetcar motorman, was downtown
with the rest of the huge crowd that night.

"The fury of the fire at the time seemed unbelievable," he later said of
this dramatic evening. "The flames seemed to leap right across the streets.
The tumult produced by the wailing of sirens summoning more supplies
and the stunning streams of high-pressure hose which seemed to be tearing loose the boarding; the babble of the curious thousands, plus the
efforts of the policemen to keep them at a safe distance, left me with a
never-to-be-forgotten impression.

"Twilight was now laying its mantle over the city and as we proceeded
nearer to the inferno, the gathering gloom further enhanced the scene.
The sky took on an orange glow, which, against the background of dense
smoke as seen from the distance, made it appear that all downtown

Toronto was ablaze. As we drew closer, the spectacle was appalling: entire blocks were on fire . . . Everything was burning on both sides of Bay, both above and below Wellington, with one exception: a huge stone building on the southeast corner of Bay seemed to resist all the fire could do. It was surrounded by flames, and for what seemed an interminable time it held out . . .

"Suddenly, as from an explosion, all floors seemed to be a blazing inferno in a single instant. This building had been the center of all eyes, as if that vast throng was willing for it to survive; but when the explosive blast ran through it, the entire mass of people gave a long drawn expression of 'Ah . . . !' The building was, I believe, the building of Wylde, Grasset and Darling, wholesale clothiers . . .

"Those were the days of the oldtime fire engines: cumbersome, steam-driven pumping machines that required three horses to draw them. These would be strategically placed and while in use had to be frequently served with coal. A special auxiliary wagon was on hand with coal; the fire engines had a siren signal and when it sounded they responded with all speed. On this night they were kept on the jump, and it was a sight to see them dashing through the streets of flame, the occupants trying to shield themselves as much as possible, then pulling up, bailing out coal at top speed, while the team stood as quiet as in the stall . . . The old steamer required a special engineer and fireman. A fire had always to be laid ready for an emergency; once called you lit up at all possible speed to raise steam and probably more often than not it wouldn't be used, but you had to have steam just in case . . .

"Motorized equipment, with all of its efficiency, never will produce the thrill of an oldtime fire turnout, with its beautifully matched teams, wonderfully trained to respond to a fire as keenly as the firemen. It was really something to see—team after team stretched out in full stride, the clanging of bells, the belching steamer with three horses pulling abreast. It was really spine tingling. No one could watch a turnout and remain unmoved."

As the great fire raged on through the night, it approached so close to the historic Queen's Hotel (located where the Royal York now stands) that its searing heat was bubbling and scorching the paint on the window sills and frames. It looked as though the familiar Toronto landmark would be enveloped by fire at any moment.

"I think the hotel was saved by sentiment," related Mr. Gerred. "The staff and guests and the public at large all pitched in to save the Queen's. It was a hot, long-drawn-out battle, in which every resource was used: pots, pans, pails, hand hoses, plus hundreds of blankets, (soaked in bath tubs) that were spread over every vulnerable spot. No one had to be invited to help—all who served did so gratis, and to their everlasting credit it may be said that if in the doing an odd bottle of whisky was used, I think even an ardent prohibitionist would shut his eyes for the occasion."

Concerning the special trains which had raced to Toronto carrying assistance, Mr. Gerred recalled: "Some time after the fire I talked to a railroad fireman who was in Hamilton and called to fire a special train into the fire-swept city. A train of flat cars had been made up containing equipment and one coach with as many of the personnel as could be spared. They were given an open line through to Toronto. The fireman said the sky was dark, but a dull glow over Toronto was their target and they aimed toward the glow. The engineer froze to the throttle, and the fireman bailed in coal. He said later: 'I've had many a wild ride, but nothing has ever approached that night.' The engineer kept the throttle open all the way, running through villages, crossing over highways, through switches, hoping every moment that the line was really clear . . ."

By the next morning the fire had been brought under control, but lying in the heart of downtown Toronto was a 14-acre desert of smoking ruins upon which the firemen were still playing their hoses. A total of 122 buildings, including 86 large commercial structures, had been destroyed and 5000 employees of these concerns were temporarily thrown out of work. One benefit of the great fire of 1904 was that it brought about the installation of improved high-pressure water mains in downtown Toronto. And, a few days after the fire, a writer in the *Globe* optimistically saw another blessing which might emerge from Toronto's great conflagration:

"Within a year the downtown district will be so changed that residents who are temporarily absent from the city will scarcely recognize the section. The skyline itself will be entirely reconstructed . . . a mighty influence on the future was furnished by one night's flames and what increases the interest and human fascination of it all is the fact that no one can tell what that influence will lead to."

Messages of sympathy poured into Toronto from all over the world, including one from the Duke and Duchess of Argyle, better known to Torontonians as the Marquis of Lorne (a former Governor General) and Princess Louise. And, as the unknown prophet of the *Globe* had predicted, a great new commercial district did rise once more from the ruins as the workmen's hammers echoed within a few days of the disaster on the work of reconstruction. Who knows? In the vision which came to this writer who wondered where the influence of the disaster would lead, is it possible that he had any inkling of the towering buildings which would one day overlook the very street upon which the flames billowed skyward on that night in 1904?

In spite of the immense destruction of the great fire, the only person who was injured on that hectic night was Fire Chief Thompson with the broken ankle which forced him out of the fight before the battle had really begun. It was a long time before he recovered from the frustration of it.

By 1907—although there were only 1500 automobiles in all of Ontario —the Toronto Police Department issued its first parking tags, displaying an early enthusiasm which has by no means abated over the years. It was in this year also that the gracious Royal Alexandra Theatre first opened its stately doors and brought many proud exclamations from Toronto playgoers who declared that it must surely be the equal of anything of its kind in New York.

Bread was five cents a loaf in that year and milk was five cents a quart. Coal sold for $4.50 a ton and you could rent a house for as little as $15 a month. You could buy a ticket for twenty-one restaurant meals for $2.75—although at least one Toronto dining place rather snootily informed its customers in a sign over its counter that napkins would not be provided anyone ordering a meal under fifteen cents. Meat was six to twelve cents a pound and semi-skilled workmen in such fields as the construction trade received wages of $12 a week. Common laborers got $8 to $10 a week, but it went a long way. Many workmen were employed that year in the building of the fine new Grandstand at the Canadian National Exhibition, which would seat 15,000.

It was the year in which Tom Longboat, the legendary Canadian Indian runner, won the Boston Marathon and came back to Toronto a hero. Born on the Six Nations Reserve near Brantford, Longboat has often been called one of the greatest long-distance runners who ever lived. He first came into prominence when he won the Hamilton *Herald*'s road race of 19 miles on Thanksgiving Day, 1906. Other victories followed and on April 19, 1907, he won the Boston classic by completing a 25-mile course in 2 hours, 25 minutes and one-fifth of a second, establishing a new record for the distance.

Few heroes or other famous folk, not even excepting Toronto's great Ned Hanlan had ever been accorded a more triumphal reception than that which the city gave the young Onondaga when he returned from Boston on the evening of April 23. When he arrived at the Union Station, he was welcomed with thunderous cheers. Then, with a Union Jack wrapped around his shoulders and another in his hands, he entered an automobile to head the parade to the City Hall. Bands played, torches flared, and representatives of every sporting association in the city was in the cortege. Thousands lined the sidewalks as he drove by. At the City Hall he was given an address of welcome by Mayor Emerson Coatsworth, who pinned a medal upon his chest.

When he lost the Marathon at the Olympic Games in England in 1908, he turned professional and raced such then world renowned track stars as Dorando Pietri and Alfie Shrubb in Madison Square Garden, New York. After age slowed Tom Longboat down, he came back to Toronto, the scene of his triumphant reception, and worked for many years as a street cleaner. He died in a humble abode at the age of sixty-two on the Six Nations Reserve where he was born.

It was in 1908 that the Toronto Street Railway finally put doors on its trolley cars and Enrico Caruso sang in Massey Hall. It was also the year in which the great Ned Hanlan died and Toronto housewives were introduced to a marvelous new household gadget called the vacuum cleaner. To guarantee a good supply of current for it and other wonders to come, Toronto during this year signed with thirteen other municipalities a contract to buy from the Ontario Hydro-Electric Power Commission electrical energy obtained from the harnessing of the mighty Niagara. Next year the people of Toronto were excited to learn that one of their countrymen, J. A. D. McCurdy, had made Canada's first airplane flight in the *Silver Dart* at Baddeck, Nova Scotia. The people didn't have to wait long to get a look at the newfangled flying machine because in August of that same year there was advertised a thrilling airplane demonstration at the Scarborough Beach amusement park, east of the city.

Charles F. Willard, an American who had been the first pupil of Glenn H. Curtiss, the great United States aviation pioneer, arrived in Toronto on August 28, with his *Golden Flyer* following him by train. The committee in charge of the flying exhibition, not having the slightest idea of what mechanical flight was really all about, had neglected to provide any space upon which the aircraft could take off or land. The only path over which the aircraft could take off was a narrow one between two buildings, leading out toward the lake. Undaunted, in the manner of most of the early birdmen, Willard arranged to have a wooden trough placed down the center of this alley to act as a guide track for the front wheel of his machine. The buildings through which he had to take off allowed barely six feet of room on either side of his wings. The track ended at the top of a three-foot-high breakwater out in the lake.

Rain delayed flight attempts until September 2. Under a lowering sky, with evening drawing near, Willard seated himself in his machine, warmed up the engine and gave the signal to let go. With a roar, the *Golden Flyer* rushed down the track toward the breakwater and from there shot out into space. The flight was billed as the grand finale of the day, but it hardly lived up to its proud advance notice. When he was scarcely airborne, the pilot nosed the craft down a few feet in the hope of picking up speed. But the engine just wasn't doing its best. After sagging along for some 300 feet, man and machine smacked into the water and it was quite dark before Willard was rescued from his cold and wet predicament.

The plane was not damaged. It had settled in the shallow water, its front wheel resting on the sand, the tail sticking high out of the water. Working like slaves, Willard and his helpers had the flying machine back in running order in five days and the intrepid pilot was ready to have another go at it. This time, small air bags were fitted to the undersides of the lower wings, in the hope they would keep the biplane afloat should it end up again in the water.

On the evening of September 7, Willard was more successful. He got his machine off the end of the breakwater at full flying speed, and to the great wonder of the assembled Torontonians, soared gracefully over the lake at low altitude. He made a wide circular flight above the water, covering a total distance of five miles in about five minutes. It had been his intention to land on the beach at Scarborough at the conclusion of his flight, but to his great consternation he found his intended landing spot crowded with spectators when he headed for it with his small gas tank almost empty. So down he went into the lake again. The air bags under the wings didn't work and when rescuers arrived they found the daring birdman sitting disconsolately in his partially submerged flying machine with the waters of Lake Ontario lapping about his neck. In four days, both Willard and his machine were sufficiently dried out to give another exhibition. Although he got off to a good start, his magneto went dead about 50 feet offshore and down went Willard into the lake *again*, for the third and final time, because on this occasion he damaged the *Golden Flyer*'s propeller. At the time, the Toronto newspapers were full of the tidings of Peary's discovery of the North Pole and Charles Willard's flying exploits at Scarborough Beach received scant press mention. But it was Toronto's first look at the airplane and it is believed that Willard's performance at the amusement park was the first advertised flying exhibition on the North American continent.

This was the year in which The Grange, magnificent home of Goldwin Smith, writer and scholar, passed after his death to Toronto, for use as an art gallery. The mansion had belonged to Mrs. Smith, who left it to her husband for his lifetime, after which it was to be given to the city. And the gold rush to Porcupine in northern Ontario got under way. In Toronto the barbershop quartets were singing "Sweet Adeline" and "In the Good Old Summer Time." If anyone saw the war clouds on the horizon, they gave them little attention and of course no one could possibly know that before long such bittersweet songs as "It's a Long, Long Way to Tipperary," "Carry Me Back to Dear Old Blighty," and "Oh, Oh, It's a Lovely War" would be the tunes of the day.

In 1910 King Edward VII died, George V ascended to the throne, Toronto's population reached 341,991 and the tranquil days were coming to an end. It was the year in which Toronto's water supply was purified after a typhoid epidemic had taken 151 lives. In Paris Madame Marie Curie had managed to isolate radium and lying up north under the craggy surface of the Canadian wilderness were tons of the strange radioactive minerals which would someday change the attitude of the whole human race toward war.

Still another gold rush was getting under way to Kirkland Lake and, as in the case of the previous discoveries, the main hub for the planning, financing, and direction of the mining developments was Toronto. From one of these Kirkland Lake mines would come the money with which gold tycoon William H. Wright would back a young Toronto stockbroker named George McCullagh in purchasing the prestigious *Globe* in 1935 and merging it in 1936 with the *Mail and Empire* to create the *Globe and Mail*. That was only one of the many ways in which new wealth from the northern goldfields would exert a profound effect upon Toronto in the years to come.

It was in 1911 that Controller Horatio Hocken (who later became mayor of Toronto) went about trying to convince the taxpayers that they should permit the building of a subway. During the previous years a New York City firm of consulting engineers, Jacobs & Davies, Inc., made a survey of Toronto's transportation problems and submitted a report to the city in which their two main recommendations were for the building of a subway and also a viaduct across the Don Valley linking Bloor Street and Danforth Avenue. The firm estimated that a subway longer than today's combined underground network could be constructed for $23,500,000. The city, said the engineers, was now large enough to be considering such improvements to its transportation system. It was suggested that, as a start, a subway could be constructed from Front Street to St. Clair Avenue for a sum of between five and six millions. (The Yonge Street subway that opened in 1954 would cost $64,000,000.)

It would therefore seem that Controller Hocken was indeed showing great foresight when he went about Toronto in 1911 pleading for the adoption of the subway proposal at every opportunity.

"I would rather see the subway project go through than be mayor," he once declared. But there seems to have been little support for his vision. Alderman Thomas Foster (who also later served as mayor) said Controller Hocken was "full of hot air" in proposing "such a hare-brained scheme."

The *Globe* called the report of Jacobs & Davies "a grievous disappointment to the citizens" and deplored its emphasis on subways. The questions of the subway and the viaduct finally went to a vote on New Year's Day of 1912. The citizens turned thumbs down on the subway but voted for the construction of the viaduct. Incorporated in the report from the New York firm was a recommendation that a second deck be built into the viaduct for the later use of a public transportation line that might run beneath the surface level that carried ordinary traffic. It now seems that Jacobs & Davies certainly knew what they were talking about, both in regard to the subway and the viaduct, because the existence of the second deck on the big bridge saved the city millions when it was utilized to carry the rails of the present east-west subway across the Don Valley.

A year later the people of Toronto went almost delirious with joy when a ceremony was held to switch on for the first time hydroelectric power from Niagara Falls. Between 40,000 and 50,000 people crowded before the City Hall to watch the inauguration. The ceremony was described in dramatic terms in next day's issue of the *Globe*:

"Striving vainly to make his voice heard above the thundering roar of thousands upon thousands of people, punctuated by piercing shrieks as women here and there in the surging crowd collapsed in fainting fits, Sir James Whitney [Conservative Premier of Ontario] last night officially inaugurated hydro-electric power in Toronto. As he pressed the button that threw the darkened streets of the city into light and set ablaze the wonderful electrical decorations about the city hall, the crowd broke through the restraining lines of police, tossing the stalwart men about like straws and forced its way like a great battering ram into the hall."

The Premier, along with Hydro Commission Chairman Adam Beck and other notables, was carried along with the crowd. The throng made its way to Mayor G. Reginald Geary's office in a noisy and happy mob. The evening had begun quietly enough with an official banquet in the King Edward Hotel, attended by civic and provincial dignitaries. About eight that evening the guests formed a parade and marched between lines of white-coated street cleaners holding torches, to City Hall. Unfortunately, the honored guests got an unexpected shower after the power had been turned on. A replica of Niagara Falls, placed over the main entrance of the City Hall, ran wild and sprayed water in all directions after the button had been pushed to turn on Toronto's new source of power.

In 1913 Toronto's fine new General Hospital was opened and the Canadian Pacific Railway completed what was then considered to be a spectacularly lofty fifteen-story "skyscraper" on the southeast corner of Yonge and King Streets. As usual, there was a deflating remark from an important visitor just as the city was becoming a little heady about its progress.

Wrote the youthful English poet Rupert Brooke, after spending a few days in Toronto: "It is not squalid like Birmingham or cramped like Canton or scattered like Edmonton or a sham like Berlin or hellish like New York or tiresome like Nice, but the depressing thing is: it will always be like it is—only larger."

That year there were 44 auto dealers in Toronto, but there were still 13 concerns offering carriage service and 37 livery stables. Old Dobbin was not yet in full retreat on the streets of Toronto and a good team and carriage were still a mark of affluence and standing in the community. Jarvis Street was a quiet and gracious thoroughfare full of substantial homes and was still considered a stylish address.

Lacrosse remained one of the city's most popular sports, so much so that R. J. Fleming gave orders to his Toronto Street Railway that any one climbing on its cars carrying a lacrosse stick should be allowed to ride free. It wasn't really a great financial burden to pay your car fare because tickets were (then) eight for a quarter. On Sunday afternoons over at the Island a kid could fill a bag with fish in no time from the waters of the quiet lagoons. Some of the luckier ones spent the whole long summer on the Island in their family cottages.

"We angled for sunfish, perch and bass in the lagoons, and trolled for pike which lurked on the edge of the weed beds," a former Island summer resident recalled of his youthful days. "We speared catfish with pronged table forks fixed to poles. We killed small frogs and caught big bullfrogs with hooks baited with bits of red flannel. The fish and frog legs we cooked over little fires of driftwood out on the ridges . . . As a special treat we would be taken to a scow moored to the shore, where they sold ice cream made from the product of Jersey cows. A saucer of the yellowish ice cream flavored with vanilla was food for the gods."

The Don River was still running fast and clean then, and people swam in it by the hundreds. Every May 24 there was a big show over in the Riverdale Park, when the militiamen assembled most of their usable artillery and fired off barrages at a great rate. The pageant was supposed to represent Toronto's brave soldiers refighting old battles.

"What old battles?" a reporter onced asked an old-timer.

"What old battles?" cried he. "Why, any old battle."

And it was a lot of fun, lying out there on the greensward while the smoke puffed from the cannon and the reverberations echoed from the surrounding hillsides. In the winter there were toboggan slides down Riverdale's slopes and merchants, including Eaton's and Simpson's, fitted their horse-drawn delivery wagons with sleighs, because when the snow came, it usually stayed on the streets right through until spring. On the frosty winter nights bands blared twice a week at the big open-air rink of the Toronto Skating Club on Dupont Street and at the Varsity Curling Rink on Bloor Street. At Christmas, the men of the family went calling and delivering gifts to friends while the women folk stayed at home to greet visitors and pour sherry in the parlor beside the friendly fireplace.

One of the favorite summer watering places was Scarborough Beach, where the great airplane exhibition had taken place. A particularly popular attraction of the place was a long chute down which you could ride in a kind of boat that shot out into the water at the bottom of its slide. On a warm summer's evening the screams of the passengers and the splash of the boats as they sped out into the water could be heard above the raucous music of the steam calliope on the merry-go-round. Twelve big passenger steamers sailed regularly out upon Lake Ontario and during what was called a "moonlight excursion" romance could blossom on the dance deck or at the rail of such fine old craft as the *Cayuga*, while the lights of Toronto twinkled in the distance across the water.

Then, one evening in the late days of a long warm summer, the unworried times abruptly came to an end. Kaiser Wilhelm of far-off Germany had marched his troops into Belgium.

Chapter 19

1914–1918

THE DAYS OF PRIDE AND PAIN

Toronto goes to war. Volunteers crowd University Avenue Armoury. Departure of Valcartier. The casualty lists come in after the Second Battle of Ypres. Colonel George Nasmith invents a gas mask. Thomas L. Church becomes wartime mayor. Canada's first aircraft factory. The flying schools. Death of General Mercer. The Patriotic Fund. Prohibition. Billy Bishop, V.C., makes a wartime visit and takes a bride. The first airmail flight. Wartime entertainment. Al Jolson at the Royal Alexandra. Toronto counts its dead.

At exactly seven o'clock on the evening of Tuesday, August 4, 1914, the *Globe* posted on its bulletin board on Yonge Street the news that Great Britain had declared war on Germany.

"For a moment," said the account in next morning's newspaper, "the big crowds stood silent. Then a cheer broke. It was not for war, but for the King, Britain, and—please God—victory . . . Toronto is British and its reception of the most sensational news in the history of the city was British. Confidence described the scene."

Heads were bowed and the crowds began to sing "God Save the King." Processions, some of them led by bands, began to appear in the streets.

"The Queen City citizens joined lustily in that old song, 'Britannia Rules the Waves,'" reported the *Globe.*

On almost every downtown street corner large and small groups stood discussing the momentous news.

"*WAR! GET POSTED . . .*" read an advertisement hastily inserted in the newspapers offering Jacks' New Encyclopedia for $3 delivered.

In the next few days volunteers by the hundreds poured into the Armoury on University Avenue to offer their services for what someone had predicted would be a "one-month war."

"The immense crowds lining the interior of the Armoury watched with keen interest the newly enrolled men drilling," said a newspaper description of the scene. "Dressed just as they came in, the men were formed into squads under a uniformed member of each regiment and instructed in the rudiments of drill for some hours. Hundreds of ladies were present in the galleries as well as the floor being completely crowded the whole evening."

On August 9, Theodore McAulay and a Mr. Puritan came winging over to Toronto in a flying boat from Niagara-on-the-Lake, on the first airplane journey across Lake Ontario, to offer their services to the war effort. Although their gesture didn't cause much excitement at the time, it was a sign of things to come, because Canada's airmen were to write in European skies one of the bravest and most valiant chapters of the war that had just begun.

Ultimately, there would be 10,000 Canadians in the Royal Flying Corps and its successor, the Royal Air Force. They would make up a quarter of the entire R.F.C.-R.A.F. fighting strength and would win a total of 495 decorations, including among their gallant ranks such illustrious names as Billy Bishop, Billy Barker, Raymond Collishaw, Clifford M. (Black Mike) McEwen, Allan McLeod, Don Maclaren, Henry (Hank) Burden, and Roy Brown, who, on April 21, 1918, would finally shoot down Germany's famed and feared "Red Knight," Baron Manfred von Richthofen, and hang the bullet-riddled seat of his airplane cockpit as a trophy in Toronto's Royal Canadian Military Institute on University Avenue.

In the days of 1914 the performers on the Keith vaudeville circuit were singing "By the Waters of Minnetonka" and "Can't Yo' Heah Me Callin', Caroline." W. C. Handy's "St. Louis Blues" was all the rage and the Irish in Toronto were applauding wildly a new number called "A Little Bit of Heaven, Sure They Call It Ireland." Fresh from *The Girl from Utah*, a new musical comedy by Jerome Kern, came "They Didn't Believe Me." Sheet music of "Sylvia" was also selling fast at Nordheimer's Music Store.

Seemingly undiscouraged by the outbreak of the war, the McLaughlin Carriage Company of Oshawa offered its fine new touring car for $1250 and sturdy Maxwells were advertised at $925. By late August, a thousand Toronto recruits were already boarding trains bound for the great military encampment at Valcartier, in the province of Quebec, while others moved out from the city to live under canvas at Long Branch. In the winter they were billeted in the Canadian National Exhibition buildings (although the original plans for all of Canada called for only one division of troops to go overseas, Toronto alone was to provide enough strength for three divisions before the war was over). In almost every Toronto household the

women were soon busy turning out bandages and other supplies for the
Red Cross. Many other young women were volunteering for nursing duty
while their brothers and sweethearts were lining up at the recruiting stations. It wasn't long before 4800 soldiers from Toronto had arrived in Valcartier and by winter, they and their comrades from other parts of Canada
were encamped in the miserable mud of England's Salisbury Plains.

Those in Toronto who couldn't carry arms were so anxious to make
their contributions in other ways that within a short time after the out-
break of war the first million dollars had been raised in the city for the
Patriotic Fund for Soldiers' Dependents, the Hospital Ship Fund, and the
Red Cross Society. The hospital ship idea, suggested by the Imperial
Order of the Daughters of the Empire, was eventually abandoned and
the funds were diverted to the establishment of the Canadian Women's
Hospital near Portsmouth, England.

Although trade for a while slumped after the declaration of war, orders
for munitions received by plants in and near Toronto soon began to take
up some of the industrial slack.

Toronto was represented in the original mustering on Salisbury Plains
by three battalions. Drafts from three older regiments were combined into
the 3rd Canadian Battalion, under Lieutenant Colonel Robert Rennie. It
was made up mainly of men of the Queen's Own Rifles, but because of
the presence of representatives from two sister regiments it was finally
named the 3rd Canadian Battalion Toronto Regiment. The 4th Canadian
Battalion was recruited partly in Toronto but mainly from towns lying immediately north of the city. It was commanded by Lieutenant Colonel
R. H. Labatt. The 15th Battalion was formed from the 48th Highlanders
Regiment, and managed to maintain its identity as such.

On November 14, Major General Sam Hughes, Minister of Militia and
Defense, came down from Ottawa to inspect the Toronto troops and military conditions as a whole in the area. Addressing the soldiers at the Exhibition Grounds, General Sam sternly warned them of the evils of strong
drink.

"I am delighted to hear that you are conducting yourselves as becomes
British soldiers," said he. "Don't be carried away by the enthusiasm of civilians who shower intoxicating liquor upon you. The one drawback to a
soldier is overindulgence in liquor. The British Army found it impossible
to keep up with the pace when drinking was indulged in, and today the
British Army is the most temperate organization in the world."

Wild rumors had been circulating about the possibility of a raid from
across the border by Germans living in the United States. And it didn't
serve to allay these jitters when, on the very next day after General

Hughes' visit, Major General F. L. Lessard, in command of the Toronto troops, called a kind of test-mobilization of the local militia, which was responsible for home defense. He was highly gratified when, within a half-hour of the appointed time 1432 men had gathered at the Armoury on University Avenue.

"We do not want to allow panic to occur in Toronto, or any other part of the Dominion," said General Lessard. "That is why I want to impress upon you the necessity of being able, within two or three hours notice, to muster in full force . . ."

General Sam Hughes, however, was highly indignant when he heard of General Lessard's action, and publicly denounced the officer. He said he had displayed "the worst military tactics possible" in needlessly alarming the people about an American-German invasion, which was absurd. And so it was. There was an invasion from across the border, all right, but it was made up of Americans who were flocking to Canada eager to join the armed forces. Two of them, Lance Corporal William H. Metcalf of Waite Township, Maine, and Captain Bellenden S. Hutcheson of Mount Carmel, Illinois, were to win the Victoria Cross while serving in the Canadian Army. The influx of volunteers from the United States became so large, in fact, that a special group was formed in Toronto, known as the 97th Battalion, American Legion, under the command of Lieutenant Colonel W. L. Jolly.

The 2200 employees of the T. Eaton Co. in Toronto who enlisted were shown particular consideration by Sir John Eaton, Timothy's son, who now sat in control of the great firm. Before each man sailed for overseas duty, his picture was taken and hung in a place of honor in the store. Married men, while on active service, were paid the full wages they had received when they left the company to fight. Single men were paid half their wages. Soldiers from Eaton's on leave overseas were encouraged to use the firm's London and Paris offices for their headquarters while in these cities. Every Christmas the company sent boxes of treats to its men at war.

A former Eaton employee writing to his old firm from Bramshott in England said: ". . . I would like just to thank you for your good wishes for my welfare, and also for the allowance you are making to my wife. It gives a fellow heart to do his bit, knowing that his wife and children are being provided for. I can assure you, you have my heartfelt thanks. I trust we shall soon see the end of this war, that I can try and repay you in a small way by giving my best services . . ."

Eaton's singularly generous gesture to its men in uniform was to cost the firm well over two million dollars by the time the war had ended.

Throughout the winter of 1914–15 there were brave huzzahs and continuing enlistments and many patriotic speeches and tearful farewells and confident predictions of early victory over the Hun. But in the spring of 1915 the full stark impact of war's awful realities made themselves felt in the intensely loyal city of Toronto, when the casualty lists began pouring in after the Second Battle of Ypres, where the Germans unleashed for the first time the horrors of poison gas upon the Canadian soldiers who only a few months before had marched away to battle to the lively music of military bands and the cheers of the populace. Many well-known Toronto names were included in the lists of those who fell in that initial dreadful onslaught of the strangling yellow clouds of chlorine. The news had a sobering effect upon Toronto and the city would receive many more such sad tidings before the war was over.

It was shortly after Germany had employed this cruel new weapon that a Toronto medical doctor, serving overseas with the Canadian troops, came up with the first effective gas mask. "It was just a simple little pad saturated with hyperchloride of soda," Colonel George Nasmith later said, "which we fitted over our mouths to counteract chlorine gas." It was crude, but it helped save the lives of many British fighting men until more refined types of masks could be developed. Thousands of Nasmith's masks were soon distributed to the Allied troops.

Various groups in the city competed with one another in raising money to buy machine guns "for our boys overseas." A woman journalist wrote in Toronto in August of that eventful year: "If you have not given a machine gun yet you had better hurry up and save your pennies or you'll be hopelessly behind the times. Everybody's doing it, doctors, lawyers, bankers, Freemasons, Varsity students, Daughters of the Empire and children of the Seven Seas are giving machine guns. The Ministerial Association of Toronto in solemn session, decided to give an extra good gun."

At Ypres, Festubert, and Givenchy that year, the soldiers of Canada demonstrated to enemy and ally alike that the country was capable of providing fine fighting men, and with the sadness brought to Toronto by the growing casualty lists was mingled a sense of new pride in the city and the nation.

While the women knitted for the troops and the recruiting banners appeared on the sides of streetcars and soldiers marched up and down University Avenue, work was going ahead that year on the building of a new Union Station on Front Street and some painters known as the Group of Seven, who would have a great influence on Canadian art, built themselves a studio on Severn Street. Toronto newspaper readers were shocked by word that the *Lusitania* had been torpedoed by a German submarine with great loss of life. It was also in 1915 that Tommy Church was elected Mayor of Toronto, an office he would hold for seven years, during which

39. The *Lady Elgin*, first locomotive to run out of Toronto, on the Ontario, Simcoe & Huron line (photographed in 1881).

40. Major General Sir Henry Pellatt.

41. Casa Loma, the castle built by Sir Henry Pellatt.

42. The first electric railway in Canada was demonstrated at the Exhibition Grounds in 1884.

43. This twelve-horse team hauling a snowplow for the street railway caused a sensation when it appeared in 1891.

44. Coach used by Toronto Railway on the Oriole Road in the late nineteenth century.

45. Horse car passes St. Andrew's Church on King Street in 1890s.

46. When the "old" City Hall was the new City Hall, 1900.

47. Crowds jam Yonge Street to celebrate British victory at Pretoria in 1901.

48. The *Luella* plied between the mainland and the Island at the turn of the century.

49. Off to a fire in the early 1900s.

time he would win a firm place in the hearts of his townsmen as the city's wartime chief magistrate. It was the year in which the people of Toronto were angered by the news of the execution by a German firing squad of Nurse Edith Cavell for suspected espionage and it was the kind of incident that gave the people an added grim resolve that the perpetrators of such an outrage must be brought to their knees. It was also in 1915 that Toronto was elated to learn that the city had now been linked by telephone with far-off San Francisco and the people agreed that the instrument invented by Alexander Graham Bell in the Ontario town of Brantford had indeed become one of the great marvels of the age.

In the early summer of that year the Curtiss Aviation School was opened at suburban Long Branch. It was a Canadian offshoot of the Curtiss Company in the United States. Although Canada had no air force of its own, those who took flight training at the Curtiss School had a good chance of joining the Royal Flying Corps or the Royal Naval Air Service when they went overseas. Along with its aerodrome at Long Branch, the Curtiss Company opened Canada's first seaplane base at Hanlan's Point on Toronto Island. During the same year the company also opened a plant named Curtiss Aeroplanes & Motors Ltd., headed by none other than J. A. D. McCurdy, who had made Canada's first airplane flight in Nova Scotia back in 1909 in the *Silver Dart* and was an old friend and associate of Glenn Curtiss. The factory turned out a number of two-seater, wheel-equipped JN Curtiss training planes, some of which were used at the Long Branch school.

When the Curtiss Aviation School began, the government paid the cost of training selected pupils, on the understanding that the graduates would proceed overseas to become members of either the R.N.A.S. or the R.F.C. Students received their examinations from officials of the Aero Club of Canada. To graduate, a student had to take off alone, fly, make a reasonably accurate figure-eight while in the air and then return to the field and make a good landing. By July 11, 1915, the first two pilots had completed their instruction at the Curtiss School and had passed their tests: they were H. Strachan Ince and Homer Smith. Among the instructors for a time at the Curtiss School in Toronto was a pilot named John Guy (Goggles) Gilpatric, who later joined the U. S. Air Force when that country entered the war. In the postwar years he was destined to become famed the world over for his creation of the rascally Mr. Glencannon, the Scottish engineer hero of an immensely popular series of rib-tickling fiction stories in *The Saturday Evening Post*. One of the the pilot-mechanics at the Toronto school was Bert Acosta, another American, who would later become renowned for his numerous flying achievements, which included a non-stop flight across the Atlantic in 1927 with Admiral Richard E. Byrd.

In November of 1915 one of the American instructors at the Curtiss School, Victor Carlstrom, created a sensation when he flew one of the school's wheel-equipped "Jennies," as planes of the Curtiss JN series were called, from Toronto to New York, making the trip of 485 air miles in easy stages with an actual flying time of six hours and forty minutes. He later set many altitude records in the United States.

During the wartime operations of the Curtiss Aviation School in Toronto it turned out fifty-four students without a single fatality or serious injury, which was quite an achievement in those early days of flying. The Curtiss airplane plant was taken over in 1917 by the Imperial Munitions Board for the manufacture of Curtiss JN4 aircraft for the R.A.F. and its name was changed to Canadian Aeroplanes Ltd. In the spring of 1917, after only three months of intensive work, there had been built a large plant covering six acres at Dufferin Street and Lappin Avenue in Toronto. It was the only airplane plant in Canada during the First World War and in the two years of its existence, operating twenty-four hours a day in two shifts of twelve hours each, with a half hour off for lunch, it turned out no less than 2900 training aircraft for the flying forces of the Empire and later the United States, when that country entered the war and needed more aircraft in a hurry.

In addition to the JN4s, the plant turned out for the American government thirty huge Felixstowe flying boats. The first of the 102-foot-wingspread aircraft was completed three months after the contract was signed and the entire thirty were delivered in the space of only seven months. Toronto was making a spectacular contribution both in men and planes to the Allied forces in the air.

"By the beginning of 1916," wrote Toronto historian J. E. Middleton, "Canada had settled down to a distinct monotony in war effort; and Toronto reflected the tendency. A battalion marching down a main street was an event of almost daily unimportance. The recruiting meetings in the theatres, on the City Hall steps, the playing of bands, the banners on the streetcars, these were the ordinary things of life. Women who knit socks in public may have been a curiosity in Toronto in 1915, but not in 1916. Every woman who could knit was hard at it all the time, and bridge parties and dances had given way to knitting parties and bandage socials."

In the first six months of that year, Canada's troops took part in two notable engagements—Saint-Eloi and Sanctuary Wood. On June 2, 1916, the city lost one of its leading soldiers, Major General M. S. Mercer, who had been a former commanding officer of the Queen's Own Rifles. He and General Victor Williams had gone up to the front line on a tour of inspection. Two hours later, the heaviest bombardment ever made by the

Germans on the Canadian lines came suddenly down on the sector. General Mercer was killed in the artillery attack and General Williams was wounded and taken prisoner. Toronto mourned the death of the man who, it was said by his admirers, was probably the most brilliant soldier the city had contributed to the war.

In the latter half of 1916 the Canadians were winning great glory at the Battle of the Somme and suffering heavy casualties. Courcelette, Moquet Farm, and Regina Trench were also added to the Canadian battle honors, but they brought great sorrow to Toronto and the rest of Canada.

As the war years went on, the people of Toronto continued to contribute their pennies and their dollars to any cause which might further the nation's effort in the great struggle. The largest amount donated to any one cause was that given to the Canadian Patriotic Fund. From 1914 to 1918 Toronto subscribed to it alone, $7,645,000. And there was no objection when City Council undertook to pay $1000 to the relatives of every Toronto soldier killed overseas.

Personifying his city's attitude toward its fighting men was Mayor Tommy Church. He was said to possess a memory for names and faces that was nothing short of uncanny. There were those who maintained that he was personally acquainted with every one of the thousands of soldiers Toronto sent to war and, although this was obviously an exaggeration, it did give some indication of the energetic way in which he tried to give the city's fighting men and their families his personal attention.

When war casualty lists arrived, usually the first caller at a bereaved home was Tommy Church, with his hand outstretched to offer sympathy and help. He didn't seem to be bothered by his partial deafness. It enabled him to complete a speech or adjourn a City Council meeting in a hurry without hearing any interruptions. The city of Toronto, the British Empire, and the Argonauts football team appeared to be the things closest to his heart.

"Mr. Church was untiring in his efforts to ease the lot of the soldier while in training and after his departure," wrote J. E. Middleton. "He was available at any hour of the day or night to give a helping hand to the desolate relatives of the man, many of whom found the going hard with the breadwinners away. When battle-broken soldiers began to return, Mayor Church was always at the railway station to greet them, and any one with a complaint found an eager listener in His Worship. One remembers seeing his high-powered motor car standing one morning before a mean house in the northern suburbs. Out of the front door came an undertaker bearing a little white coffin. There were only two mourners: the father, a wounded soldier, and the Mayor of the City."

The mayor, wearing a straw boater cocked at a jaunty angle on his head in the days of summer, was indeed a familiar sight on the station platform whenever a group of soldiers left Toronto or came back from overseas.

In the fall of 1916, the great drought arrived in Toronto and the rest of Ontario as the provincial government imposed prohibition. The understanding was that whether it continued or not would depend upon a referendum to be held after the soldiers returned from the war, but it would be some years after hostilities ceased before Torontonians would be able to legally slake their thirsts once more.

On April 6, 1917, the United States entered the war and the new marching songs were "Good-bye Broadway, Hello France!" and George M. Cohan's "Over There." Victory bonds went on sale in Toronto and the rest of Canada that year and the Canadian fighting men carried out their historic storming and capture of Vimy Ridge in one of the great battles of the war. But it was an expensive victory and among the casualties were many from Toronto. It was the year in which a great explosion in Halifax Harbor killed 1800 and injured 4000. It was also the year in which Canada's foremost flying ace, Major William Avery Bishop, wearing the ribbons of the Victoria Cross, the Distinguished Service Order, the Military Cross and numerous other decorations, visited Toronto in the autumn during a leave from overseas duty.

Although the slim, unassuming twenty-three-year-old pilot, whose score of enemy aircraft totaled seventy-two by the end of the war, didn't seem to relish playing the part of the public hero, he was given wild acclaim wherever he appeared. Said a writer in the *Globe*:

"If I am any judge of expressions I should say that Bishop would rather be most anywhere else than where he is at the moment. He was more rattled at meeting that enthusiastic, admiring crowd than he would have been suddenly meeting an enemy aviator while turning a corner among the clouds. Though I had seen many receptions of this kind I admit that this was the first one that gave me a real thrill and I cheered for all I was worth . . ."

It was during this leave that he married a Toronto girl named Margaret Burden who was a granddaughter of Timothy Eaton and a sister of one of Bishop's close friends and flying comrades, Henry Burden, who was also an air ace and eventually a holder of the Distinguished Flying Cross. The marriage took place, of course, in Timothy Eaton Memorial Church on St. Clair Avenue.

As the war dragged on through the remainder of 1917 and into 1918, conscription arrived, although it allowed many exemptions and, by March 1918, the draft law had produced a total of no more than 22,000 reinforcements in all of Canada. The people of Toronto read of the last great counterattack of the Germans at Passchendaele, in which troops from their city were heavily involved. Some idea of what these fighting men faced in those grim days may be gained from a description by Kim Beattie, historian of Toronto's 48th Highlanders:

"The mud sea . . . was awful beyond words. Derelict guns, bodies, bloated horses and broken timbers were scattered wherever they looked. Had the plank road and duck-walks vanished into that quagmire they would still have been traced by the debris and the dead that flanked them.

"On the day that the 1st Division attacked, half the battalion was detailed to the task of stretcher bearing. Carrying stretchers is an arduous job at any time, but at Passchendaele, where a man could only move a yard or so at a time without sinking to his thighs, and where the shells fell always about them and burst in the mud, it was work that defies description. Eight, ten and twelve men to a stretcher and all exhausted before one load was given into the hands of the C.A.M.C.

"One sergeant, remembering a stretcher-bearing detail at Passchendaele, said this: 'It was the dirtiest job that ever I ordered men to do. They slaved like men, but I hoped it would never be so bad again. It was slippery, as were the stretchers and the wounded—what with mud and blood. They sank to their waists. The poor wounded lads fell off at times and had to be fixed and put on again. It took hours for a trip.'"

Such was the horror and the hardship faced by the young men of Toronto and the rest of Canada who had jauntily stepped up to the recruiting tables (some of them set out right on the city's main thoroughfares) to lightheartedly embark upon the Great Adventure a few short years before.

Out at the Canadian National Exhibition Grounds that year they held a motorcar race and one of the feature attractions of the event was a contest between a car handled by a racing driver named Gaston Chevrolet and a low-flying airplane piloted by a woman aviator from the United States named Ruth Law. Because the airwoman had to fly so wide on the turns, the motorcar won the race by one-third of a lap.

It was during this final year of the war that Canada's first airmail flight took place, carrying letters from Montreal to Toronto. The historic event happened in an almost accidental manner and it is perhaps even doubtful that its full significance as an indication of things to come was fully appreciated at the time. Captain Brian A. Peck, attached to the aerodrome which had by now been established at Leaside, a Toronto suburb, wanted to pay a weekend visit to his home in Montreal and managed to persuade his superiors to allow him to fly a Curtiss JN4 training plane to the city and put on a little aerial display as a possible spur to recruiting.

Continuous rain during the stay in Montreal washed out the recruiting flight but Captain Peck got in his visit home and was preparing to return to Toronto when he was presented with a novel idea by George Lighthall,

president, and Edmund Greenwood, treasurer, of the Montreal branch of
the Aerial League of the British Empire. They suggested that he carry
with him on his flight back to Toronto a batch of mail. Peck was more
than willing, and contact with post office officials soon completed the arrangements. They authorized Mr. Greenwood to act as local postmaster
for the day and on June 23, 1918, he did the rubber-stamp canceling of
120 letters taken at random from the regular mail to Toronto. Captain
Peck was prevented from getting away by bad weather that day but he did
manage to wobble into the air the next morning.

One of the reasons why his take-off was so sluggish was that, besides carrying full gasoline tanks and one passenger, Corporal E. W. Mathers, he
had aboard a secret cargo stowed in the front cockpit with Mathers and
the mail. It seems that a lieutenant in charge of stores at Leaside was
about to get married. Ontario was "dry" and Quebec was still "wet" in
those days and Captain Peck had been asked to bring back a little something for the celebration. When he landed in Toronto the sack of mail
was proudly presented to Postmaster W. E. Lemon of Toronto, but Captain Peck naturally made no mention of the case of Old Mull which had
reposed on the lap of Corporal Mathers all the way home during the flight
that made Canadian history.

In the grim and somber years of World War I those at home in
Toronto occasionally tried to take their minds off the ebb and flow of battle and the ever-growing casualty lists by attending shows at the city's several theaters. Besides the posh legitimate theater affectionately called the
Royal Alex, on King Street near Simcoe, there was the Grand Opera
House on Adelaide Street and the Princess, which was on the south side of
King Street one block east of the Royal Alex. For those with differing
tastes, there were the vaudeville houses. There was Shea's Victoria, one of
the Keith big-time vaudeville houses, at Victoria and Richmond Streets,
and Loew's on Yonge Street, which ran both moving pictures and
vaudeville.

Later on, Loew's opened on the floor above its theater another vaudeville house named the Winter Garden and known more popularly as "the
roof garden." Ten acts of vaudeville were offered each week night evening
at the Winter Garden and down in the orchestra pit leading the band at
that time was Jack Arthur, who became known over the years as "Mr.
Toronto Show Business" and staged the great spectacles which later took
place before the Grandstand of the Canadian National Exhibition. Over
on what was then Terauley Street (and is now Bay Street) was Shea's
Hippodrome, featuring both vaudeville and movies. There were two burlesque houses, the Star on Temperance Street between Yonge and Bay,
and the Gaiety on Richmond Street just west of Bay.

What were called the "deluxe" Toronto movie theaters during this war-time period were the Regent on Adelaide Street and the Tivoli on Rich-mond Street, which were opened just east of Yonge Street in 1917. At the Regent, Jack Arthur's twenty-piece orchestra—the largest movie house or-chestra in those days this side of New York—played synchronized music to a celluloid romance called *Little Lady Eileen*. At first the Toronto thea-tergoers didn't heavily patronize the movie houses, after the novelty had worn off. For one thing, the pictures were not very good and, for another, they still had about them some of the aura of the nickelodeon days, which caused some of the upper crust of Toronto to avoid them as gauche and vulgar entertainments. But when D. W. Griffith's *The Birth of a Nation* played as a road show with reserved seats at Massey Hall, even some of the society matrons turned up along with those who belonged to the common herd.

In those days of 1918 Al Jolson was knocking 'em cold in a show called *Sinbad* at the Royal Alex with such lively songs as "Rock-a-Bye Your Baby with a Dixie Melody" and of course such lusty war songs as "Hinky-Dinky Parlez-vous" (also known as "Mad'moiselle from Armentières") and Ir-ving Berlin's "Oh! How I Hate to Get Up in the Morning," were being played and sung all over the city. "Roses of Picardy" caused many a lonely wife or sweetheart to dab her eyes as she thought of her man in the far-away battle trenches of France.

But then, early one Monday morning, November 11, 1918, the war came to an end. The news had reached Toronto before dawn and when its people awoke that morning there was wild rejoicing and dancing in the streets and burnings of the Kaiser in effigy and tears of relief among thou-sands of families who had loved ones overseas. People dashed down the street dragging behind them old saucepans and wash boilers and tinware and bells of all sorts, anything and everything that could make a joyful noise. By order of Mayor Tommy Church a steam whistle was set to blast-ing shrilly at the City Hall and downtown on Bay Street the ticker tape started tumbling to the roadway from the upper floors of office buildings. Motorcars crawled along the main thoroughfares bulging with overloads of passengers and several more hanging to the running boards. Young ladies doused passers-by with talcum powder and in the hotels, all would have certainly been a shambles had the city not been dry. Hoarse quartets sang "Pack Up Your Troubles in Your Old Kitbag and Smile, Smile, Smile."

But, when the rejoicing was over there was this sad fact to contemplate: Although some 60,000 would be coming home to make new lives, 10,000 of the flower of Toronto's young manhood would be left behind to sleep forever in the war cemeteries of Flanders fields.

Chapter 20

1918–1927

THE ROARING TWENTIES

The postwar slump. The housing shortage. The visit of Edward, Prince of Wales. The Great Toronto–New York Air Race. The Dumbells. The disappearance of Ambrose Small. Dr. Frederick Banting's great discovery. The fun at Sunnyside. Toronto gets a radio station. Foster Hewitt broadcasts the hockey games. The Toronto Transportation Commission takes over the street railways. More mining strikes pour stream of gold into Toronto. The "sheiks" and the "flappers." Maple Leaf Baseball Team wins Little World Series. Ted Rogers and his batteryless radio. Toronto movies start to talk. George Young's conquest of the Catalina. Mazo de la Roche and the White-oaks of Jalna. The new Union Station. Prince of Wales visits again, with Stanley Baldwin.

Although the months which followed the end of the First Great War were filled with joyous homecomings of Toronto's soldiers, it was also a period of painful change from a war economy to a peacetime one. Some munitions workers in the city were given their final pay checks within a week of the Armistice. Soldiers who had seen years of military service and times of great peril, now had to make the difficult transition to a civilian life and peaceful pursuits they had almost forgotten. It would take almost two years before the economy would be sufficiently adjusted and strengthened to take up the slack left in the immediate wake of the war and many of those who had fought to preserve their country and their way of life found that in many respects the old ways had vastly changed during their long absence overseas. Unemployment was widespread and many of Toronto's men met real hardship for a time. Prices were high because of a scarcity of peacetime goods and wages still lagged far behind. Living conditions were complicated because of a lack of housing. The war had stopped most building and a shortage of dwellings created considerable congestion as two or more families crowded into a house which had formerly sheltered but one. And even the cost of a "bathroom flat" was now more than the former rent of a house with eight or nine rooms. Under the new pressure for housing, it was feared for a while that Toronto might become a nest of tenements. But this evil was to a large extent averted by strict building by-laws and a deeply ingrained Toronto tradition that a man should have his own house and garden. Few communities of similar size anywhere in North America could boast so many owner-occupied homes and this has been the situation in Toronto even up to the present time.

In 1919 Sir Wilfrid Laurier, one of Canada's greatest Prime Ministers, died, and so did Sir William Osler, a distinguished student of the University of Toronto, who became world-renowned as one of the most highly respected physicians of his time, despite the fact he had once advised that the best cure for the common cold was to hang your hat on the bedpost, get under the covers with a bottle of rum, and imbibe from it until you could see two hats hanging before you.

Another important event of that year was the arrival in August of Edward, Prince of Wales. Although his was the third Toronto appearance of a direct heir to the Throne, none of the previous Royal visitors even approached this Prince in the hold he held upon the affections of the city's people. After all, this shy young man had on several occasions shared the recent hardships of the soldiers at the front and many of Toronto's returned fighting men cherished among their favorite anecdotes of the war years the recollections of how they had once encountered His Royal Highness slogging through the mud somewhere on the battlefields of France.

"Here was a young man who knew the surly savagery of the trenches," wrote J. E. Middleton. "Who was full brother to every man who had worn khaki. He was a sporting Prince, a steeplechase rider, a lover of boxing, and withal as modest as a university freshman . . . Is it any wonder that men and women alike cheered this gay, blithe Personage without a surname, and cried God bless the Prince of Wales? A thousand years of tradition were behind him, an aeon of aristocracy, yet in his manner he was like those cheery subalterns who had marched away from this city by the hundreds and thousands."

Still wearing khaki uniform during most of his public appearances, the Prince of Wales officially opened the Canadian National Exhibition that year. At a dance at the Royal Canadian Yacht Club over on the Island, he caused great excitement among canoeists paddling with their sweethearts near the club pier when he suddenly wandered out on it alone to have a quiet smoke away from the throngs of socialites gathered within the graceful building.

Among the then currently popular musical numbers to which the Prince danced with the breathless local belles were "I'm Always Chasing Rainbows," "Sunrise and You," and "After You've Gone." The girls who were lucky enough to be asked for a dance by the dapper and handsome heir to the British Throne were assured of a firm place in Toronto society for years to come.

The Prince was virtually a chain smoker. It was rigid custom, in those days, never to light a cigarette, cigar, or pipe at any public dinner until a toast had been offered to the King. After one such function during the Prince's visit to Toronto, one of his table mates related that, nervously waiting to light up his cigarette, the Prince had whispered: "By Jove I hope they hurry up and get the business over about the Old Boy! I'm simply cracking for a smoke."

He visited the hospitals, sending some toys ahead to sick children and he heartily greeted disabled veterans when he arrived in their wards. When he took a twenty-mile drive through the city on August 27 to bid farewell to Toronto, the sidewalks along the route were lined with 50,000 people lustily cheering their handsome young visitor.

"I leave Toronto very happy," said he, in his parting speech to Mayor Tommy Church.

During his Toronto visit the Prince had turned up at the Leaside aerodrome to wish Godspeed to the contestants in "The Great Toronto–New York Air Race," sponsored by the Canadian National Exhibition. The competitors were flying about as curious a collection of assorted aircraft as had ever been assembled at one event. Most of them were military types left over from the war and they ranged from small former training planes to surplus bombers. The course for this early international race covered a circuit to New York and return or from New York to Toronto and return. The pilots were allowed to make their own choice of starting points and both American and Canadian contestants could begin the race from either city. The winner was to be judged on elapsed flying time for the round trip of approximately 1142 air miles. Among the contestants seen off by the Prince of Wales were Colonel Billy Barker, V.C., Lieutenant C. A. (Duke) Schiller, who became one of Canada's most famed and colorful bush pilots, and Major Rudolph W. (Shorty) Schroeder, an American who later was the first U.S. pilot to fly a plane into the vicinity of the stratosphere at an altitude of seven miles.

Many of the aircraft cracked up along the route but no one was killed.

"You could follow the course easily just by keeping an eye open for the wreckage along the way," Duke Schiller later recalled. "And headwinds!

Sometimes it was downright discouraging to see those freight trains passing you by."

Those who had to fly across the lake fitted themselves with inflated tire
inner tubes for life preservers before venturing out over the open water. A
U.S. pilot, Lieutenant Colonel H. B. Claggett, had been entrusted with a
letter from President Woodrow Wilson to the Prince of Wales. When he
crashed at Albany, it was passed on to Lieutenant B. W. Maynard for delivery to the Prince. But Maynard ended up far off course at Windsor, Ontario.

Remarked a waggish fellow contestant: "Maybe Maynard had heard
about the royal castle at Windsor, England, and simply made a slight mis-
calculation in the locality."

At any rate, the letter finished the rest of its journey by train and
presumably caught up with the Prince eventually. When Major Jack W.
Simmons, who had managed to complete the flight from New York, came
in for a landing at Leaside, a smoke pot was set off to show him the direction of the wind. But the resultant smoke screen so obscured the Major's
vision that when he skimmed low over a horse and wagon his lower wing-
tip caught the harness and completely stripped it from the animal without
injuring either the horse or his flying machine. Major Schroeder was the
winner of this historic event in the city that would some day be the home
of the Canadian International Air Show, visited each year by aircraft and
pilots from all over the world.

Captain Merton Plunkett, who had formed a soldier theatrical troupe
to help brighten for the Canadian troops the cruel gray days at Vimy
Ridge in 1917, had kept the gang together after the war and in 1919 their
show was packing them in at the Grand Opera House. They called themselves The Dumbells and so much did nostalgia exist for the old war days
that the show repeatedly went on the road across the nation and continued to keep Canadians laughing for nine years after the Armistice. It was
said that The Dumbells earned $500,000 during the time they kept their
show together, which was by no means peanuts for a Canadian theatrical
group in the days immediately after the war.

It was near the close of this first year after the war that there occurred
what is still regarded as perhaps Toronto's most celebrated and baffling
mystery and was the subject of a guessing game that went on in the city
for many years. Even today the disappearance of Ambrose Small is still an
occasional topic of newspaper items which invariably stir up discussion of
the case once more. At least two generations of Torontonians could usually get a laugh when they suggested that some new building excavation
would probably reveal the whereabouts of Ambrose or cracked that when
a heavily laden desk drawer or clothes cupboard was cleaned out it

wouldn't be surprising to find the long-missing Mr. Small. His name became almost synonymous in Toronto with anything or anybody that went missing.

It was perhaps one of the curious quirks of fate that had Ambrose Small not disappeared, very few people in Toronto would ever have been aware he had been there in the first place. He was a small and unimpressive little man, with a droopy mustache and such a passion for anonymity that when he owned race horses he would not permit them to be run under his own name. Although he was very wealthy, he was extremely frugal. He owned Toronto's Grand Opera House and a string of other Canadian theaters, yet his idea of a handsome gift to show his appreciation of the work of some leading lady who had appeared in a performance on the stage of the Grand was to present her with a small box of chocolates. He liked to gamble, but did it in an unobtrusive way.

On December 2, 1919, after selling out his theater chain for $1,750,000, he went downtown in the morning and deposited a cheque for $1,000,000 in his bank. Meeting his wife at noon, he took her out to lunch. Then he went back to his office in the Grand Opera House on Adelaide Street. At about seven o'clock that evening, he bought a New York newspaper from his regular newsboy near the theater and sauntered off. He was never seen again.

The mystery, which was sensational enough in itself, brought a new rash of headlines in newspapers all over Canada when, about three weeks after Ambrose Small disappeared, John Doughty, his secretary for many years, also vanished. A subsequent check of a safe deposit box held by Mr. Small revealed that Victory Bonds worth $105,000 had vanished as well. Detectives traveled thousands of miles following false leads on both the missing Mr. Small and his secretary. Doughty was finally picked up in an Oregon lumber camp and brought back to Toronto to stand trial on charges of theft and conspiracy to kidnap. He was convicted of the theft charge and sent to prison for four years, but the conspiracy to kidnap charge had to be dropped for lack of evidence.

Almost every other day for months a new theory arose and was duly described in the newspapers concerning the disappearance of Mr. Small. Was he murdered? If so, what could the motive have been, because, except for Doughty's running off with the bonds after Small's disappearance, he didn't seem to have been robbed. And no one could think of any enemies who hated him enough to kill him for spite. Was he kidnaped? Well, there had certainly been no ransom demands. Had he disappeared on his own volition? Then why did he not take any of his fortune with him nor make any apparent attempt to tidy up his affairs before running off? But the newspaper conjectures concerning his strange disappearance continued: he had been kidnaped and murdered: he had been spirited to a foreign country and there put to death: he had run away with a woman: his body had been buried in the Rosedale Ravine: his body had been burned in a coal furnace. In June 1920, his widow offered a reward of $50,000 to anyone who would locate him alive and $15,000 for the finding of his body. The rewards were never collected.

Even the great magician Harry Blackstone—who should certainly have been an authority on disappearing acts—made his contribution to the mass of theories some years after the theater magnate had disappeared. Blackstone, who had played many times on the stage of the Grand, was a close friend of Small's and had once even accompanied him to London, Ontario, after Small had sold a theater in that city. Small collected the money for the sale in cash and, because he was afraid he might be recognized during the journey back to Toronto and robbed, he had Blackstone accompany him and carry the money from London while Small sat in another seat in the railway coach. The incident serves to illustrate that Small and Blackstone were closer than mere casual business acquaintances.

At any rate, Blackstone later told a Toronto reporter that some years after Small had disappeared the magician had gone one night to a gambling casino during a visit to Tijuana, Mexico. "The place was very crowded," he related. "After I'd been playing at one of the tables for a while, I looked across the room and found myself staring face to face with Small! I waved and yelled 'Hi Amby' and he appeared to recognize me, because he waved back. I'd know him anywhere. As I pushed my way through the crowd toward him I noticed a couple of men move in beside him. By the time I got across the room he was gone . . . but I swear it was Ambrose Small I saw there that night."

In Toronto today, the discussion on whether Ambrose Small is still alive —he would now be well past a hundred years old—has largely given way to arguments about whether flying saucers are real. But for many years the talk in Toronto concerning Small's whereabouts was every bit as mysterious and fascinating as today's conjectures about the possible existence of little men in ships from outer space.

Around two o'clock on a November morning in 1920, a young doctor who had been in civilian practice only four months since returning from the World War, arose from his bed where he had been restlessly tossing for some hours and wrote seventeen words in his notebook. The lines which would go down as being among the most important ones ever written in medical history read as follows:

Ligate pancreatic ducts of dogs. Wait six to eight weeks for degeneration. Remove the residue and extract.

Dr. Frederick Grant Banting, at the age of twenty-nine, was on his way to making a medical discovery at the University of Toronto which was so important that it has been estimated that it has already saved more lives than were lost in both World Wars. Millions of diabetics would soon hear that a new lease on life had been given them by the discovery of insulin in Toronto. For some it would indeed mean that they would be hauled back from death's very door. For others it would mean the difference between misery and happiness, sickness and health.

Dr. Banting worked out his theory at the University of Toronto laboratories in collaboration with Dr. John J. R. Macleod and Dr. Charles H. Best. Not a cent for the proprietary rights on the great discovery would go to Dr. Banting or his colleagues. It was a boon that was to be shared with diabetic sufferers all over the world. Few scientists have received such rapid and enthusiastic recognition for their discoveries as did Dr. Banting. His finding that use of a pancreatic hormone obtained from animals helped diabetics was greeted at first with considerable doubt by medical authorities, but its speedy and obvious benefits soon won it general acceptance. Honors were heaped on Dr. Banting. Jointly with Dr. Macleod, he was awarded the Nobel Prize for Medicine and Physiology in 1923. Medical men in many countries hailed the young Canadian's discovery as the greatest since those of Pasteur. The Canadian Government granted him an annuity of $7500 to enable him to pursue an uninterrupted program of research. Eventually there was a research laboratory erected on College Street which bears his name. Close by is another research building carrying the name of Dr. Banting's colleague, Dr. Best. Dr. Banting was to be knighted in 1934. He had been wounded in the arm in the First World War and it is perhaps a matter for conjecture to think of how much human misery might have been endured for a longer period had the enemy bullet been a fatal one. Yet, he was to lose his own life at the age of forty-nine in the Second World War when an airplane carrying him on a special military medical mission to Great Britain crashed in the Newfoundland wilderness in 1941.

In 1922 Toronto's new playground and watering spot of Sunnyside opened. It was located along the lakeshore at the western end of the city and it was an even more exciting place than had been Scarborough Beach, the popular eastern mecca for summertime fun for so many years. Scarborough was still operating then, but within four years it would be closed. During the thirty-four years in which Torontonians flocked by the thousands to Sunnyside's attractions, it became a kind of summer tradition in the city. All through the months of winter its booths and rides would lie deserted and drifted with snow. But around early April, Sunnyside would begin to stir and show signs of life again as painters and carpenters and amusement operators began to prepare for May and especially Victoria Day, May 24, when things would really get rolling.

In fact, even during April, Sunnyside became the center of Toronto's interest on Easter Sunday, because it was along its two miles of boardwalk that the annual Easter parade took place. The young blades wore new suits, topcoats, and neatly dented pearl gray snap-brim hats and the finery of their girl friends was topped by the latest creation in Easter bonnets. Torontonians, both young and old, turned out by the thousands to join the Easter strollers along Sunnyside's boardwalk while the often chilly but always refreshing breezes blew off the lake. So firmly was the boardwalk established in the affections of Torontonians that even the city's officials, renowned for their admiration of the practical and the utilitarian, staunchly refused when, from time to time, it was suggested by some kill-joy that the promenade should be paved. Objection was sometimes made to the cost of regularly replacing the planks on the long thoroughfare. A parks commissioner with the highly appropriate name of Walter Love, said he wouldn't think of replacing the boardwalk with a layer of cold cement, because it would undoubtedly take all the glamour and romance away from it.

"Just what makes two hearts beat in three-quarter time to the rhythm of klunking feet on boards civic officials have no idea," remarked the *Telegram*, "but they are ready to resist efforts to replace the boardwalk with any substitute."

Which should have been enough to give the lie to those who complained that Toronto authorities were never known for allowing sentiment to interfere with their judgment of what was economical and sensible for their city.

Spread along the lakeshore strip were numerous hot dog stands, candy floss booths, popcorn counters, and ice cream vendors. There were also such games of chance as a "fish pond" in which the customers could angle with a line baited with a magnet. When you dropped it into the water, you could bring up a metal disk bearing a number. The higher the number the bigger the prize and sometimes the fishermen would try for hours. There were also a ferris wheel, a merry-go-round and the stellar attraction of the park, a roller-coaster known far and wide as the Sunnyside Flyer. Strolling along on a balmy summer's evening, with the lake breezes spiced by whiffs of hot dogs, popcorn and candy floss, you could hear the shrieks accompanying the rattling plunge of the roller-coaster as breathless damsels clung to their heroes during the thrilling dives into the valleys.

Sol Solmon, the impresario who operated the Sunnyside Amusement Company, figured there was an early crowd, a middle crowd and a late crowd. The early crowd was made up of parents with their children. The middle crowd, which spent the most money, was made up of young swains taking their lady loves on a night out at Sunnyside. If the girl friend admired a Kewpie doll, a young man would keep trying to win at the games until he'd shot his bankroll or come up lucky. The late crowd was usually smaller and more boisterous, and consisted mainly of young sports and their girls who wanted to take one final fling at Sunnyside before going home. It was the men in this final wave of customers who usually clustered around a device which had a weight that ran on a track up a graduated pole with a bell on the top. The idea was to mightily smite your target with a kind of sledgehammer. The harder you hit it, the higher the weight bounced up the pole and if you were really powerful and handy, you could sometimes ring the bell at the top and thus win the admiring glance of your sweetheart or maybe someone else's sweetheart, for that matter. It was usually the mighty *klumps* of the hammer blows and the occasional ring of the gong that were the last sounds heard at Sunnyside as the booths were closing and the calliope of the merry-go-round became silent at the end of another exciting summer night down by the lakeshore. On week nights some of the booths and amusements stayed open after midnight, but on Saturday nights everything closed sharply at the stroke of twelve, in order not to disturb the jealously guarded peace of the Toronto Sabbath.

One Easter Sol Solmon tried to work up a little added interest in the Sunday fashion parade by offering prizes totaling $25 for the best-dressed strollers. But Sol was immediately pounced upon before Easter Sunday arrived by the Lord's Day Alliance and the police, who warned him that such commercialism on the Sabbath was highly illegal. So Sol hastily erected a sign beside the boardwalk that Easter Sunday which read:

No Prizes on Account of Law.

From time to time there were other attractions at Sunnyside besides the games, rides, and refreshment booths. There were concerts at an open air bandshell called the Orthophonic and all through the summer there were quite important softball games at the diamond just east of the amusement area. Although a fence was erected around the baseball field and admissions were charged for some of the games, plenty of dead-beats would save money by gathering at the railing up on the south side of King Street where you could look down upon the game from the top of the slope above the railway tracks. One night, as an extra super-colossal spectacle Sunnyside's promoters towed an ancient sailing ship up from the harbor and set it afire out on the lake in front of the amusement strip.

But among the most popular and frequent Sunnyside attractions during the summers of the 1920s and '30s were the itinerant flagpole-sitters, who would set up housekeeping on their lofty perches and stay there for days. Ben Kayfitz, who worked at Sunnyside during his summer vacations in those days, later wrote:

"At all hours of the day and night there were small knots of the curious gathered under the lofty eagle's nest, impelled by a driving curiosity—a rather indelicate one, if the truth be known . . ."

Beauty contests to choose Miss Toronto were also held at Sunnyside for some years. But the main road entering the city from the west ran smack through the middle of the Sunnyside amusement area and as traffic grew heavier and dwellers became more numerous in the western suburbs and drivers more impatient, there was an increasing clamor to eliminate the Sunnyside bottleneck. And the roadway *was* constantly sprinkled with strollers on summer evenings. So in 1956 they tore Sunnyside down and now some of the newcomers to Toronto, speeding into town along the Gardiner Expressway, are probably not even aware that down below them there was once a magic place much beloved by the Torontonians of yesteryear. Those of us who knew it, of course, imagine that sometimes on a summer's night we can still hear laughter and the shouts and smell the savory aroma of boiling weiners, for hot dogs that sold for a dime. Or maybe hear again the sound of an orchestra wafting out on the warm evening air the strains of "Breezin' Along with the Breeze" as a new Miss Toronto daintily makes her bow to the admiring throng.

A few months before Sunnyside was unveiled in that year of 1922, another exciting happening in the field of entertainment took place. On March 28, if you had a quiet room and a crystal set and pressed your earphones hard against your head, you could hear Toronto's first radio station, CFCA, operated by the *Daily Star*, sending its initial program out over the air. One of the announcers on CFCA in those days of the early '20s was a cub reporter from the *Star* named Foster Hewitt, who described such events as the hockey games in the Mutual Street Arena. He was later to become perhaps the most familiar voice in all of Canada as year after year he brought the excitement of the big-league hockey games to ardent fans in just about every city, town, and hamlet in the whole country, over the Canadian Broadcasting Corporation's national network. When he started out, his job was both hard and hazardous. There was no broadcasting booth from which to cover a game in those days. Hewitt had to sit right out on the rail, ducking wayward pucks, while shouting his lungs out into an ordinary telephone microphone.

The promotion-minded *Star* saw to it that when something important was being broadcast on CFCA during the daytime, great loudspeaker horns and a radio were installed in school auditoriums in the city. At first most of Toronto's radio listeners had only crystal sets. After all, KDKA

Pittsburgh, the continent's first radio station, had then been on the air for only a couple of years and sometimes it could be picked up in Toronto if you had a good antenna. As time went on, tube-equipped radios began appearing in some of the city's more affluent households and envious neighbors and friends were often invited in to hear the new electronic marvel, which sometimes emitted more sqawks and crashes of static than music or intelligible words.

It was in this year that the newly formed Toronto Transportation Commission, which had taken over the old Toronto Street Railway Company in 1921, introduced double-decker buses on some of its runs and residents who had been overseas said the town was beginning to look more like London every day. Exciting news was coming down from the northern border between Quebec and Ontario, where the mining activities in the Noranda-Rouyn area had attracted a lot of attention on the financial pages of the city's newspapers. More gold in Ontario was always good news in Toronto, where the stock was being traded on the Mining Exchange more briskly each year.

By 1924, the first dial telephone appeared in Toronto and it was in that year also that the Toronto Granites won the Olympic crown and brought great joy to their hockey-loving townsmen. Next year a new gold rush, to Red Lake in northwestern Ontario, got under way and with a war surplus Curtiss JN4 airplane he had obtained as a trade-in on a car, Hamilton auto dealer Jack V. Elliot and some other pilots using the same old reliable machines, flew in prospectors and supplies to the Red Lake camp and the exciting and romantic era of the bush flier was under way in Canada. Before long Canadian bush pilots, most of them veterans of the aerial battles of the World War, would be hauling everything from heavy mining machinery to live cattle into the frontier goldfields and setting world records for annual tonnages of freight transported by air.

It was in 1925 that Tommy Church finally relinquished the mayor's chair and it would be many years before this record of seven consecutive terms in office would be broken. But it would not be long before his townsmen sent the redoubtable Tommy up to Ottawa as a Member of Parliament. Torontonians soon pinned the casual name "Tommy" on the next incumbent when Thomas Foster succeeded Tommy Church as Mayor. Perhaps it made easier the transition from Tommy Church, who had became a kind of Toronto institution, to Tommy Foster, who became known as "the watchdog of the civic treasury," a phrase that had a nice ring to it in sane and solid Toronto.

But the 1920s were not completely sane, of course, even in Toronto. It was the era of the flapper and the sheik, a gay blade who wore his hair plastered down smoothly with *sideburns* and sported bell-bottom trousers and tried his level best to look as much as possible like Rudolph Valentino, the great lover of the silent screen, who devastated his worshipers in Toronto and elsewhere by dying suddenly at the age of thirty-one in August 1926. The ukulele and the coonskin coat were symbols of the age and the bootlegger flourished in Toronto as he did in United States cities.

In 1925, they began building a Cenotaph, in memory of Toronto's war dead, in front of the City Hall. The then spectacularly tall Northern Ontario Building was opened on Bay Street and within it were located the new offices of those who were riding the crest of the boom in gold. Next year, in 1926, the impressive Maple Leaf Stadium on Fleet Street was opened and the Maple Leaf Baseball Team showed its appreciation of its fine new home by winning the Little World Series.

At the Uptown Theater on Yonge Street, moving pictures were starting in 1927 to utter their first faltering words. The novel attraction at the Uptown, in fact, was so reluctant to come right out and say something to Toronto audiences that it didn't provide any sound until the last one and a half reels. During the previous part of the picture, Jack Arthur and his orchestra provided their usual music synchronized to the mood of the picture.

"The picture," Jack related afterward, "was called *Mother Knows Best*. They hadn't really caught on yet how to regulate sound. In the talkie part at the end, there was a scene in which Mother was dying, and her final gasps were so thunderous that it must have been quite easy to hear them right out on Yonge Street."

Torontonians were thrilled in May of that year by the news that a modest, lanky young man by the name of Charles A. Lindbergh had flown his *Spirit of St. Louis* from New York to Paris non-stop. A new Toronto radio station, the only one of that period which still survives, opened on February 9 with a musical presentation from the orchestra pit of the Uptown Theater. Not surprisingly, the conductor who raised his baton as the orchestra went on the air in CFRB's first broadcast was Jack Arthur, who seems to have been associated with so many of Toronto's important entertainment events over the years. CFRB's first studios were in Ryan's Art Galleries on Jarvis Street. (Thomas Ryan, the sportsman and art dealer who owned the building, had overlooked a possible fortune by forgetting to obtain a patent on five-pin bowling, when he invented the game in Toronto back in 1908.)

The proprietor of the new radio station also had to *his* credit an invention, one that revolutionized the infant radio industry. After tinkering around with radio since his childhood and being one of the first Canadian "ham" wireless operators to make a transmission across the Atlantic to Scotland, Earnest S. (Ted) Rogers had devised in 1925, at the age of twenty-five, a radio that plugged into the socket of the ordinary household electrical supply. His new radio made obsolete the old equipment that required a large array of batteries for its operation, and he went on to make his fortune with the Rogers-Majestic radio company and established CFRB, the last two letters of which stand for "Rogers Batteryless," which was what young Ted first called his new kind of radio. Toronto's electronics genius died just a few years after his triumphs, at the age of thirty-eight.

Just a month before CFRB's opening, an event took place in far-off California that sent all of Toronto into a great dither of joyful pride. A seventeen-year-old kid from Toronto's Cabbagetown district (said to be so named because the early residents of modest circumstances had planted cabbages even on their front lawns as a way of stretching their meager grocery budgets) had set out for California some weeks earlier on an ancient motorcycle to take a try at the $25,000 marathon swim between Catalina Island and the mainland. The event was sponsored by chewing gum magnate William Wrigley, Jr., and had attracted entries from all over the world. When George Young's old motorcycle broke down in Denver, Colorado, he managed to hitch a ride the rest of the way to California with a honeymoon couple.

On January 15, 1927—15 hours and 46 minutes after the great Wrigley marathon had begun—the unknown youngster from Toronto walked out of the water on the California mainland stark naked and under the glare of many searchlights, the only one in a field of 102 of the world's best swimmers to complete the cruel test of swimming skill and endurance. Hardly anyone in Toronto had ever heard of George Young until his name suddenly blazed into the headlines all over the world. Hastily assembled committees prepared to give him a rousing Toronto reception and a fund was started to buy him a house. But George Young took his time about coming home, staying in the United States long enough to pick up $5000 in theater appearances and take a small part in a movie. When he finally did get back to Toronto that year, the local boy who had so suddenly skyrocketed into fame was given one of the biggest welcomes the city had ever offered a celebrity. Along Queen Street, 150,000 people jammed the sidewalks to see him make his triumphal ride downtown from Sunnyside Station.

The next Wrigley marathon swim was staged at the CNE. It was held over a 21-mile course and the people of Toronto settled back confidently to see their hero win all over again from an international field of competitors. But George Young was pulled out of the water when he developed cramps after completing only five miles of the home town race and those who had worshipped him were suddenly saying he was a bum. The event was won that year by Ernst Vierkoetter, billed as the "Black Shark of Germany."

The 1928 Wrigley marathon was the first of a series of such swims which would go on at the CNE right up until 1965. But George Young won only one of them, a 15-mile event held in 1931. In 1933 he went down to Philadelphia, where he got a minor job in a railway shop. During one CNE season he came back home to appear in a sideshow swimming tank, but by then he had been all but forgotten by the city which for a brief time had idolized him.

Another Torontonian who won more lasting world-wide fame in 1927 was novelist Mazo de la Roche, who during that year was awarded the $10,000 *Atlantic Monthly* prize for her *Jalna*. It was her third novel and the first of the long and popular series about the Whiteoaks of Jalna. She did much of her writing in a bed-sitting room on Yorkville Avenue and was to write eleven more of the Jalna stories, which were translated into fifteen languages. The fictional Jalna was believed to have been based on an area around Clarkson, just west of Toronto. Miss de la Roche was one of Canada's most internationally successful authors, but the more she won fame and fortune, the more retiring she became, although she occasionally turned up at the Queen's Hotel, her favorite Toronto hostelry, for dinner in its quiet old dining room. She died at her home on Toronto's Ava Crescent in 1961 at the age of seventy-six.

Toronto's new Union Station on Front Street finally opened in 1927 and residents agreed that the impressive building was a fitting terminal for a city that had reached a population of 569,899. Canada was celebrating its Diamond Jubilee of Confederation that year and attending the ceremonies was the Prince of Wales, who came back for another Toronto visit. With him were Prince George and British Prime Minister Stanley Baldwin. The Royal visitors opened the new Princes' Gate at the eastern entrance of the CNE Grounds during their stay in Toronto and on the evening of August 8, 1927, were entertained at a state dinner in the King Edward Hotel. As the glittering assembly of guests observed the Prince of Wales and Mr. Baldwin sitting at the head table that night, they of course had no way of knowing that within a few years a historic clash of wills between the British statesman and Toronto's favorite Prince would result in the abdication of Edward VIII, King and Emperor, to marry "the woman I love."

Chapter 21
1927–1939
THE DEPRESSION YEARS

Stormy Sam McBride. Still another Toronto sculler wins championship of the world. The passing of the Queen's Hotel. Opening of the Royal York. R-100 flies over Toronto. The lofty Bank of Commerce Building. Conn Smythe builds the Maple Leaf Gardens. The hard times. Toronto celebrates 100th birthday. President Roosevelt sends back Upper Canada's mace. The deceit of Norman "Red" Ryan. The Moose River mine. The long hot summer. The Stork Derby.

In the Toronto civic election of January 1, 1928, a scrappy politician named Sam McBride, a doughty fighter with florid features and an impressive mane of white hair, defeated Mayor "Honest Tom" Foster, "the watchdog of the treasury." Foster, who had been so grudging with the city's money that he once suggested that rather than go to the expense of enlarging its police force Toronto should just reimburse any citizen who was robbed, had come by his parsimonious ways naturally. Born in Uxbridge, Ontario, he had arrived in Toronto as a butcher's apprentice, finally established his own butcher shop in Cabbagetown and then, through shrewd investments in Toronto real estate, became a wealthy man. It was said that he would walk half a mile to the nearest dairy store to buy only half a pound of butter at a time and he wore celluloid collars for economy's sake. But, as will be related later, when he died in 1945 he left one of the most interesting wills in the city's history and one that would bring many benefits to the community where he had made his fortune. Sam McBride, his successor, was one of the most colorful of Toronto's mayors. He had had a long and stormy career as an alderman and a controller before becoming the boss man at City Hall. Back in 1916, during a passionate debate, he had grabbed a fellow alderman by the throat and backed him against the wall of the Council Chamber. At various other times in his political career he had struck another alderman in the face with a sheet of folded paper; threw a tin of canned tomatoes across the Council Chamber and, after biting off a piece of raw carrot, had thrown the remainder of this vitamin-rich vegetable at the gentlemen of the Fourth Estate assembled at the City Hall's press table. Once he barred the reporters of the *Telegram* from his office, although he was fond enough of newspapermen to move that their request for a larger press room be granted.

Sam McBride was a boisterous and fearless political battler and liked nothing better than to mix it up on an election platform with his opponents. Sometimes an audience at an election meeting would be treated to some special fireworks, such as when Sam arose from his chair on the campaign platform one night and collared another alderman, pushing him across the stage until he was pinned against a window at the back. But that was Sam, and even his most ardent political opponents never held a grudge against him for long, because they recognized his courage and quickness to forgive his own enemies.

Another Olympic hockey title was brought back to Toronto in 1928 by the Toronto Varsity Grads. And that year still another Toronto oarsman, Joe Wright, won the Diamond Sculls, symbolic of the world's rowing championship, at Henley in England. Another Ontario gold rush got under way, this time to Pickle Lake in the northwest wilderness of the province. And a reminder to the mining capital of Toronto that gold could be an expensive thing in more ways than one occurred when a disaster at the Hollinger mine in Timmins that year took thirty-six lives. The first honest-to-goodness full-length talking picture opened in Toronto, *The Jazz Singer* starring Al Jolson, and by this time even the more culture-conscious theatergoers of the city were beginning to admit that movies might be a kind of art form, after all.

It was in 1928 that the wreckers began to pull down the Queen's Hotel, that stately landmark of a more placid age. It was being removed to make way for the Royal York Hotel and many Torontonians heaved a sad sigh and shed a tear at its passing. Wrote Toronto journalist Nathaniel Benson a few years later:

"I well remember dining at the gracious and restful Queen's Hotel with a rich young American businessman. He assured me that there were no such slow-paced dinners, such wine cellars, such veteran servitors or red velvet comfort anywhere else on the continent . . ."

The Queen's long reigned supreme as the hotel *par excellence* of Toronto. It had been the favorite rendezvous for statesmen, actors, princes, and many other members of the titled gentry. In its Red Parlour, Sir John

A. Macdonald had held meetings with his stalwarts of the Conservative Party. It was said that the manager of the hotel once approached Sir John A. on the stairs after one of these meetings of the Conservative faithful and accused him, with well-feigned indignation, of trying to turn his hotel into a furniture factory.

"I hear," he told the startled Sir John A., "that there is cabinetmaking going on in your room." Whether this gave Canada's first Prime Minister the idea of writing "cabinetmaker" behind his name on a register during one of the Charlottetown conferences leading to Confederation—or the hotel manager later cribbed the phrase from Sir John A. himself—history does not record.

The Queen's had been the first hotel in Canada to use hot air furnaces for heating and to provide running water in all its rooms. It was also the first hotel in Toronto to install a passenger elevator and its telephone was the first to be used for business purposes in the city.

But when Governor General Viscount Willingdon officially opened the Royal York in June 1929, after the huge hotel had been completed in less than two years, Toronto was dazzled by its size and opulence. And small wonder. The magnificent edifice had cost the Canadian Pacific Railway $18,000,000, a sum thirty-five times the total assessed value of all the property in the entire community when Toronto became a city in 1834! The newspapers assured the citizens that Toronto's new hotel was the largest and finest in the whole British Empire. (Although the Queen Elizabeth Hotel in Montreal threatened this proud title for a while, the Royal York's addition of a new 400-room wing in 1959 made the claim safe again. With 1600 rooms, the Royal York is in all the world second in size only to the 3000-room Conrad Hilton Hotel in Chicago.) Throughout the years since opening its doors, the Royal York has certainly carried on in worthy fashion the tradition of the Queen's as a center for the social life of the city and a lodging place for the famous who visited Toronto.

Although swank new hotels are now popping up in Toronto by what seems to be the dozens, the Royal York's general manager, Angus MacKinnon, has so endeared himself over the years to the great hostelry's international clientele that from Rome to Rangoon he is spoken of as "the chap who keeps the hotel in Toronto." Even yesterday's Ely Playter could hardly have been more solicitous of the welfare of his guests than is Mr. MacKinnon, who has been with the hotel, in one capacity or another, since it opened.

There would be many tales told around the Royal York about such personages as Canadian-born Lord Beaverbrook, the British press baron, who was dining in the stately Imperial Room one evening when he was called

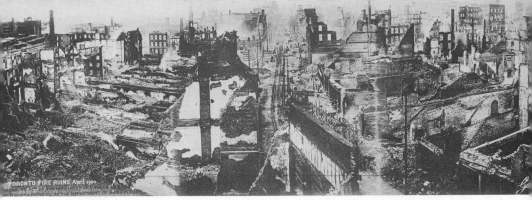

50. Front Street looking west from Yonge Street after the great fire of 1904.

51. Docks at foot of Yonge Street, 1907.

52. Toronto is now port of call for ships from all the world.

53. Bay Street looking north from Temperanc Street in 1910.

54. Edward, Prince of Wales, with Mayor Thomas L. Church during visit in 1919.

55. In the 1920s the lake excursion steamer *Cayuga* was a favorite craft for moonlight cruises.

56. Double-decker buses appeared on Toronto streets in 1921.

57. The burning of the *Noronic*, September 17, 1949.

58. Marilyn Bell, the high school youngster who was the first person to swim across Lake Ontario, seen with Mayor Nathan Phillips and trainer Gus Ryder.

59. All that was left of Raymore Crescent after flood waters of Hurricane Hazel had swept by, carrying scores on this street to their deaths in 1956.

60. Frederick G. "Big Daddy" Gardiner, the man whose determination and aggressiveness as Chairman of the Council molded the new Metro Toronto, fights back tears as he raises his hat to Yonge Street parade in his honor upon his retirement in 1961.

to a telephone located near the headwaiter's desk beside the entrance. As Beaverbrook stood at the telephone, impeccably clad in white tie and tails, a merry group of diners arrived. "Could you show us to a table near the entrance?" asked the host of the party, deftly slipping a bill into Beaverbrook's hand. The story goes that, with great composure, his Lordship pocketed the money and led the party across the room to a point where it could be taken in hand by one of the regular dining-room captains.

But on October 25 of that same year in which the Royal York opened there occurred a day that would later be known as "Black Friday" in financial circles everywhere. On that day the stock market crashed, and though it might not have been realized by many in Toronto at the time, it was a sign of the coming of the lean days of the Great Depression, which would last for many years.

Next year, on October 4, the British dirigible R-100 flew majestically over Toronto after its first journey across the Atlantic and there are still those who witnessed the event who say it was the most impressive sight they ever saw in the city—or over it, to be more correct. Cameramen caught pictures of the giant airship sailing high above the new Bank of Commerce Building on King Street, which, when completed, early in 1931, would allow Toronto to claim not only the largest hotel in the British Commonwealth, but the tallest office building as well. The 36-story structure towered 476 feet high and for many years its observation platform would be one of the prime tourist attractions of the city. Toronto was growing up, in more ways than one. It was the year in which the T. Eaton Company opened a large new store at College and Yonge Streets and its Toronto customers nodded knowingly when they saw the low building covering such a large area. They figured that Eaton's was laying the foundation for a larger store in expectation that the main activities of the city would move farther northward. But some one was wrong, because Eaton's have so far refrained from piling any more levels atop what has become known as the College Street store and great redevelopments are taking place in the downtown area.

It was on May 16 of that year that a prospector who had been searching in the northland for seventeen years found pitchblende on desolate Great Bear Lake, far up in the Northwest Territories. The discovery of this new source by Gilbert A. LaBine shattered Belguim's world monopoly on radium, used extensively in the treatment of cancer, and forced down the market price from $70,000 to $25,000 a gram. As he later sat in his newly established Toronto head office, he never dreamed that before long uranium from his Eldorado mine would be used to arm the bombs that fell

in 1945 on Hiroshima and Nagasaki, ending the war with Japan but opening a new uneasy era in human affairs which would become known as the
Atomic Age.

It was also in 1931 that Major Conn Smythe realized his fondest dream
by watching the opening of the new Maple Leaf Gardens on the corner of
Carlton and Church Streets. During the ensuing years, the great sports
palace would be called "the house that Conn built," and for very good
reason.

Conn Smythe was born not more than a hundred yards from the future
site of his great arena, on February 1, 1895, and was destined to greatly en-
liven his home town's sports scene—and that of Toronto generally—for
many years. His father had been a Toronto newspaperman. When young
Conn was only seventeen, he displayed the typical Smythe audacity by
going up to homestead on a hundred acres of northern Ontario bush near
Cochrane. He had cleared two acres of his land when he came back to
Toronto on a visit, and during his absence a forest fire destroyed his humble buildings on the property. He sold his holdings for $300 and when an-
other bush fire a year later killed the man who had bought it, Conn
Smythe said it must have been his Irish luck that saved him from being
the victim. He used the $300 to enroll in the civil engineering course at
the University of Toronto.

But while he was still a nineteen-year-old undergraduate, the First
World War broke out and Conn promptly joined up as a gunner. He won
the rank of major before the war was over and was decorated with the Military Cross for bravery at Vimy Ridge. After serving fourteen months in
France as an artilleryman, he joined the Royal Flying Corps in 1917 and
was shot down in no man's land between the trenches, where he was captured, and spent another fourteen months in a German prison camp. He
returned to the university to take his final year after getting back from the
war and then went into the sand and gravel business. But, like so many
other young Canadians, he was quite mad about hockey and had coached a
University of Toronto team that won the Olympic title at Antwerp, Belgium. During later hockey tours in the United States he caught the eye of
Colonel John S. Hammond, who was looking for someone to assemble a
new professional hockey club, the New York Rangers. Smythe took the job.
But Hammond, disturbed by Conn's volcanic eruptions when things went
wrong, fired him before the season was over. The man who was to become
known to Canadian sportswriters as the "Little Pistol"—he was five-foot-
seven of dynamite—took his dismissal as a serious personal affront. If he
couldn't direct the Rangers, he brooded, he'd get a team of his own. Talking some businessmen into helping him with the idea, he bought the St.
Pats, Toronto's entry in the National Hockey League, for $160,000. Then,

undaunted by the depression which was bearing down upon Toronto as the '30s began, he set out to build a fitting home for the hockey team that had now become the Toronto Maple Leafs. In those lean times, he had to finance his arena in any way he could. He got some money out of hard-headed local financiers, and contractors, carpenters, and masons got part of their pay in stock of the Maple Leaf Gardens, which was certainly a good thing for those who hung on to it, because this stock later sold for more than thirty times its original value. With Smythe breathing down their necks all the time, the builders got the $2,000,000, 12,586-seat arena erected in just five months from the time the first sod was turned.

Conn Smythe, if he had any animosity toward the management of the New York Rangers, certainly got even with them five years after his dismissal, when his Maple Leafs took the Stanley Cup from the Rangers in three straight games in 1932. Wherever Conn went on the hockey circuit, there was usually some fireworks. He had a sign hung in the Gardens' dressing room which read as follows:

THE TORONTO MAPLE LEAFS
DEFEAT DOES NOT REST LIGHTLY ON THEIR SHOULDERS

Hockey is a rough, body-contact game, as it is played on this continent, and Conn was once quoted as saying "If you can't beat 'em in the alley, you can't beat 'em on the ice." Once, after a particularly lively Donnybrook during a game, Conn rubbed his hands thoughtfully. "We'll have to stamp out that kind of thing," muttered the Little Pistol, "or people are going to keep on buying tickets."

Among those who deplored the aggressive attitude of the scrappy major was the late Frederic McLaughlin, owner of the Chicago Black Hawks, who issued a statement calling for more decorum in the game. When Conn Smythe made his next public appearance, during a game in Boston between the Maple Leafs and the Bruins, he startled all present by turning up wearing a top hat and tails. Carrying a large bouquet of thorny roses, he strode through the corridors of the Boston Garden tipping his hat and bowing politely to the fans. He seemed to particularly like needling Boston. On the eve of one clash between the Maple Leafs and the Bruins, he inserted a four-column-wide advertisement in the Boston newspapers which read: *If you're tired of what you've been looking at, come out tonight and see a decent team play hockey.*

If, as some critics say, Toronto has lacked certain color, it most certainly wasn't the fault of Conn Smythe, as colorful a citizen as you'd find in any man's town.

The years of depression were long and hard. Many a proud family breadwinner who had never in his life asked for help had to join the line-

up at the counters of a city office that became known as "the Pogey," to
register for relief. Soup kitchens flourished all over town for the single
unemployed and among the buildings which were utilized as flophouses
for the idle drifters who passed through Toronto in search of work was the
old St. Lawrence Hall, once the focal point for the wealth and glitter of
Toronto society and the scene of so many gala occasions in the life of the
city. Now, in the hall where Adelina Patti and Jenny Lind once sang,
there hung the heavy smell of disinfectant and the steel bunks extended
row on row while hopeless men sat on them and mumbled to one another
in flat monotonous voices.

Evictions for non-payment of rent or mortgages were common all over
the city. Often a family would return to its home to find all of its belong-
ings heaped on the front lawn, and a padlock on the door. Sometimes the
unemployed gathered in menacing rings around some neighbor's lost
home and the bailiff had to call for help from the police. Even more common than the evictions were the suspensions of electric or water service because the bills hadn't been paid.

OAKVILLE VETERAN'S WATER CUT OFF read an indignant
headline in the *Globe* after the public utilities department of the neighboring town halted a householder's service because he couldn't pay his
bill.

Thousands of the unemployed mustered in Queen's Park to protest
their lot and speakers damned capitalism from a bandstand right behind
the Legislative Buildings. They were joined by other groups of the
unemployed from all over the country to form what was called a Hunger
March to Ottawa and during the days of preparation for this trek there
were sometimes riots in Queen's Park which required the services of the
mounted members of Toronto's police force to restore order. Up on the
Holland Marsh, a few miles north of the city, vegetable-growers on some
of the richest land in the country had little to eat except potatoes, carrots,
onions, and cabbages, and were becoming destitute in the midst of their
rotting crops because there was so little sale for their products and the
commission merchants sometimes ended up charging the *farmers* for loads
of vegetables that didn't sell. Some Toronto organization finally bought
many carloads of the Holland Marsh vegetables to send out to the Western Prairies, where there was not only economic depression, but also severe
drought.

In the Toronto newspapers such classified ads as this were common: "$1
daily—Young man, 28, single, good education and appearance; bank
ledger-keeper experience; also chauffeur's and taxi license. Desires position."

Prices for goods and services were low enough, if only you had the money to buy them. A six-room house on Boulton Avenue was advertised for $15 a month and for $50 a month you could rent a 10-room house at Bloor Street and Spadina Avenue. Bungalows were being sold for $150 down and prime sirloin beef from prize stock that had been exhibited at the Royal Winter Fair could be had for 25 cents a pound. Sugar was 10 pounds for 46 cents; tea was 35 cents a pound and coffee 39 cents. A young fellow could take his girl to the movies and have a dish of ice cream on the way home for a total expenditure on the whole night out of not more than 50 cents.

When the people of Toronto who had been through it all later thought back upon the lean years of the '30s, they would remember perhaps more of the good things than the bad ones and among the very best things of that period were, of course, the radio programs which helped brighten the depression days. Toronto stations carried the dance music of Bert Niosi from the Palais Royale down by Sunnyside and the dulcet strains of Luigi Romanelli's Orchestra from the King Edward Hotel. Archie Cunningham entranced his listeners with his numbers on the piano from a Toronto radio station called CKCL. But one of the most popular radio programs of that time—which would have an extremely loyal following for twenty-two years—was a show that started out every weekday at 1:15 P.M. on the CBC station like this: First would come a loud knock on a door. Then a voice calling "Who's there?" And in a hearty chorus from the entire cast would come the words: "It's the *Happy Gang!*" Bert Pearl was the master of ceremonies, Kathleen Stokes sat at the organ, Blaine Mathe played the violin and Bob Farnon the trumpet. The Happy Gang's lighthearted interval became a sound as familiar to Toronto as the striking of the clock in the City Hall tower.

In 1934, with its population having grown from 9000 in 1834 to 629,285, Toronto celebrated the 100th anniversary of its incorporation as a city. In view of the depression, the city fathers were careful not to make any improvident expenditures of public funds, but they did line up a program of events that would extend through spring and summer of that year. On the stroke of midnight on March 6, 1934, a lone flaming rocket streamed skyward from the lake front near the Canadian National Exhibition Grounds. It was the signal to light up an oil-soaked pyramid of two hundred resin and tar barrels on historic Gilbraltar Point on Toronto Island. As thousands of people lined the waterfront, a hundred more rockets flashed into the night sky from the Island at fifteen-second intervals. When the pyrotechnics were over, a crowd of 12,000 gathered in the Coliseum on the CNE Grounds to take part in a prayer of thanksgiving and listen to a sermon by the Reverend Dr. J. H. Cody, president of the University of Toronto. The service was carried by radio throughout the nation. On hand for the ceremonies was William Lyon Mackenzie King, a grandson of Toronto's fiery first mayor. This descendant of the little rebel of the 1830s had been twice Prime Minister of Canada and was destined to assume the high office again the following year. Mr. King occupied a box in the Coliseum with ten other descendants of the colorful champion of civil liberties who had thrown Toronto into such a turmoil nearly a century before.

In May a four-day military pageant was held, opening with a parade through the city led by the Governor General's Body Guard in their scarlet tunics. Even by that time, Toronto was becoming more cosmopolitan in its nature and many who marched in the parade wore the costumes of their overseas homelands. But to inject a dash of rugged Canadianism into the affair more than 200 of the marchers were garbed in the costumes of lumberjacks, miners, and fishermen. Floats in the parade represented various historical incidents. The Governor General of Canada, Lord Bessborough, arrived to dedicate a restored Fort York, which was declared a national shrine. As 6000 gathered at the old fort to take part in the ceremonies, the famed Nova Scotia fishing schooner *Bluenose*, a likeness of which now adorns the back of the Canadian 10-cent piece, glided gracefully out through the Western Gap, just as the ships of sail had done during the days when Simcoe was building his little backwoods town.

The weather was warm and fine much of the time that summer and bright sunshine blessed most of the outdoor events. President Franklin D. Roosevelt had ordered the release of Upper Canada's little captured mace from its long-time resting place in the Naval Academy at Annapolis, Maryland. That summer, in a glittering and impressive ceremony, U. S. Admiral William D. Leahy arrived aboard a gunboat and returned the symbol of British parliamentary authority to the Honorable Herbert A. Bruce, Lieutenant Governor of Ontario. The countries which had bled through a great war together were now firm friends.

Britain sent Field Marshal Viscount Edmund Allenby and Sir Reginald Tyrwhitt, Admiral of the Fleet, to the Centennial ceremonies and a demonstration in precision flying was given over the city by seven pilots of the Royal Air Force in 200-miles-an-hour Hawker Fury fighter planes. Willoughby J. Cole, of Southampton, England, a descendant of John Graves Simcoe and Colonel Gabriel de Taffanel, Marquis de La Jonquiere, a descendant of the governor of New France who had ordered the building of Fort Rouille, also participated in the ceremonies. Special telephone lines were installed in Mayor William J. Stewart's office to permit leaders in other municipalities to directly extend anniversary congratulations. Many pageants displaying the city's history were conducted during the year as historians, poets and artists went to work depicting the past and future of their city.

Orators who tried to arouse visions of the Toronto of the future didn't do too badly as prophets, although they were perhaps a little modest in their predictions. They said that by the time another century had gone by, Metropolitan Toronto would have a population of 2,500,000 and the area from Highland Creek to Hamilton would be blanketed with urban development. There would be more television sets in the Toronto of 2034 than the city had telephones in 1934. Widespread automation and more leisure time for workers was foreseen and it was predicted that a network of subways and large-scale apartment complexes would make Toronto into a vast metropolis with a 50-mile radius. It would appear that the crystal balls being used by the civic officials weren't so very cloudy while they were making these optimistic guesses about the Toronto of the future.

Although 1935 came and went in Toronto without any particularly noteworthy events taking place, 1936 turned out to be a year of high excitement on several occasions. King George V died when his life came "peacefully to a close" at Sandringham Palace and before the year was out many Torontonians sat with tears in their eyes as they heard over their radios the historic address to his people in which Edward VIII announced his abdication from the ancient Throne of England so soon after beginning a reign which started with the high hopes of his devoted subjects in the city in which he was such a familiar and beloved figure.

At the beginning of that year the night assistant manager at the Nealon House on King Street was being frequently greeted by the customers of the beverage room as though he might have been a big-league hockey player or a football star. "Hi, Red!" they'd call out and the tall, handsome Norman Ryan would wave back cheerfully at the sound of his nickname. Red Ryan was indeed a celebrated resident of the city in which he was born. Only the summer before he had been released from Kingston Penitentiary after serving only eleven and a half years of a life sentence for bank robbery. Red had been in trouble off and on ever since he'd been a kid. He had been serving a sentence when the First World War broke out and he had convinced the prison authorities that he'd be of more use to King and country in the Army than behind bars. But not long after he'd arrived overseas, he deserted from the Army and, according to the story he later told, joined the French Foreign Legion for a while and, in turn, deserted from that. He knocked around the world for a few years, during which he took a whirl at crime in Australia. When the war was over he came back to Toronto and it wasn't long after he returned that he was sentenced to twenty-five years of imprisonment in Kingston Penitentiary for robbing a bank.

In November 1923 he and some companions went over the wall at Kingston and entered into a new series of bank robberies which placed them high on the lists of the continent's most wanted men. Ryan was arrested later that year in Minneapolis, Minnesota, and sentenced to life imprisonment when he was brought back to Canada. It was not long thereafter that Red Ryan, the notorious bank robber, appeared to undergo an impressive change in attitude.

Reports kept coming out of Kingston Penitentiary of how Red Ryan had undoubtedly become a reformed man in one of the most dramatic alterations of character in Canadian penal history. It was announced that after many long hours of experiment, he had developed a pick-proof lock for mail sacks and those who read the news said that surely a man who had performed such a public service could be reclaimed and returned to society. Said one hardened old Kingston con, who had heard one of the many lectures on the futility of crime Red had been giving his fellow inmates:

"He talks to them like a Dutch uncle. If I was a bank president, I'd make him chief guard!"

Newspaper reporters arranged to see this remarkable example of reformation.

"I want to carry a dinner pail again," said Red. "Tell those young men who are slipping backwards on life's highway to keep to the straight and narrow."

He was described as one of the most kindly and conscientious attendants in the prison hospital. When Warden J. C. Ponsford retired from Kingston Penitentiary, Red Ryan, his most model prisoner, sent him a note.

"I would feel rather ungrateful," he wrote, "if I failed to show my keenest regrets and genuine sorrow the news of your retirement has caused."

As the obviously intelligent and changed man went quietly about his prison duties in Kingston, a public clamor for his release began. Toronto ministers called for his parole in sermons from their pulpits.

"He became a model prisoner, indeed eventually Kingston's show piece," columnist J. V. McAree later wrote in the Globe and Mail. "Every visitor whom he met seems to have been impressed by him . . . One inspector continued to harbor doubts about Ryan's sincerity and for this heresy lost his job. Everybody who knew about this heartily approved, for there was a time when to doubt Ryan's honesty was a kind of blasphemy."

Finally, with an alert ear to the public's sympathies, Prime Minister Richard B. Bennett himself came down from Ottawa in 1935 to have a half-hour interview with the by-now nationally famous inmate of Kingston's grim gray Portsmouth Penitentiary. It wasn't long after this that Red Ryan received his parole and the public applauded the government's display of clemency toward such a worthy prisoner.

When he walked out of Kingston's gates on July 23, 1935, he warmly shook hands with the warden.

"If I ever go wrong again, I deserve to be shot," he declared. "For me to go back to a life of crime would be the biggest blow the ticket-of-leave system ever got."

Two top reporters of the Toronto *Star* were right there waiting for Red to drive him home and, incidentally, to keep him out of the clutches of rival Toronto newspapers. The *Star* had become renowned for such enterprise and reporters Athol Gow and Roy Greenaway got some choice quotes from their famous passenger on the way home. Toronto welcomed Red Ryan with open arms. Pictures of him were all over the newspapers. Wrestling promoter Frank Corcoran, a big-hearted Toronto sporting man, gave Red a night job at his Nealon House and a Weston car dealer employed him during the daytime as a salesman . . . and Red was certainly a salesman.

During some of his spare time—but, evidently, not all of his spare time—he went about the city lecturing boys' clubs on the folly of crime. At some of the hockey matches in the Maple Leaf Gardens he sat in the boxes with politicians and magistrates. His autograph was much in demand and it was suggested by someone that he be appointed a member of a Royal Commission on prison reform. Between his night job at the hotel and his daytime car-selling position, he earned $500 a month, which was a small fortune in those depression days. But, after all, celebrities come high.

Then, on Saturday afternoon May 23, 1936, in Sarnia, Ontario, two masked thugs stepped into a liquor store and pointed their guns at the clerks. One of them carried two pistols, a .45 and a .38. As they went about following the order to hand over the money, one of the clerks stealthily stepped on a special alarm button that rang a bell in police headquarters. The police quickly arrived on the scene and, as they rushed into the store, one of the thugs fired point-blank at Constable John Lewis and killed him. The robbers then tried to race down the stairs to make their escape, but before they had covered more than a few steps they were bowled over by a blast of gunfire from the other officers. Both gunmen died within a few minutes and when the mask was pulled from the face of the one who had shot Constable Lewis, it was discovered that it was Red Ryan, the freed model prisoner from Kingston Penitentiary. The other was an underworld pal of his by the name of Harold Checkley.

Four people, including the driver of the hearse, attended the burial of Red Ryan in Toronto. Thirteen days after the funeral, police ballistics experts announced that it had been one of the guns carried by Ryan in the

Sarnia robbery attempt that had been used early in 1936 to shoot down in cold blood a Markham garage man and town councilor named Edward Stonehouse, after he and his son had surprised some burglars in his premises.

Red Ryan got the wish he had so fervently made when he said good-by to the Warden of Portsmouth. He did go wrong again, he did get shot and he did deliver the biggest blow the ticket-of-leave system ever got. The number of paroles dropped sharply the following year.

Over in the newsroom of the *Star*, Roy Greenaway and Athol Gow set aside a manuscript which they had been rewriting from a biography Toronto's most famous criminal had prepared during his years in prison. The tentative title: *Crime Does Not Pay*.

Red Ryan had contributed an impressive last chapter to this work on the bloody steps of the liquor store in Sarnia. But the book was never published.

It was during the same spring of the same eventful year that another newspaper story broke in Toronto which would keep the city's people in a frenzy of excitement for days. On April 12, 1936, Dr. D. E. Robertson, chief surgeon at Toronto's Hospital for Sick Children, Alfred Scadding and Herman Magill were out in Moose River, Nova Scotia, to inspect an old gold mine with the intention of finding out whether it was feasible to reopen it. They descended to the 141-foot level and were looking about the shaft when suddenly, with a thunderous roar, a rock slide trapped them in the depths of the earth. A short time later there began one of the most dramatic rescue operations in Canadian history. Calls were hastily sent out, by those who began the work, to Nova Scotia's renowned "draegermen," coal miners who were specially trained in the hazardous tasks of rescue. As newspapers carried the story of the trapped men, a kind of hysteria began to grip the Canadian people and especially those of Toronto.

Over the radio network of the CBC came the grave and sonorous voice of announcer J. Frank Willis, describing the work of rescue right from the scene. It was his terse, regular bulletins, eagerly listened to in every Toronto household possessing a radio, that created, as much as any other factor, the growing sense of tension which gripped the Toronto populace.

On April 18 the rescue workers managed to sink a drill hole into the portion of the mine which held the trapped trio and on the next day faint voices from the depths of the earth indicated that at least some of them were still alive. Cocoa and brandy were lowered down the drill hole and the trapped men received their first nourishment in seven days. One of the factors which made the rescue attempts so dramatic and so greatly increased the tension of the newspaper-reading and radio-listening public, was that the ever-present danger of fresh rock slides constantly threatened both the trapped men and those who were trying to reach them. At one point the going was so delicate that rescuers pawed away at the soil with their bare hands rather than risk setting off another slide by the jar of picks and shovels.

On Monday, April 20, Scadding shouted up the drill hole that Magill had died. He also told those on the surface that it wasn't likely that he and Dr. Robertson could last for much more than about another ten hours, because of the rate at which water was rising in their prison. Rescuers redoubled their efforts, tortured by the thought that if they moved too slowly they might not reach the men in time and if they moved too fast they might set off another slide. All of these harrowing facts were duly passed on to the anxious public by J. Frank Willis, whose deep-voiced and solemn delivery seemed to match so perfectly the grimness and the urgency of it all. The bulletins came on the air from the mine site more and more frequently as rescue work progressed and soon a large portion of Toronto's population was sitting up half the night listening to them. The drama being enacted at Moose River was a constant subject of excited conversation all over the city.

On Tuesday it was duly reported in one of Frank Willis' regular bulletins that Dr. Robertson, the eminent Toronto physician, had asked for a fountain pen to be lowered down the drill hole in order that he could draw up his last will and testament. The draegermen and the rest of the rescuers—some three hundred in all—kept working like slaves in circumstances of great peril.

"Do you want to live on this earth all your life?" scornfully asked one grimy miner when he was advised to slow down and take it easy because of some suspicious-looking loose rock in the area where he was feverishly working.

By Wednesday afternoon, it looked as though the dog-tired rescue workers were going to accomplish their mission of boring from an old shaft nearby into the spot where the men were trapped. But there was still some tricky rock to contend with. Nevertheless, Toronto's Wednesday afternoon newspapers, assuming that the men would soon be saved, screamed RESCUED in boxcar letters on their front pages. It was not, however, until 12:44 A.M. Atlantic Standard Time on Thursday, April 23, that Dr. Robertson was finally brought up to the surface, followed by Scadding at one o'clock. Led by some members of the Salvation Army, that stalwart organization which so often turned up in places where it saw a need, the weary rescue crews doffed their hats and sang "Praise God from Whom All Blessings Flow."

The people of Toronto, having followed every minute of the last few hours of the rescue, ran out into the streets laughing and crying. The bells in the City Hall wildly pealed out a thankful clamor for the rescue of Toronto's two citizens who had undergone such a cruel ordeal.

REALLY RESCUED read the banner line on the extra edition the *Globe* got out that morning. "The Old Lady of Melinda Street" could not help needling its impetuous contemporaries.

In July of that summer of 1936, Toronto sweltered through one of the greatest heat waves in its history. Some one fried an egg on the City Hall steps and at night people left their stifling houses by the thousands to sleep on the grass along the lakeshore at Sunnyside and in the Canadian National Exhibition Grounds. After the hot and smothering blanket had lasted for more than a week, ambulances of the Public Health department began to work steadily all through the night and day, rushing to hospitals those who had collapsed from the heat. Torontonians began dying by the dozens, so many, in fact, that the newspapers gave up writing separate stories on the victims and merely ran casualty lists, like those of wartime, on their front pages.

It was at the very height of the depression that the city which prided itself in its sane and sensible ways was the scene of an event so utterly wacky that newspapers from all over the continent sent reporters to embarrassed Toronto to record the details. October 31, 1936, had been set as the deadline, in the will of Toronto lawyer Charles Vance Millar, for the payment of $500,000 from his estate to the Toronto mother who had borne the largest number of children during a ten-year period after his death in 1926. The eccentric lawyer also left in his will stocks in breweries and race tracks to local ministers of the church. As the pay-off day drew near, the mothers who were running neck-and-neck or baby-and-baby were solemnly interviewed by newspapermen. A Mrs. Matthew Kenny, a plump little woman who then appeared to be right in there among the top contenders, gravely informed reporters who asked to speak to her husband one afternoon that he was upstairs sleeping because, at this critical phase of the contest, he needed all the rest he could get.

When the time did arrive to distribute the money to the winner of what had become known all over North America as the Millar Stork Derby or the Maternity Sweepstakes, the whole thing descended into a brawl among many contenders and a court case that went on for almost two years. Finally the money was divided equally between Mrs. Arthur Timleck, Mrs. John Maclean, Mrs. Alfred Smith, and Mrs. John Nagle, each of whom had borne nine children during the ten years following Millar's death. For the lucky families it was a fantastic windfall, coming as it did in the midst of the depression when some of the fathers were out of work. But the *Globe and Mail* probably spoke for a large number of the more staid citizens of Toronto when it said in an editorial following the distribution of the Millar fortune:

> Nothing about the notorious Millar will stipulations and the nauseating details of recent contentions and litigation is more welcome than the apparent ending of the sorry business. There will be general hope that the battling claimants are appeased by the money grants received, and that nothing further will be heard, in court or elsewhere, of the will and the uproar it created. Also, there will be fervent hope that no other wealthy man will get it into his head to do likewise with his money. Even the humorously cynical Charles Millar could not have anticipated the situation that has arisen as a result of his strange bequest: mothers contending for the rights of legitimate and illegitimate children, wrangles about birth registrations, and awakening of the sordid impulses that the expectation of money can arouse . . .

Hectic 1936 would be a year that was long remembered in the bustling city on the Bay.

Chapter 22
1939–1945
THE SECOND WORLD WAR

The coming World War casts its shadows. The "old sweats" of 1914–18 hold giant Toronto reunion. The first visit of a British sovereign. Toronto's men march off to battle. New encampments at the CNE. No. 110 City of Toronto Squadron is first R.C.A.F. unit to arrive overseas. The city is stunned by casualties at Dieppe. Toronto produces huge armada of warplanes. Bren machine guns by the thousands. Casa Loma's secret war plant. The young "war guests" from Britain. Toronto hails the news of victory.

As the late 1930s carried Toronto, Canada, and the world along toward the testing time that would begin in 1939, there was an uneasy feeling that some day a confrontation with the Axis allies would have to come, but this mood of vague apprehension had for most become almost a way of life. Toronto radios sometimes carried the peculiar fluttering sounds of relayed short wave broadcasts from far-off Berlin, in which Hitler raved and the great *"Heils!"* of the Nazi faithful came ebbing and flowing from loudspeakers like the sound of some angry sea beating against a distant shore. Mussolini swaggered and held up his fist in the Fascist salute while diminutive Haile Selassie, Lion of Judah and Emperor of Ethiopia, sat in refuge in London and dreamed of the day his country would be free from the oppression of its Italian invaders. In 1937 the Liberals, under their colorful leader Mitchell F. Hepburn, returned to power in Ontario. A new tailored-to-measure national airline called Trans-Canada came into being. In the fall of the previous year, young George McCullagh, a handsome and audacious former promotion man and financial writer for the *Globe*, who had gone out on Bay Street, made a fortune in the brokerage business and then came back to buy the paper with the backing of mining tycoon William H. Wright, had merged it with the *Mail and Empire* to form the

Globe and Mail. A new airport was opened on Toronto Island, which would later serve as a training base for the fugitive members of the Royal Norwegian Air Force, after that country fell to Hitler's legions.

William Lyon Mackenzie King was again Prime Minister of Canada, for the third time, and often during his visits to Toronto he would go over to Bond Street to pay a quiet little pilgrimage to the home of his fiery rebel grandfather. Mr. King always had a great respect for his ancestors and it was even whispered that he sometimes sought through mediums the advice of those who had gone to the Great Beyond. The house in which William Lyon Mackenzie had died had not, at that time, been taken over as a historical monument and it was a seedy and broken-down little dwelling that was regarded as a shrine by few other than Mr. King.

The story is that on one of his visits to Toronto, the rather prim bachelor Prime Minister took a couple of friends up to Bond Street to show them the last home of his famous grandfather. The three men arrived in a chauffeur-driven limousine that halted across the road from the old Mackenzie home. Emerging from the car, they all doffed their hats and stood respectfully gazing at the house while Mr. King described its background. They were staring at the house and listening intently to Mr. King when, to the consternation of them all—and particularly that of the Canadian Prime Minister—a painted woman furtively pulled open the curtains at the window of an upper room of the grubby little place and impatiently waggled her finger at the trio to come right on in, instead of standing out there inviting the attention of the police.

In 1938, the year Germany seized Austria and brought one step closer the conflagration that was to set the whole world aflame, the Canadian Corps held a great reunion in Toronto. The old sweats were looking a little grayer and a lot thicker around the middle, but before long some of them would be back in the service of the King. Veterans from every part of the country swarmed all over Toronto and their colored berets bobbed through the streets by the thousands. Youngsters who watched their hijinks and wondered what it must have been like to fight in a war, were soon to find out.

The great new Cunard liner *Queen Mary* made a record transatlantic run that year. Soon she would be donning a grim coat of battleship gray paint in New York harbor, to begin her career as a troopship. Toronto, the mining center of Canada, heard the interesting news that an important iron discovery had been made at Steep Rock in the Ontario bush.

In the green and mellow spring of 1939, Toronto had the first visit in its history of a British sovereign. King George VI, a shy young man on his first great Commonwealth mission, stepped off the Royal train at the flag-bedecked North Toronto railway station on Yonge Street just below St.

Clair Avenue. At his side was Queen Elizabeth. Although female members of the Royal family—and especially Queens—are almost invariably referred to in newspaper reports as looking "radiant" when they appear upon the scene, it was certainly the only fitting word to describe Her Majesty. Her sunny smile and the peculiar way in which she waved her hand quickly won the hearts of the people of Toronto, as it did those of the other towns and cities in Canada. The King was rather solemn and grave, but the Queen—whom, every one agreed, looked *much* more beautiful than in her pictures—was lively and vivacious at all times. Often she nudged the King to bring his attention to some special group and occasionally tears sprang to her eyes as she was touched by some particularly moving gesture of the Toronto subjects of her slim, quiet husband. In the still intensely loyal City of Toronto, the people nodded their heads and said that this was indeed a striking demonstration of the value of the Monarchy, a system in which the people made proud the King and the King made proud the people.

After Prime Minister King, who scarcely left the side of the Royal couple during the entire Canadian tour, had introduced to Their Majesties the Lieutenant Governor of Ontario and Mrs. Matthews, Premier and Mrs. Mitchell F. Hepburn and Mayor and Mrs. Ralph Day, the King inspected the Guard of Honor while the last booms of a Royal salute rang out from the guns of the 21st Medium Battery of the Royal Canadian Artillery. Then they drove off to the City Hall. As he mounted the steps to the reception platform, which was decorated with an immense blue drapery bearing the arms of Canada in color and topped by a huge Royal crown, the King halted and briskly saluted the Cenotaph erected to the memory of those Toronto thousands who had died in the First World War.

After the ceremony in front of the City Hall, the King and Queen were driven to the Legislative Buildings at Queen's Park, past cheering thousands. Heralded by a fanfare of trumpets, the Royal car pulled up in front of the massive old building, which was bedecked with many pennants bearing the crosses of St. Andrew and St. George. After Premier Hepburn had read the province's official address of welcome to the Royal couple in the Assembly Chamber, he presented to them seven Ontario holders of the Victoria Cross. They were Sergeant Colin Baron, Private Thomas W. Holmes, Captain B. H. Geary, Major E. J. Holland, Lieutenant Walter Bayfield, Sergeant H. H. Robson, and Captain Charles Rutherford. The spectators in the crowded galleries applauded enthusiastically. This was the kind of scene that was dear to the hearts of Torontonians. Though modern cynics may smile at this fierce loyalty to the Crown that had always been one of Toronto's most striking characteristics, this sentiment was one of the strongest fibers in weaving the fabric of the city's greatness in that day's Canadian scheme of things.

When the ceremonies in the Assembly Chamber had been completed, the King and Queen were escorted to the Lieutenant Governor's suite in the Legislative Buildings, where they met Canada's world-famed Dionne quintuplets and Dr. Allan Roy Dafoe, who had brought them into the world and cared for them since then. The "Quints" had been brought down from Callander in a special train. The five little girls lined up before the King and Queen and made their carefully rehearsed curtsies. Then six-year-old Cecile ran over to the Queen and stood in front of her, holding up her arms. The Queen knelt down, and Cecile put her arms around her neck and gave her a big hug and a kiss. Instantly her sisters rushed over, childishly ignoring the protocol called for on such a great occasion, and the Queen gave each of them a kiss. But then Cecile, evidently not wishing to see the King forgotten, ran over to him and held his hand. He leaned down and whispered something to the child and they both laughed.

After the ceremonies at Queen's Park, the Royal couple proceeded to Riverdale Park, escorted this time by the mounted soldiers of the Governor General's Horse Guards, resplendent in their scarlet tunics, their pipe-clayed gauntlets and their burnished helmets. In the vast natural amphitheater formed by the surrounding green hills of the park there extended a sight the like of which had never before been seen in Toronto. Down on the flat, where ancient guns had been fired in the early part of the century to celebrate "old battles" every May 24, were assembled 75,000 Toronto school children. Sitting or standing on the grassy slopes were 100,000 more of Toronto's people. As the glittering calvalry accompanied the Royal car into the great bowl of Riverdale, a thunderous cheer arose from the assembled throng.

Later in the day the King and Queen were on hand at old Woodbine Race Track on Queen Street to personally present, for the first time in the long history of the classic Canadian horse race, the Royal guineas to the winner of the King's Plate. Originally it had been called the Queen's Plate, when first it was run back in 1860 in the days of Victoria, but never before in all of its long history had the event been attended by the ruling Sovereign. The race was won on that mellow day of May by Archworth and, somewhat to the consternation of the vast array of gray-toppered owners, Jockey Club officials and many other dignitaries assembled at the Woodbine that day, the colt's owner stepped up to receive the purse of fifty guineas from the King's own hand, wearing an ordinary business suit. It would not be known until later that the reason young George McCullagh appeared in such casual attire was that it was only at the very last moment that his dying mother had persuaded the publisher of the *Globe and Mail* to leave her bedside at London, Ontario, and drive to Toronto just in time to see his horse win the historic race.

On their farewell drive through the city that day the car bearing the King and Queen stopped at Christie Street Military Hospital, where, assembled in the yard, in bleachers and beside the path, stood three thousand veterans, nurses who had served overseas and Silver Cross mothers who had lost sons in the great conflict that was supposed to end all wars. Assembled at the front of the gathering, in wheel chairs and hospital beds, were two hundred veterans who were still suffering the pain of wounds received on the battlefields of France a whole generation before.

King George and Queen Elizabeth departed from Toronto at the Union Station on Front Street and, as they walked toward its doors, the Queen suddenly spotted the thousands who were leaning out of every south window of the lofty Royal York Hotel and excitedly stopped His Majesty to point them out to him. He stood there for a few moments smiling and waving up at them and then the grave young Monarch and his gracious and lively Queen turned away and continued to their train, the great blue steam locomotive of which would proudly bear for many years a Royal crown on its front.

That fall, just as the people of Toronto were preparing for the Labor Day holiday, came the Second World War. It was a warm and pleasant weekend, as far as the weather was concerned. On that Saturday, September 2, Germany marched its armies into Poland and the defenders of that unfortunate country tried to push back the invading tanks and armored troop-carriers with cavalry mounted on horses. But this war was not to be like any other, as new wars seldom are. *Blitzkrieg* was a word that would soon become common in the headlines of the Toronto newspapers.

On that Saturday the Germans hastily closed their display at the Canadian National Exhibition, in which colorful posters invited Toronto tourists to come sailing on the Rhine or visit the Black Forest. Some visitors from Toronto would indeed see these tourist attractions, in a few years, but they would get there the hard way. A loud cheer went up from a gathering of bystanders as workmen lowered a sign reading, GERMANY from the top of the exhibit.

But there would be very little more cheering in Toronto that weekend or in the days to follow. The same old familiar things were happening—except in one respect. Recruits were lining up once more at the doors of the University Avenue Armoury, guards were being posted at Hydro installations, everything was almost a playback of that August 25 years ago—yet, this time there were no gay parades in the streets or choruses of "Rule, Britannia!" There was just a quiet acceptance of what everyone had known was really inevitable. The memories of the last World War were still too vivid to permit the lighthearted approach to world conflict that had featured the beginning of the Great Adventure back in 1914. In this war there would be sober resolve and great organization and complex weapons and terrible death tolls among both soldiers and civilians, but there would be few gay, jaunty songs like "Pack Up Your Troubles in Your Old Kitbag" or "Mad'moiselle from Armentières."

Ontario Premier Mitchell F. Hepburn ordered four aircraft of the Ontario Provincial Air Service—a bush fire-fighting organization—to commence regular patrols of critical areas, such as those embracing Hydro installations and the Welland Ship Canal, to keep an eye out from the sky for possible saboteurs. Sentries stood on guard at the headquarters of the Royal Canadian Navy Volunteer Reserve and at the Armoury, from the vast interior of which there sounded the muffled wail of the bagpipes as the 48th Highlanders once more mustered their men. Other units of the Toronto garrison, such as the Governor General's Horse Guards, the Royal Regiment of Canada, the Queen's Own Rifles, the Queen's York Rangers, the Irish Regiment of Canada and the Toronto Scottish also proceeded full speed with their mobilization. More than a thousand recruits were sworn in during that first weekend.

On Sunday morning Prime Minister Neville Chamberlain of Great Britain issued his terse announcement: "This country is now at war with Germany." The King who had so recently visited Toronto said: "In this grave hour, perhaps the most fateful in our history, I send to every household of my people at home and overseas this message: For the second time in our lives, we are at war . . ."

Although Canada itself was not yet officially at war and would not be until the formal declaration had been made at a special session of Parliament at 10:23 on the following Saturday evening, everybody knew Canada was in it. But somehow the full import of this awful fact didn't really sink into the minds of many of the people of Toronto on the fateful Sunday morning in the midst of the Labor Day holiday weekend. Such things as the outbreak of a great world war take a while to be completely realized.

But it wasn't long before the full stark impact of the new and grim state of affairs was impressed upon them. That evening, while listening to their favorite Sunday night radio programs in the quiet comfort of their living rooms, they were startled to hear a broadcast interrupted for a special news bulletin. The liner *Athenia*, bound for Montreal with 1400 passengers, including 120 Torontonians, had been torpedoed by a German submarine 200 miles west of the Hebrides. Even Toronto's young people, who knew little or nothing about the old war, began dimly to realize that this, then, was the way war was to be. Some of the city's young men made in their minds a solemn resolve, that very evening, to present themselves at a recruiting station next day. Many of their people, from their city, were clinging to life rafts on the bleak Atlantic that night and the thought of it brought to their hearts a peculiar kind of cold anger they had never felt before.

As the Canadian National Exhibition neared its end, next day, Midway impresario Patty Conklin quickly scrapped a show called Cleopatra and put in its place a display of old weapons and other relics from the First World War.

High above the CNE waterfront, Flight Lieutenant Ernest McNab of the Royal Canadian Air Force put through its paces before the great crowd a swift new fighter aircraft called the Hawker Hurricane. This airplane and its noble successor, the Spitfire, would next year stem the tide in the skies over London during the historic Battle of Britain and Ernie McNab and his young Canadian comrades would be included among the select and gallant group to which Winston Churchill paid tribute so eloquently when he uttered the stirring words: "Never in the field of human conflict was so much owed by so many to so few."

On the last day of the last "Ex" Torontonians would see for five years, a bull threw a press agent, and this unusual twist won some ink in the local papers for the enterprising publicity man who had tried to ride the animal as a stunt at the rodeo which was going on in the Coliseum. Soon this huge building would be known as the Manning Pool, where recruits were accepted and processed by the thousands. During the first war the CNE had been able to continue its two-week run each year while the soldiers were camped elsewhere under canvas. This time the buildings would be used by the military the year round.

Henrich Boediwein, a former member of the famed Baron Manfred von Richthofen's *jaegstaffel*, turned up at a Toronto registration center to signify that he was ready to fight for his adopted land, but requested that his services not be used in direct conflict with his former countrymen. Old Canadian warbirds were soon back in uniform, this time in the blue-gray of the Royal Canadian Air Force, which would finally be fighting under its own standard, although many of its members would be scattered through squadrons of the Royal Air Force from time to time. William Avery Bishop donned the uniform of an Air Vice-Marshal and his flying comrade and fellow winner of the Victoria Cross in the old war, William G. Barker, would also undoubtedly have reappeared in the R.C.A.F. had he not been killed nine years earlier while demonstrating a new training plane at Rockliffe Airport near Ottawa.

Meanwhile, came news from overseas that one of the first raids of the Royal Air Force against enemy territory had merely dropped propaganda leaflets on the Ruhr Valley urging the Germans to rebel against Adolf Hitler. It would not be long before it was admitted that something more potent than pamphlets would have to be dropped upon the Reich before the Germans changed their minds about their leader.

No. 110 City of Toronto Squadron of the R.C.A.F. was destined to be the first Canadian air unit to go into action against the enemy. It had originally been designed to act as an army co-operation squadron, equipped with slow-flying Lysanders. It disembarked in England on February 25, 1940. Later, after only two weeks of additional training, some of its men would be pressed into action as fighter pilots during the Battle of Britain. The squadron's insignia was an eagle's head in front of crossed tomahawks and bore the motto: "*Percussuri Vigiles*" ("On Watch to Strike").

One of its pilots, Flight Lieutenant "Bitsy" Grant, was to establish something of a reputation as a train-buster, bagging fifty-eight locomotives in occupied France before he was killed in September 1943.

The first of Canada's ground troops had already landed in England in December 1939, the vanguard of 300,000 from the cities and towns and farms of the nation. Among them were many young men from Toronto. And there were many who had most definitely passed the full bloom of youth. Major Conn Smythe, M.C., turned his back on his beloved Maple Leaf Gardens to head up the 30th Battery of the Royal Canadian Artillery, which soon became known as the "sportsmen's battery" because of the number of athletes and other sports figures it contained. Sports columnists Ralph Allen of the *Globe and Mail* and Ted Reeve of the *Telegram*, who may have thought Smythe was occasionally a trifle opinionated and even truculent as the head of their city's hockey team and sports palace, regarded the Little Pistol highly enough when the country was at war and the chips were down to join up with his battery. When the battery was later obliged to build some shelters, during a spell of guard duty on the Pacific coast before proceeding overseas, Allen, who was probably the world's worst carpenter, superintended the construction by his crew of a woefully wobbly structure which staggered in all directions. As Major Smythe made his rounds to inspect the work, he paused in wonder before Allen's production.

"Well!" said the Little Pistol, "it looks not unlike the Taj Mahal, Corporal Allen . . ."

Major Gregory Clark, M.C., of the First World War, and Major Bert Wemp, D.F.C., of the same vintage, went hotfooting it back overseas as war correspondents—Clark for the *Star* and Wemp (a former Toronto mayor) for the *Telegram*. Bert Wemp's standard opening question: "Is there anybody here from Toronto?" became a familiar greeting wherever

Canadians were stationed. Ralph Allen was later released from the Army to become the *Globe and Mail*'s war correspondent.

Canadian troops including the 48th Highlanders, the Hastings and Prince Edward Regiment and the Royal Canadian Regiment—all containing a goodly number of soldiers from Toronto—crossed over the English Channel to France on June 13, 1940. Within four days they were desperately retreating through Brest on the way back to England, being strafed unmercifully all the while by the Luftwaffe, which was then flying high in more ways than one.

After Dunkirk came the long lull that was to be known as "the phony war," during which time Canadian fighting men were forced to cool their heels in England, bored and frustrated. But they picked up a new language—English—which they thought they had known all the time. Movies became flicks, pies turned into tarts, drivers drove lorries instead of trucks, soldiers went prowling about London not on a subway but in the tube—and they learned not to become excited or take anything for granted just because the barmaid in a pub called them "dear."

Then, suddenly, on August 19, 1942, it was no longer a phony war, as far as Canada was concerned. On that day five thousand Canadians, comprising five-sixths of the attacking force, went ashore in France at Dieppe. When the brief, fierce action on Dieppe's pebbly beach was over 3350 had been killed, wounded, or taken prisoner.

It was after this tragic fiasco that the casualty lists began appearing in the Toronto newspapers as in the sad days of 1914–18. Yet, it did bring a proud thrill to all of Canada when it was later announced that two of its brave men who went through hell that day in the death-box of Dieppe had been awarded the Victoria Cross. They were Captain John Weir Foote of Madoc, Ontario, a gallant padre who refused to leave the beach and was taken prisoner with the wounded he sought to comfort and Lieutenant Colonel Charles Ingersoll Merritt of Vancouver who led his men across a bridge that was being heavily swept with gunfire and was littered with the dead.

At home in Toronto, the wheels of industry were spinning night and day in the production of weapons of war. Under Phillip C. Garratt, who had been a pilot in the First World War with the Royal Flying Corps (and whose doctor father had patched up the first victim of a Toronto electric streetcar) the de Havilland Company was moving into production. During the lean years after its establishment in Canada in 1928, de Havilland had kept its handful of employees working at the job of assembling and repairing aircraft made by the parent concern in England. Before the war had ended de Havilland's Toronto plant would have a staff of 8000 at its peak and would turn out 1520 Tiger Moth trainers, 375 twin-motored Ansons and no less than 1032 Mosquito light bombing and re-connaissance aircraft. The speedy Mosquito was the aircraft that had a good deal to do with the turning of the tide in the air war and Toronto's contribution to this accomplishment was a great one.

Plants large and small in the Toronto area were playing a vital part in the struggle. Massey-Harris turned from the production of farm machinery to the manufacture of such articles as aircraft parts. The John Inglis Company's payroll swelled to 17,000 workers who turned out more than 100,000 Bren machine guns as well as such vital items as engines for de-stroyers and corvettes. Research Enterprises manufactured critical and complicated range-finders, prismatic gun-sights and other precise military optical equipment which would have been considered far beyond the reach of Canadian technicians only a few years earlier. When radar arrived, the plant also turned out many units of this remarkable invention.

Even within the turreted walls of Toronto's prime curiosity, Casa Loma —although it wasn't revealed until after the war—technicians were working under heavy security precautions producing highly secret anti-submarine devices.

On the sea, where, before the war had ended the country would have 90,000 officers and men serving in the Royal Canadian Navy's 375 fighting ships and smaller craft, Toronto was heavily represented. Lieutenant Commander William Sclater, in his book about *H.M.C.S. Haida,* the Tribal class destroyer which covered herself with perhaps more glory than any other Canadian warship, describes a scene aboard the vessel when her officers were guessing the reason for a sudden cancellation of shore leave at Plymouth:

" 'Maybe it's the invasion,' said a brash young officer brightly and then subsided as he realized the amused contempt aroused by his suggestion.

" 'Tell him, somebody,' said a lounging senior, 'or is he too young to know?'

" 'What's the use?' another asked, 'he wouldn't understand anyway.'

" 'Oh, is he from Toronto?' rejoined the first speaker sweetly.

"At that about half the wardroom, to whom that much-abused city was home, piled on the speaker simultaneously and he disappeared beneath a mass of struggling bodies, arms and legs."

H.M.C.S. Haida, preserved as a permanent reminder of Canada's part in the war at sea, now lies berthed at Ontario Place.

Before the war had been long under way, many of the thousands of British children who had been moved to Canada were living with Toronto families. They were called "war guests" and some of them stayed in the city several years and, to Toronto ears, seemed to begin losing much of their English accents—although their parents would later say they'd picked up *Canadian* accents. Nelson Quarrington of the *Telegram*, who was one of the finest newspaper photographers who ever worked in the city, took a picture of one tot shaking hands with a policeman as he arrived at the Union Station in the early days of the war. When the youngster was returning three years later, the imaginative Quarrington got the same policeman and photographed him saying goodbye to the same youngster at the same place. When the *Telegram* published the two pictures side by side in the closing years of the war, showing a much taller young fellow returning to England, it provided an almost poignant indication of how swiftly the grim years of strife were rolling by.

There was rationing, of course, and tips were published on how to stretch your meager butter allowance by adding gelatin and there were no cuffs on the trousers of suits because, as it was pointed out, fifty-four pairs of saved cuffs were almost enough to make a battle dress for a soldier. Kate Aitken, a woman broadcaster in Toronto, gave weekly menus on her program which could be produced on the current rations and the women of the city hoarded their precious silk or nylon hose for special events and wore cotton or rayon ones the rest of the time.

"Make do, remake, eat it up, wear it out," advised the Consumer Branch of the Wartime Prices and Trade Board. Liquor got down to one small "mickey" a month and one tippler sadly complained that he *spilled* that much pouring the first drink in the morning. There was a "dim-out" in the later years of the war to conserve Hydro power to turn the wheels of industry which were so busy all over the Toronto area. The civilian population of the city never approached the British public's level of austerity, of course, but it did have to tighten its belt.

Then, as the early months of 1945 arrived, there came news of more and more victories for the Allies. Now, as well as the casualty lists, there began to appear names of those who had been liberated from German captivity. Soldiers of the once mighty *Wehrmacht* were surrendering by the millions and almost every day the newspapers told of a new batch laying down its arms. On May 1, Hitler committed suicide in his bunker in Berlin and when the news hit Toronto papers there was an item from Moscow which said the Russians believed it was only a trick. But it was real, all right, as were the pictures of Italian partisans stringing the bodies of Benito Mussolini and his mistress up by the heels.

As victory seemed to be approaching, Judge W. T. Robb, chairman of the Liquor Authority Control Board, sternly announced that all liquor stores and beverage rooms in the city would be closed if and when the great day arrived. When it did come, on May 6, the people of the city went wild. Skyrockets flared above the rooftops and tens of thousands crowded the City Hall square. Dancers attached paper streamers to a star-

61. The first St. James Church.

62. The present St. James Cathedral stands on the site of the first.

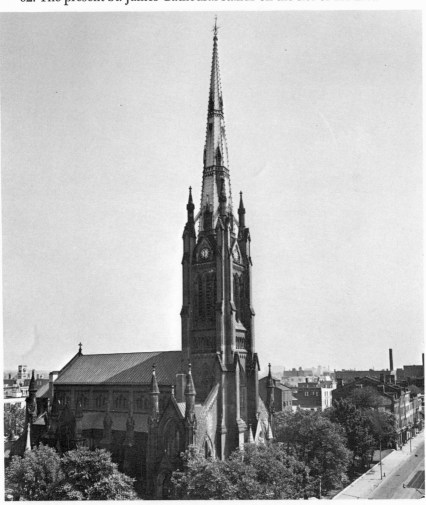

63. Toronto Island is still a quiet retreat from the uproar of the nearby city.

64. Canadian National Exhibition is world's largest annual fair. Prince's Gate entrance is shown in foreground.

65. Animals are displayed in natural settings such as this at the new Metro Toronto Zoo, one of the finest on the continent.

66. Completed Eaton Centre (left foreground) is shown superimposed on general view of downtown Toronto's impressive skyline.

67. City Hall, opened in 1965, is still one of Toronto's most spectacular structures.

tled Toronto policeman and used him for a maypole as they circled round and round while he stood there peering out from under the tall helmet which the city's constables still wore in those days. Cheering people moved through the streets aboard crowded automobiles loaded down to the axles. The jubilant Mr. and Mrs. Mike Olynick, who had a baby girl that day, named her Victoria.

During the long and bitter struggle, in which Canada had more than a million men under arms, Toronto did its share. Three of its sons—Corporal George Topham, Major Frederick Albert Tilston, and Flight Lieutenant David Ernest Hornell (of suburban Mimico, now part of Metropolitan Toronto)—won three of the sixteen Victoria Crosses awarded to Canadians in that war. Many of Toronto's youth were among the 40,000 Canadian dead.

Perhaps as a sign of the swinging days to come, four thousand young "hepcats" crowded into Maple Leaf Gardens that month to "stomp" to the music of visiting Gene Krupa and his band.

Chapter 23

1945–1966

A Time of Change

The curious will of Thomas Foster. Opening of Sunnybrook Military Hospital. Mary Pickford visits her old home town once more. The great postwar wave of immigration. The spread of the suburbs. The bars open in Toronto. The new CNE Grandstand. The tragedy of the Noronic. The building of the subway. Metropolitan Toronto. Marilyn Bell swims Lake Ontario. Hurricane Hazel, Toronto's greatest disaster. The new City Hall. The six cities of Metropolitan Toronto.

As Toronto's fighting men began to return to their city during the months following the capitulation of Germany and Japan, they found the same old problems which had been encountered by their fathers when they came back in 1918–19. For one thing, there was a tremendous shortage of housing, and there was naturally the painful process of personal adjustment from the ways of war to those of peace.

In the year the war ended Toronto heard the details of the curious will which had been left by its former Mayor Tom Foster, who had died at the ripe age of ninety-four. He gave $500,000 to the University of Toronto for cancer research and then distributed the remainder of his estate in a number of remarkable ways. He provided for the upkeep of the great $200,000 mausoleum he had built for himself and his family at his old home town of Uxbridge. It was called the Thomas Foster Memorial and it had been built along the lines of a miniature Taj Mahal, which the one-time Cabbagetown butcher had seen during a visit to India. In his will he requested that the memorial be held "as a place for religious or commemorative services in honor of the pioneers of the district and the ancestors of the people living in it." Although he had been a lifelong Presbyterian, he left $5000 each to the Anglican and United Churches but only $3000 to his own. He set up a fund, the income of which was to be used each year for the holding of a picnic for Toronto school children and stressed that "the Mayor, or some prominent clergyman of the City of Toronto make a short public address at the picnic explaining by whom and in what manner the picnic was provided." This annual affair still takes place.

He also provided a sum of $5000, the income of which was to be used for the feeding of birds in Toronto, and the annual income from a further bequest of $100,000 for the purchasing, planting, and maintenance of trees alongside the main arterial highways leading into Toronto ". . . to the intent that parties approaching the city may do so over beautifully treed roadways." He also provided money for the erection of flagpoles in the city and a fund to help newsboys get into business.

Also—horror of horrors!—he left some money to be shared among the Toronto mothers who had borne the most children in the ten years following his death. It was only the modest sum of $2500, however, and didn't start another frantic Toronto stork derby such as that set under way in 1936 by the will of Charles Vance Millar. The sum was later divided between seven Toronto mothers with a total of fifty-four children.

In 1946 the great new Sunnybrook Military Hospital was opened and the Grandstand burned down at the Canadian National Exhibition. Mary Pickford, "America's Sweetheart," came back for another visit to her old home town and Toronto's Archbishop James C. McGuigan became a Cardinal of the Roman Catholic Church. The people of Toronto were pleased at the news that a hero of the Second World War, Field Marshal the Earl Alexander of Tunis had become Governor General of Canada.

Although no one had yet written a love song about Toronto, Lister Sinclair in 1946 brought smiles to some Canadians—and particularly to those in Toronto—with a musical play broadcast over the Trans-Canada network of the Canadian Broadcasting Corporation. It had a song called *We All Hate Toronto*, which ran like this:

> In Toronto the Good, it's quite understood; that
> sin is a thing to bewario.
> If you are bad be sure to be sad, for nothing is
> fun in Ontario.
> The people are pure and vengeance sure descends
> on a budding Lothario.
> The same is true of anyone who, prefers not to
> drink in a dairyo.
> They let him drink beer, but make it quite
> clear, it's really a crime in Ontario.
> In short you might say, if life is a play, Toronto's
> the censored scenario.

Which prompted an ex-Torontonian by the name of Ken Johnstone to spring loyally to his home town's defense with the remark in the Montreal *Standard:* "The Toronto citizen, despite the mantle his city would drape upon him, is a pretty good guy when you get him with his hair down."

It was not long after this that a Toronto woman newspaper reporter proved beyond any doubt that Torontonians didn't spend all their time hanging around dairyos when she came up with the startling intelligence that some one up at City Hall had figured out that the city's residents consumed no fewer than 527,530,600,000 glasses of water annually!

But in this year something happened that was to bring about a profound change in the personality and character of the city that had for so long been almost more British than Britain. Surveying their homelands which had been devastated in two great wars, some of the long-suffering little people of Europe—and some professional and business people as well —began looking for a place in which they could escape Europe's old spites and bitterness and build for themselves and their children a new life in some new land. Canada put out the welcome mat for immigrants and of all the provinces of Canada, none was more enthusiastic in its invitation than was Ontario. And as Ontario's largest city, Toronto naturally became home for a large proportion of those who came to live in the province. At first it was just a trickle and then it grew to a flood as hundreds of thousands of what were called New Canadians poured into the city.

Many of them were delighted with what they saw. A. C. Baxter, just two weeks out from Scotland, wrote in 1952 in a Toronto newspaper:

"Here is a man who has fallen in love with a city—the great big bustling, bursting, beautiful city of Toronto. I am a New Canadian, but already this is not your city only—it is also my city.

"There never was another city like Toronto," Mr. Baxter rhapsodized. "In no city that I know—and I have been in many—is there the same feeling of energy and greatness . . . Canada is on the march and here in Toronto we can see and hear the heartbeat of the giant itself . . . I wonder if Torontonians themselves realize the greatness and beauty of their city. This beauty is not that of Paris or Budapest or Prague or of Edinburgh, but the beauty is here to see. It is the beauty of prosperity and progress, the beauty of great factories and mighty apartment blocks— symphonies in stone and melodies in mortar."

As new suburbs sprouted up all around Toronto in the postwar years and the great exodus from the inner city got under way, the New Canadians moved into the old houses left behind by their former Toronto owners, until whole great sections of the city had been taken over by newcomers from Europe. Some of them were willing to live two, three, four, and even five families in a house, until they could establish homes of their own. But they brought new cultures and skills and a fresh vitality to the city and when the new Toronto began to be built, it was the brawny little Italian immigrants who could often be seen doing most of the labor on construction sites large and small.

By 1967, more than one-third of the entire population of Metro Toronto would be of other than British extraction and most of them would be jammed into the area that lay within the borders of the old city. They spread mainly westward from Yonge Street and for miles along such thoroughfares as Dundas and Bloor and College Streets and even St. Clair Avenue there extended signs advertising *fornitura* stores and *liquidazione* sales and movie house marquees offering such attractions as *Il Ponte Sul Fiume Kwai* and on the warm Sunday afternoons of spring little groups of Italians gossiped on every corner. The Italians made up the largest racial group among Toronto's immigrants from the Old World and such names as that of Alderman Joseph Piccininni were becoming more common upon the Toronto political scene.

In 1961, when the results of the Canadian census appeared, it revealed these remarkable figures concerning the racial extraction of Metro Toronto's population:

British	1,107,203
French	61,421
German	80,300
Italian	140,378
Jewish	53,123
Netherlands	33,434
Polish	58,578
Russian	14,186
Scandinavian	16,050
Ukrainian	46,650
Other European	136,610
Asiatic	20,534

Thus, in scarcely a decade and a half, had Toronto's whole racial character and makeup drastically changed. And it was indeed a fantastic change from the days when a candidate for civic office stood little chance of being elected if he failed to gain the support of the Loyal Orange Lodge and Tory Toronto was British to the core.

In 1947, cocktail bars opened in Toronto and those men of the church who had for so long zealously guarded the city's morals and preserved its notoriously quiet Sundays acted as though a bolt of lightning from Above might come down at any moment and smite the wicked place. It had become like "Sodom and Gomorrah before their destruction" they said and the drinking places opening up along Yonge Street were "hatcheries of

Hell." And one elderly lady sat at a bar on King Street enjoying the delicious thrill of carefully ordering different interesting-looking drinks as she worked her way right through the list, meticulously crossing them out as she polished them off.

In 1948 Mayor Robert H. Saunders, one of the most popular and capable chief magistrates the city ever had, resigned to become new chairman of the Ontario Hydro Commission. In 1955 he would die in an airplane crash and be deeply mourned by the people of the city on the street corners of which he once sold newspapers as a boy. It was also in 1948 that the Canadian National Exhibition opened a huge new $3,500,000 Grandstand to replace the one that had burned.

In the next year Toronto experienced the worst tragedy by fire in its history and it was a peculiar disaster in that it was all over before most of the people in the city knew anything about it and when the death toll was counted there wouldn't be a single Toronto name on the casualty roll.

On September 16, 1949, the Canada Steamship Lines excursion steamer *Noronic* docked in Toronto. The 6905-ton, 362-foot-long vessel had been built thirty-six years earlier in Port Arthur and was once regarded as the queen of the Great Lakes passenger fleet. She carried to Toronto that day 542 passengers on a gay holiday voyage to the Thousand Islands. Most of them were from Cleveland and Detroit.

On that pleasant early autumn day, the passengers thronged ashore to go sightseeing in Toronto, but most of them were back aboard the ship by midnight. Although it was later revealed that a passenger had mentioned to a bellboy some time shortly after 1 A.M. that he smelled smoke, an alarm wasn't turned in until 2:38 that morning. Although the firemen responded immediately, by the time they had arrived the *Noronic* was an inferno and there was nothing that could be done to save her. Although most of her passengers were removed to safety down ladders and gangplanks, 119 of them died when they were trapped in the flaming ship and for days the charred bodies lay in a temporary morgue at the CNE Grounds awaiting the completion of the difficult task of identification. On December 9 of that year the gaunt, fire-blackened hull of the *Noronic* was towed away to a Hamilton scrapyard and her owners eventually paid $2,150,000 to the families of the dead.

On September 8, 1949, to the skirl of the bagpipes, work had commenced on the Yonge Street subway. From that day Toronto's main stem would be a shambles for almost five years, during which time pedestrians had to pick their way through a chaos of barriers and clamoring construction equipment. Month after month the pneumatic drills and pile drivers set up such a horrible din that one Yonge Street merchant sadly shouted: "We have to use sign language to sell anything to our customers."

A startled elderly Toronto dowager was heard to say, as she peered suspiciously down into one of the many gaping caverns which opened on Yonge Street: "*Well!* I certainly hope they know what they're doing."

Most of the time they did, but sometimes they didn't. Communications were frequently cut off in some Yonge Street section as the great metal beasts chewed up telephone cables. The job had been proceeding only two months when a steam shovel took a bite out of a water main, setting off a gusher that tossed one workman eight feet into the air and flooded the basement bar and grill of a Yonge Street establishment with three feet of water. Fascinated Torontonians observed the uproar and clutter on Yonge Street and wondered whether they'd ever get the thoroughfare put back together again. Stocky little workmen recently arrived from Italy were also doing much of the slugging on this job, as they had on other construction projects throughout the city.

In that year Toronto novelist Hugh Garner wrote in a magazine article about his city that it had "the best street cars and the most stuckup prostitutes in the world." He was willing to concede that Toronto indeed had more than its share of snobs and killjoys, but pointed out that "it also has a lot of tough, hard sentimental little people and their descendants who came from Cheapside, Glasgow's Gorbals, Belfast's Falls Road, Lancashire cotton towns, the ghettos of Warsaw and Pinsk and the narrow alleys of Milan and Budapest . . ."

As for Toronto's notoriously quiet Sundays, said Garner, the reason the people preferred them that way was because they were recovering from hangovers from the Saturday night before and greatly needed their sleep.

In 1951 a gang of thugs led by Alonzo Boyd robbed fourteen Toronto banks and killed a city detective before they were placed behind bars. Next year the Toronto Transportation Commission was hit by a strike and Torontonians became quite chummy as they shared the inconvenience and their cars with each other.

It was in 1953 that an experiment of interest to the whole continent made headlines when Toronto joined the suburban communities of Leaside, Mimico, New Toronto, Weston, Forest Hill, Long Branch, Swansea, East York, Etobicoke, North York, Scarborough, and York to create a vast new metropolitan area. Although the neighboring municipalities would retain their independence in many matters, they were to pass over to the Metropolitan Government such major regional services as police and fire protection, road building, water supplies, public housing and similar responsibilities. The new Toronto set-up, first of its kind in North America, gave Metropolitan Toronto a population of 1,174,002. In charge of it all was Metro chairman Frederick G. Gardiner, who became a kind of super mayor without being elected. His appointment by the provincial government to the important job proved to be a fortunate one, because

the chairman who was to become known as "Big Daddy" Gardiner was a
scrappy and pugnacious bulldog of a man who had just the right tempera-
ment to push through the various tricky requirements of amalgamation,
unruffled by sometimes heavy criticism and the regional jealousies which
were bound to accompany the execution of such sweeping change. Big
Daddy became a kind of municipal dictator—and that was exactly what
the job required. It would be hard to think of any one who could have
better done what needed to be done, if the daring Toronto experiment
was to succeed.

In 1954 they finally got the Yonge Street subway open. Standing side by
side and smiling triumphantly, Ontario Premier Leslie Frost and Toronto
Mayor Allen W. Lamport, on March 3, pulled the switch that set the system in motion.

More than 100,000 delighted Torontonians took a ride on the four-and-
a-half-mile line on the very first day. Said the *Globe and Mail* next day:

"There was a holiday atmosphere in the stations and on the spick and
span trains. Businessmen left office chores to join stenographers and
housewives, and a substantial number of young fry who should have been
in school, in the thrill of riding from terminal to terminal in as little as 15
minutes.

"When the Eglinton station slid into view, many of the passengers on
the first train north from the Union Station found it hard to believe that
they had reached journey's end. Many of them remained in their seats and
travelled all the way south again . . ."

One of the first passengers on the new line, ninety-year-old James Kerr,
regaled reporters with his memories of how the old horse-drawn cars used
to move about the snow-covered streets of Toronto in winter and of how
nice it was of a summer's evening, to take a ride on one of the old open
cars.

As it turned out, there was to be more than the opening of the new subway to make 1954 a memorable year in Toronto. For a long time the Canadian National Exhibition had been staging marathon swims along the
waterfront and the novelty had definitely worn off these tests of strength
and endurance. What the "Ex" needed was something brand new and
spectacular in aquatic events and CNE sports director George Duthie
finally came up with a dandy. He invited the famous U.S. marathon
swimmer Florence Chadwick, who had conquered the English Channel,
the Strait of Gibraltar, the Catalina Channel and the Hellespont, to come
up to Toronto and take a try at swimming right across Lake Ontario, a
feat that had never been performed.

There was a great deal of fanfare when Miss Chadwick entered the

water on the New York side of the lake on September 8, and started out
for Toronto. Receiving little attention that night were two Canadian
swimmers who were so imbued with national pride that they decided to
try the swim even though they hadn't been invited and Miss Chadwick
had been given by the CNE a guarantee of $10,000 for her appearance.
One of them was Winnie Roach Leuzler, a marathon swimmer of some
note in the country. The other was a sixteen-year-old diminutive Toronto
high school girl by the name of Marilyn Bell. Although she had won the
women's event in a marathon swim at Atlantic City not long before, she
was relatively unknown in her native land and even in the city where she
had been born and raised.

Marilyn slipped into the bone-chilling waters of the lake from a log re-
taining wall near Youngstown, New York, at 11:07 that night and as she
stroked her way toward Toronto she was accompanied in a boat by the
man who had trained her and had great faith in her. Gus Ryder was perhaps Canada's most able swimming coach and had trained hundreds of
kids in the water.

A few hours after they had started out, both Florence and Winnie
Roach Leuzler had to be pulled out of the water. But tiny Marilyn Bell
kept right on swimming toward a place in Canadian sports history. Shortly
after it became known that the two well-known swimming stars had given
up and that a Toronto school girl was still out there in the darkness of the
night stubbornly swimming toward Toronto, a peculiar thing happened. It
began slowly, as the radio bulletins told of Marilyn's steady progress, and
then a great wave of emotion seemed to grip the people of traditionally
sober Toronto. Soon the whole city was wild with excitement. There was a
two-way radio in the boat accompanying Marilyn and offers of rewards
began rolling in from well-wishers ashore. Merchants promised her household equipment and clothing and from Paul Rice, up in Huntsville, there
even came an offer of a two-week-all-expense-paid holiday in any Muskoka
resort she cared to choose after she'd got dried out. The CNE sent word
that they were giving her at least $7500 (it was later upped to $10,000)
and at the show in front of the Grandstand cowboy Roy Rogers asked the
vast crowd to join him in a silent prayer for Marilyn. By dusk of September 9, as Marilyn continued to pull steadily closer to the Ontario shore, a
kind of hysteria swept the city. Rockets flared into the sky and Torontonians by the hundreds of thousands came down to the waterfront to
peer out into the darkness, crowding the Lake Ontario shore for miles.

As Marilyn Bell approached the actual finish of her great swim, just before eight o'clock that evening, bedlam broke out. A small armada of craft
of all kinds followed her in, adding the din of their whistles and sirens to

those that were sounding on shore. Car horns set up a thunderous clamor. Marilyn was too close to exhaustion at the end of her almost 23-hour, 40-mile swim to pay much heed to the great ovation.

"I have no recollection of actually touching the breakwater," she said later. "Before I was aware I was on land again, the last thing I remembered seeing and hearing was my coach, Gus Ryder, saying from the boat 'swim for the yellow building, swim for the yellow building!' I was amazed when I listened to the broadcast recordings of the finish and heard all that pandemonium—the horns blowing, the people yelling and shouting . . ."

A crowd of 100,000 jammed in front of the bandshell at the CNE when later she was officially presented with a cheque for $10,000 and Dr. Leslie Bell led his great choir in the singing of a specially composed song called "Marilyn."

Prime Minister Louis St. Laurent sent her a message of congratulation and Ed Sullivan invited her down to New York to appear on his television show. Movie offers also started coming in, but Marilyn just went back to school. Newspaper editors voted her Woman of the Year in a Canadian Press poll and her picture went up in the Sports Hall of Fame at the CNE. In later swims she conquered both the Juan de Fuca Strait in the Pacific and the English Channel and today she is a happy housewife in Levittown, Pennsylvania, where she is known as Mrs. Joseph di Lascio.

In the fall of 1954 there occurred a disaster in Toronto which in one curious respect resembled the tragedy of the *Noronic*; it occurred during the night and the bulk of the city's people weren't really aware of it until the following morning, when it was all over. This time it was water, instead of fire, that created the horror which took place on the night of October 15 and in the early hours of the next morning.

There had been a great deal of rain in the city that fall and the ground of what might be called the surrounding Toronto watershed had absorbed just about all of the moisture it could really hold. Thus did nature conspire to set the stage for disaster in Toronto as a new tropical hurricane named Hazel crept up the eastern seaboard of the United States, where it killed thirty-nine people in New England after pummeling Haiti and causing more than a hundred deaths on the island. By the time the edges of Hazel had reached Toronto, she had lost most of her peak wind velocity, but she burdened the glowering skies above the city with millions of tons of water. The rain descended upon the city in great sheets all through the afternoon and the evening, but when the people of Toronto heard it pelting upon the rooftops as they went to bed they didn't think much about it, except to regard it as a kind of nuisance, like any other heavy storm. However, as Toronto slept that night, the normally placid waters of the Etobicoke, Humber, and Don Rivers were beginning to

angrily swell and lash at their banks as an unprecedented four inches of
rain fell in a few hours over the vast area that was drained by these
streams. Up on the Holland Marsh, forty miles north of the city, many of
the farmers' houses were already floating about in the new lake which now
covered the fertile low-lying acres which had been drained for agriculture.

Rampaging down toward Lake Ontario, the waters of the rivers ripped
out virtually everything that stood in their way along their banks, uproot-
ing trees and tearing to bits forty bridges. On Etobicoke's Raymore Drive,
which hugged the Humber River, a whole section of the street suddenly
disappeared in the raging waters, carrying fifty-four people to their deaths.
Five firemen, trying to rescue some youths from the top of a car, drowned
as their boat overturned in the Humber's madly swirling torrent.

On that following tragic morning Toronto and the area immediately
surrounding it counted a death toll of eighty-one persons and property
damage of $25,000,000. Yet fully 90 per cent of the people of the city had
no idea of what had happened until they glanced at their morning newspaper or turned on their radios at breakfast time. And when they did hear
the news, it just didn't seem possible. Floods that took many lives and
caused great destruction were things which occurred in other far-off places
—never in Toronto! Yet, difficult as it was to fully comprehend, the city's
greatest tragedy had come so stealthily in the night that even some of
those who lost their lives were carried to their doom while peacefully
sleeping in their beds.

In September 1956, Mayor Nathan Phillips announced that an international contest would be held to obtain a design for a new City Hall for
Toronto. It was a great day for the mayor, because he had been trying for
a long time to get a new municipal building under way. In December of
that year, by a rather close vote of 32,000 to 27,000, the citizens put their
OK on the spending of $18,000,000 to build the new edifice if and when a
design was chosen. Some of the city fathers didn't like the way the competition was being handled. Controller William Allen thought it should
be limited to Canadian architects and Controller Ford Brand suggested
that instead of a new City Hall, an extension should merely be put on the
old one. Even famed U.S. architect Frank Lloyd Wright got into the act
when, upon hearing the details on the Toronto contest, he remarked that
it would appeal only to hungry and untried men. Few established and in-
ternationally recognized architects, said he, would bother entering such a
competition.

As it turned out, the design selected from 532 entries from forty-two
countries was that of a comparatively unknown Finnish architect named
Viljo Rewell. Although he had done some distinguished work in his native
Finland, he had no international reputation. He had been vice-president

of the Institute of Finnish Architects and was for a time superintendent of the Museum of Finnish Architecture. His design for Toronto City Hall was selected by a committee of which Professor of Architecture Eric Arthur of the University of Toronto was chairman.

But when Rewell's winning design was publicly unveiled, there were loud cries of ridicule and protest. Controller Roy Belyea called it "a monument to one of the dizziest times in civic history." "Big Daddy" Fred Gardiner, the blunt Metro Chairman, at first called it a Taj Mahal and an extravagant attempt to build a stairway to the stars. (Later, however, he changed his mind and admitted it was "a unique and outstanding building.")

Alderman Frank Nash cried the taxpayers had been hoodwinked and when some one suggested a cocktail bar in a proposed restaurant in the building, Alderman George Ben said its twin towers should be called Sodom and Gomorrah, a term that had been used before when strait-laced Toronto became a little frisky. The doughty Controller, Allen Lamport, who had earlier been one of Toronto's more colorful mayors, said he'd scrap the plans for the new City Hall if he were elected mayor on his try in 1960, but he lost out to the incumbent Mayor Phillips that year.

And it *was* a startling kind of building when you first saw the pictures of it. The reactions of the man in the street were quite mixed. Some thought it was wonderful and others thought it looked like a streamlined privy with two curved walls shielding what looked like a seat in the center. The east tower, with 27 floors, would be 325 feet high and the west tower, with 20 floors, 260 feet high. Between the towers would stand the great dome of the Council Chamber, which would be 150 feet in diameter.

As the storms of controversy raged around the design, Mayor Phillips, sturdy champion of the spectacular City Hall, blithely turned the first sod to start construction of the building on his sixty-ninth birthday, while the assembled spectators sang "Happy Birthday to you." Nate Phillips looked out from under his mane of snow-white hair and smiled triumphantly. The great space in front of the remarkable building is now called Nathan Phillips Square and the tribute is well deserved because no one was more responsible than the veteran Toronto politician for pushing the fine new City Hall through against a great deal of opposition. The chief magistrate, who sometimes referred to himself as the "Old Gray Mayor," beat Tommy Church's record by holding the office for eight years and before that had been an alderman for twenty-eight years. During his long public service he became greatly beloved by the people of his city, even if he did sometimes inject terribly corny stories into his informal speeches. He also had a habit of mispronouncing the names of visiting dignitaries. Once he addressed Russian Ambassador Aroutinian as "Rootin' Tootin'" and industrialist George A. Stringfellow as "George A. Stringbean."

Nathan Phillips was finally toppled by Donald Summerville, a young man who was to die in office of a heart attack after taking part in a benefit hockey game.

Once the new City Hall project got under way it spelled the doom of the ancient and rather grubby establishments which had grown up around the old building. Across Queen Street were burlesque houses and pawnshops and cheap restaurants. It was in one of these burlesque houses, then called the Roxy, that the proprietor Abe Appleby was found shot dead beside the safe in his upstairs office one Sunday morning back in 1935. On Sundays the Chinese community sometimes took over the Roxy to stage one of their plays and on this particular morning the weird singsong of the actors was sounding from the stage while, unknown to either the performers or the audience, the body of Mr. Appleby was being carried down the stairs and the police were beginning their investigation of his murder, in an atmospheric setting that might have been taken straight from an Edgar Wallace detective thriller.

Another old and colorful part of Toronto that came tumbling down to make way for progress and Nathan Phillips Square was a lower section of Elizabeth Street which contained much of the city's long-established Chinatown. Once it was like a trip to the Orient to wander along this strange street with its seedy-looking little restaurants, its Chinese drugstores (where the middle-aged could buy ground rhinoceros horn to restore virility) and the strange flat ducks hanging from hooks in the windows of the exotically stocked grocery shops. Chinatown still exists in Toronto and there are world-travelers who insist that its restaurants provide the best Chinese food to be found anywhere. But its establishments are now more scattered and Chinatown lost much of its rich Eastern atmosphere when the bulldozers obliterated lower Elizabeth Street.

The new City Hall opened (at a cost of $25,000,000) in all of its breath-taking splendor on September 13, 1965, and set off a whole week of ceremonies celebrating the great event. On Monday there was the formal opening and a pageant and band concert featuring the Navy, the Army, and the Air Force. Each evening a display of fireworks lit the sky over downtown Toronto. On Tuesday there was a concert and display by the Toronto Symphony Orchestra, the Canadian Opera Company, and the National Ballet of Canada. On Wednesday there was square dancing in which the fiddle-music that had delighted the pioneers in little York of long ago sounded out once more in the splendid modern surroundings. Thursday there was an Education Night, Friday a pageant called Nation

Builders, presented by the Community Folk Art Council and on Saturday night there was a near-riot called "Toronto A-Go-Go" in which the young swingers took over and one of the throng of teen-agers got stabbed. Very much on hand at all these functions was Mayor Philip Givens, who had succeeded Don Summerville.

As autumn gave way to winter in Toronto, the colorfully garbed skaters turned out on the rink in front of the new City Hall and glided around the ice to the music that came from a public address system. Those who stood on the sidelines witnessing the blend of old and new, created by the toques and scarves of those enjoying Canada's ancient national sport against the streamlined modern background, agreed that after all the arguments and the protests, Toronto had indeed acquired a bright new heart for an exciting new city.

At the end of 1966, acting on a Royal Commission report prepared by municipal expert H. Carl Goldenberg, Metropolitan Toronto abolished the numerous communities which had gone to make up the original amalgamation, creating instead a borough system which, in effect, on January 1, 1967, established a Metropolitan Toronto consisting of the original city and the five new ones of Scarborough, Etobicoke, York, East York and North York, all under a Metro Toronto Council of which William Allen, successor to Fred Gardiner, became chairman. William Dennison, who had served many years on City Council, became the new Mayor of Toronto when he defeated Philip Givens in the 1966 election.

Chapter 24

The Reborn City

Metro Toronto, with a population of 2,628,000, sprawls across 240 square miles. Toronto International Airport. A harbor for ships of all the world. Reclaiming the waterfront. King Street, where the very old and the very new stand side by side. The quandary of Yonge Street. The horrendous traffic jams. Peculiar Yorkville. Toronto, financial, industrial and cultural heart of Canada. A city beginning to find a soul.

When Dr. Henry H. Scadding, one of the city's earliest and most respected historians, wrote *Toronto of Old* in 1873, he used the literary device of taking his readers on an imaginary stroll through the streets of his little community, proudly pausing here and there to point out some special landmark or building, describing its background and the worthy deeds or lamentable follies of those who had built it or dwelt or worked in it. Although Dr. Scadding's detailed description of these places and people might occasionally have grown a little wearisome to the ears of his companion, it is unlikely that the sightseer's feet would have given out, because, in those days, most of Toronto's more interesting areas could be seen during a comparatively brief walk. The city then covered about seventeen square miles, but most of the points of interest could be observed in the area extending from Front Street north to Queen Street and from the Don River west to Spadina.

A modern Dr. Scadding and his rubber-necking companion would require a sports car with the gas tank brimming full to cover the present Toronto and it's likely they would even then be obliged to make at least one or two stops at filling stations along the way. What is now called Metropolitan Toronto extends over an area of 240 square miles and contains a population that approaches 2,250,000.

If I were guiding a visitor today, I would like to have him catch his first sight of my city in the exciting way in which I have often seen it—at night, from an altitude of several thousand feet, while approaching it from the south by air. Long before we crossed Lake Ontario we would see Toronto sprawling down there on the northern shore, its millions of lights glowing like a vast scattering of bright jewels spread out upon a field of purple velvet. The great central bulk of this sea of glittering lights extends so far to the north that it seems almost to bend over the horizon. But you will note that at least a sprinkling of suburban lights stretches all along the lakeshore to the west until they join the glowing mass of Hamilton. To the east there also extends an ever-widening and sparkling ribbon that is scarcely broken between Toronto and Oshawa, 32 miles away. Someday, in the not too distant future, the traveler approaching Toronto at night by air will probably see a clustering of lights so broad and solid between Hamilton, Toronto and Oshawa—a distance of 78 miles—that the stranger might easily mistake it for one huge community. In recent years this path of light along the Lake Ontario shore has been spreading like a kind of grassfire and most Torontonians have given up guessing where it will end. They only know that their city is growing by great and startling leaps and bounds, in every direction including up—save the south. And even in this direction there are advances, from time to time, as more land is reclaimed from the lake.

The flying visitor to Toronto gets his first down-to-earth view of the city at the huge International Airport, one of the most imposing in the world. The landing field itself covers an area of 4400 acres and one section of the streamlined terminal has, among other things, a main lobby larger than Salisbury Cathedral, curtained with 36,000 square feet of glass drapes, $150,000 worth of its own art and sculpture, a sundial 20 feet high, 112 washrooms, five emergency power stations, a heating and cooling system big enough for a town of 1500 homes and an eight-level indoor parking area.

The aeroquay (now called Terminal One) is designed in such a way that the routes to the loading areas spread out like the spokes of a wheel, cutting to a minimum the walking distances between ticket counters and the awaiting aircraft. (Someone measured the line of ticket counters and found that they extended for a sixteenth of a mile. A walk around the glass-walled concourse covers a distance of one-third of a mile.) Often visitors to the airport who aren't going anywhere or meeting anyone come out just to park their automobiles in the 2500-car-capacity garage over the terminal and dine and dance in the Aeroquay Restaurant and Lounge, with its soft lights, its discreetly moving waiters and its superb view across the bustling airport.

A second vast building, called Terminal Two, was opened on June 15,

1972, at a cost of $53 million. A much more austere structure than the original aeroquay, its cavernous interior and long hauls between ticket counters and boarding areas at first brought numerous howls of complaint from air travelers. But some of the more awkward wrinkles in the new building were finally ironed out, at least to the point where not so many passengers were experiencing the suspicious feeling that they were actually *walking* halfway to their destinations after paying full fares for their journeys. Some idea of the size of Terminal Two may be gained from the fact that it took five acres of carpeting—or roughly enough to spread over three average-sized football fields—to cover its floors.

But even with these extra facilities, the present airport is beginning to encounter further problems with overcrowding, both within the terminal buildings and on the runways where the big airliners taxi out for take-off. The number of passengers it now handles each year is approaching 11 million. It has been estimated that by 1980 this figure will have grown to 15 million and perhaps to 50 million by the year 2000.

For a time it looked as though a huge new airport would be built on 18,000 acres of farmland in the Pickering area, northeast of Toronto. But sustained and vigorous opposition from residents of that locality finally caused the project to be abandoned—at least temporarily. Many residents of Metro Toronto—and particularly those living near the present busy airport—are still hoping the plan for Pickering will be revived. In common with most of the residents of many large North American cities, the people of Toronto and its surrounding areas may want a new airport—but not within many miles of where *their* homes are located.

Upon reaching the Gardiner Expressway on our drive into town from the airport, we go whizzing eastward into the heart of the city, traveling for much of the distance over an elevated dual highway under which, near Strachan Avenue, there still huddle the ancient and tiny buildings of old Fort York. For a while it seemed they would be destroyed to make way for the expressway, but it was finally decided to skirt them.

As we turn northward up York Street, after leaving the expressway, one of the first impressive buildings we see, at Front Street, is the huge 1600-room Royal York Hotel, one of the largest in the world. At one time, not so long ago, the Royal York dominated the Toronto skyline in this part of town. Now it seems to huddle far below the great towers of commerce which in recent years have sprouted up beside and behind it.

Directly across the road, on the south side of Front Street, stands the Union Station, with its impressive forty pillars and wide portals. For a while the fifty-year-old building was threatened with destruction, to make way for a vast development in the area to be known as Metro Centre. News of the station's impending fate brought loud cries of outrage from those who were anxious to preserve Toronto's more important landmarks, and an organization was formed to fight the would-be wreckers to the last ditch. But the station's staunch defenders might have saved their effort, because the plan for the Metro Centre foundered and it was no longer necessary to remove the fine old building. Instead, it was remodeled and improved to continue in its original role as a railway terminal.

Should you stop at the Royal York during your stay in Toronto—or check in at the Harbour Castle, down closer to the lake and only one of eight major new hotels that opened their doors in Toronto in 1975 alone —you will be able to see from the windows of their upper floors on the south side a magnificent view of Toronto's busy seaport, lying so far from the ocean.

Down there in the harbor you will see flying from seagoing freighters the flags of many distant countries—Japan, Britain, Norway, Sweden, Denmark, Holland, Germany, Israel, Russia and a dozen other lands . . . With the opening of the St. Lawrence Seaway, Toronto, 1300 miles from the Atlantic, became an important port for the vessels of all the world. Once more the ancient water highway up and down the St. Lawrence has become a busy route for the transportation of goods to and from Toronto, as it was when the *voyageurs* carried their trading supplies and furs in their great freighter canoes and bateaux to and from old Fort Rouillé. You will note that new and streamlined ferries hustle back and forth across the Bay between the Island and the mainland, still carrying passengers over the same route followed by Michael O'Connor's four-horsepower *Sir John of the Peninsula.* The Island still fulfills its traditional role as a playground for the people of Toronto, as it did when Mrs. Simcoe first galloped her spirited horse along the sandy strip of what was then a peninsula. Here and there, upon the broad bosom of Toronto Bay, dainty craft from the Royal Canadian or the National Yacht Clubs unfurl their billowing sails to remind us of the windjammers which once provided most of the traffic entering or leaving Toronto's harbor. No longer in the dead of winter does the Bay freeze solidly enough across its entire surface to permit "a concourse of the beau monde of both sexes in carioles and sleighs" as it did during the fox hunt described in the *Upper Canada Gazette* of 1801. Some of the Island's dwindling residents cross to and fro on special water transport provided throughout the winter.

But Toronto Island, that almost incredible haven of nearby tranquillity which has for so many years been home to a small residential community across the water from the southern threshold of the bustling city, is also going through the sometimes bewildering flood of change that has marked Toronto during the hectic sixties and seventies. Many families once passed along from one generation to another the now rather quaint-looking small frame dwellings that line tree-shaded streets overlooking the waters of Lake Ontario and Toronto Bay. It was a village, quiet and seemingly rural, which had by some miracle been protected by a comparatively short stretch of water from noisy downtown Toronto almost as effectively as if it had been located 100 miles away from the hurly-burly of the great city.

There were no motor vehicles, except those required for various essential community services, such as fire protection, garbage pickup and ambulance service. The Islanders moved about in their idyllic retreat slowly and quietly, on foot or on bicycles. Those who worked in the city commuted back and forth on the regular ferry service. At the end of each summer's day, they were able to ride away from the city's heat and din while being bathed in the cool breezes off the bay, as the boats chugged toward a green and peaceful little refuge shared with old and familiar neighbors. It was probably too good to last, in a modern world, even though it did manage to survive for a remarkable length of time, considering the vast and rapid transformations that have come to the Toronto area.

Some of the tightly knit community of Islanders are still hanging on, stubbornly fighting Metro Toronto's efforts to expropriate the last of the private holdings to make way for more recreational parkland. Thirty years ago about 2000 people lived on the Island during the summer months, and some of them all year around. By 1977 there were only about 700, and they faced eventual eviction from their 254 remaining houses.

Even though this is an age in which private property owners are more and more expected to surrender some of their personal comforts and privileges to the over-all public good, those with a feeling for things of sentiment and nostalgia cannot help sympathizing with the remaining Islanders in their fight to hold on to that which is sadly slipping away. Recent statistics show that more than 1,200,000 visitors from the mainland ride the ferries to the Island each year.

Over to the east of the Island group a new man-made peninsula extends for three miles out into Lake Ontario. It was started about twenty years ago and gradually lengthened by dumping up to a thousand truckloads of landfill each day, provided by such huge excavation projects as the subway and the basements of numerous new hotels, office buildings and apartment blocks around the city.

The slender neck of land—part of 2000 immensely valuable acres added to the Toronto shore line since 1910 by reclaiming them from the lake— may be used as still another area of waterside playgrounds for the benefit of the people of Toronto.

At the western extremity of Toronto Island may be seen the airport for land- and water-based aircraft, which sits right on the front doorstep of the metropolis. Few cities in North America can boast of such a handy airport. It is capable of accommodating all but the larger passenger aircraft and will undoubtedly grow in importance as Toronto's rapid expansion creates more demand for the kind of flying facilities which allow the sportsman pilot or airborne commuting businessman to disembark from his aircraft and be in the heart of the great city in a matter of only a few minutes.

Its long shore line should have been one of Toronto's greatest blessings and glories, but over the years a civic interest that seemed to be preoccupied with the economic rather than the aesthetic aspects of urban life allowed a large portion of this splendid waterfront area to get away from us. We took the great lake, with its cool summer breezes and sparkling vistas of wide blue waters, far too much for granted. As a result, all kinds of industrial encroachments were allowed to take place, year after year, particularly along the eastern portion of the shore. Railway yards, coal yards, oil refineries and similar stinking and grimy enterprises managed to insert themselves between the people of the city and the stretch of lake front that provided one of the community's most precious legacies passed on from those who first selected the site of Toronto.

In a new, more forward-looking city, there appears to be a fresh, keen consciousness of what the lake means to its residents. It is an attitude that has been a long time in coming and now, as a result of former neglect, will take a long time to convert into reality. But at least a good start has been made and considerable progress has already been achieved. Numerous plans for a restored waterfront have been introduced and then apparently shelved.

There was to have been, for example, a great Metro Centre project built in the area now occupied by miles of railway tracks close by the waterfront. The present CN Tower, in fact, was to have been a focal point for the $1 billion development, which was to have contained office buildings, hotels, homes, shops and green park areas—a whole new lakeside city within a city. But the Toronto authorities and the railways couldn't get together on a rather complex set of land swaps and the project was shelved. The brave and spectacular sketches of how the new community would look—almost like illustrations from a science fiction yarn about life in the twenty-first century—are now gathering dust in the files somewhere.

In October of 1972 the Liberal government in Ottawa, in the closing stages of a hot election campaign, promised Toronto a great new lakeside park. It would be called Harborfront and would consist of 86 acres of shore line worth $30 million. But the federal gift has been the subject, so far, of a great deal of confusion as to just when and how this dream of a fine new lakeshore playground for the people of Toronto will be achieved.

Meetings in which the public has been invited to take part have been held in search of advice on how to utilize the area in the best possible way. Some suggestions from the floor during these public forums have sometimes seemed a little zany. They have ranged all the way from making the central section of the waterfront zone into a newer and larger version of Ontario Place, right down to converting one of the harbor slips into a huge water bed, where playful citizens could frolic to their hearts' content. One speaker suggested that the CN Tower be made into a mammoth sundial. Another liked the idea of an international gambling casino being built at Harborfront. Still another thought one of the big grain elevators standing at the water's edge should be converted into a cathedral!

Yet progress *is* being made. Of the twelve-mile strip of waterfront that extends from the Humber River eastward to the R. C. Harris Purification Plant, ten miles have been set aside as functional parklands to which the public already has a promising amount of access. It seems likely that year by year—now that the new resolve and the new land are there—Toronto will slowly but surely retrieve for recreational purposes the excellent waterfront that once seemed to have been lost to it forever.

A kind of keystone and impressive symbol of things to come in the redevelopment of Toronto's waterfront is Ontario Place, the 96-acre cultural and leisure complex located on three man-made islands lying in Lake Ontario just off the grounds of the Canadian National Exhibition. To provide a breakwater behind which to dump 2.5 million cubic yards of fill into the lake to form the islands, three old lake steamers, ready for the scrapyard, were towed to the site, loaded with rocks and sunk. They looked a little forlorn and unpromising at first, with parts of their rusty superstructures still showing above the surface. But it was not long before the mounds of earth deposited behind them began to take on the appearance of real, honest-to-goodness islands.

By opening day for Ontario Place, on May 22, 1971, the new islands displayed, in addition to a five-pod pavilion, 17 acres of green and well-trimmed lawns, more than three miles of pathways and 30,000 trees, shrubs and plants. The $32.5 million complex, owned and operated by the Ontario government, has been described as a "fun place" for both young and old and has turned out to be a highly successful tourist attraction.

The main structure is the Ontario Place Pavilion, consisting of five steel and glass modules suspended 100 feet above the lake. The pavilion, which was awarded the 1973 American Design and Steel Institute's citation for excellence, contains 250,000 cubic feet of "experiential" theaters and various restaurants.

Located just to the south of the pavilion is perhaps the most exciting feature of Ontario Place. Called the Cinesphere, it is a huge, globe-shaped motion picture theater seating 800. Upon its giant curving screen, which is

60 feet high and 80 feet long, startlingly realistic movies are projected by means of a process called IMAX, which is claimed to be "the world's most sophisticated development to date in high fidelity, large format and high stability motion picture presentation." Naturally, nothing less than epic-sized subjects are shown on the vast screen. One of the most popular of these was *North of Superior*, in which for the first time the scenic grandeur of the country lying above Canada's largest lake was displayed on film in the kind of gigantic dimensions of sight and sound that could do proper justice to such a beautiful and rugged land.

Another popular feature of Ontario Place is the Forum, an amphitheater built in the classical Greek tradition of theater-in-the-round. It can seat 2000 under its vinyl canopy and, in favorable weather, an additional 6000 on the grassy slopes that surround its 75-foot-diameter circular stage. During the summer months the Forum presents symphony, opera, ballet, rock, jazz and country music, featuring talent of both local and international fame.

On one fine and memorable summer evening, several thousand music lovers sat around on the grassy slopes, under the stars, listening to the Toronto Symphony Orchestra perform Tchaikovsky's sometimes hectic and clamorous *1812 Overture*. At the place in this composition where the booming of cannon is usually simulated by the deep voices of bass drums being mightily smitten, the audience was treated to the real thing. The distinguished Canadian destroyer *H.M.C.S. Haida*, now on permanent display at its moorings in Ontario Place, fired blank charges from its deck guns at intervals exactly synchronized with the musical score. On that balmy evening, members of both the orchestra and the audience had to agree, with happy grins, that Ontario Place was *indeed* a fun place, when you could enjoy an experience like *that!*

Although the actual waterfront is today a little farther away from the heart of downtown Toronto than it was in earlier times when it lay close by Front Street, it is still within an easy stroll of the lakeshore. King Street, which was regarded as the city's principal thoroughfare in the past, has not really lost any of its prestige, in spite of the tremendous changes that have taken place in the city over the years. To this day it retains a curious mixture, embracing some of the very oldest and the very newest of Toronto's more important and interesting buildings.

Just below King, on Bay Street, may be seen the Toronto Stock Exchange, second to that of New York in the volume of shares traded each year. On the face of the handsome building a frieze containing figures in low relief depicts Canada's transition from an agricultural nation to an industrial and mining country. If you happen to be near the intersection of King and Bay Streets shortly after five o'clock in the afternoon you may feast your eyes upon some of the most attractive young women in Canada as the secretaries and stenographers from the surrounding office buildings pour out to catch the rush-hour subways, streetcars and buses. Glancing up Bay Street as you cross it at King, you see the old City Hall, its tower sitting there like some ancient grandfather's clock in the shadow of the new and spectacular City Hall, which, through newspaper photographs and travel posters, has become familiar to people throughout the world who may never see Toronto itself.

There are still many Torontonians who have an abiding sentimental attachment to the old City Hall, although there are others who have always considered it ugly. Those who defend it say they would particularly miss the clock and maintain that the failure to include a civic timepiece in the new City Hall was a grave oversight. A town hall just isn't a town hall, they say, if it doesn't have a clock. The great bells of the old clock, which first rang out at midnight on December 31, 1899, to usher the twentieth century into Toronto, has a slow and ponderous voice, which sounds out with many mighty clangs the quarter hour, the half hour, and the hour. There are still those who remember the high and haughty arrogance of the old clock when it commenced a long procession of clangs and bongs, marking the hour of 11 A.M., just as Edward, Prince of Wales, during a visit in the late twenties, stepped up to the microphone on the City Hall steps to begin an address to the citizens of Toronto. For what seemed like hours the Prince had to stand there, waiting patiently with his speech in his hand. Even the voice of a Royal visitor had to remain silent when the old clock was speaking in the reverberating tones which have become one of the most familiar sounds of the city.

Crossing over Yonge Street, it is hard to realize that this teeming thoroughfare in the heart of Toronto was once a muddy road on the western edge of the Town of York. It has always been a busy and interesting street but it could never be called an elegant one. Once its overhead wires and projecting shop signs made it seem extremely narrow and seedy, but now that the wires have been concealed underground and the signs of its business establishments have been placed flush against their fronts, the street seems to have widened a bit. The removal of the streetcars from Yonge after the opening of the subway for a while gave it an additional look of airiness.

Just what to do about Yonge Street has for years been an extremely hot subject of discussion in a Toronto trying rather desperately to adjust itself to a new character without being quite sure just what that character should really be. There were those who maintained that the garish and honky-tonk atmosphere that had been taken on by a downtown portion of the street was a civic disgrace and an abomination. And it had, in many respects, become an area as loud and gaudy as the Midway at the Canadian National Exhibition—but with far more sex attractions than those offered by the most brazen hootchy-kootchy show that ever appeared at the CNE.

Blaring rock music and the hoarse harangues of pitchmen boomed out from the loudspeakers in front of various seedy Yonge Street establishments and on some evenings the panhandlers were outnumbered only by the hookers. For a time there seemed to be a body rub parlor and/or a blue movie peep show every few doors. On the crowded sidewalks it was almost impossible for a pedestrian to move far without having a leaflet shoved in his hand advertising the shady glories to be found behind the mysterious curtains of Ali Baba's Harem or some similar playroom for the lascivious.

But in recent years the city authorities have tried to crack down more heavily upon such enterprises, by means of tougher licensing requirements and other regulations. This civic resolve was abruptly strengthened, in the summer of 1977, when a twelve-year-old shoeshine boy named Emmanuel Jaques was lured from his stand near the corner of Yonge and Dundas Streets for sexual purposes and brutally murdered in an apartment situated above one of these sleazy dives. The tragedy seemed to bring home to people, with a new and stunning clarity, the sad state of degradation to which this section of one of their city's principal thoroughfares had fallen.

In recent years there have been several hopeful experiments in transforming a section of Yonge Street between Queen and Dundas Streets into a pedestrian mall during the summer months. It seemed a fairly bright idea when the project began. Some thought the casual feeling of togetherness on such a mall would be a wonderful thing in a city where the downtown area had not previously been marked by a great deal of friendly sociability among pedestrians. But others looked upon the innovation as a somewhat shabby and pathetic attempt to create an atmosphere that somehow did not fit the locality.

The mall's detractors were not much impressed by the potted trees and sidewalk chairs and tables, which did look a little as though they had hastily been hauled out onto Yonge Street for some kind of open-air rummage sale. There was something improvised and temporary about the appearance of the whole scene that prevented some of the beer drinkers at the sidewalk cafes from ever truly relaxing—particularly the older patrons, who felt that after all, damnit, it took more than a few tables and chairs and the odd potted tree to change Yonge Street from being *Yonge Street*, where public drinking, right out on the pavement, had always been dangerous sport indeed. There was always the haunting and uneasy feeling that somewhere in the distance the sirens of the approaching police cars were wailing, just below the twanging guitars of the wandering street minstrels.

68. Ontario Place, situated on the Toronto waterfront beside the CNE grounds, is a prime tourist attraction.

69. Ontario Place's Cinesphere, which shows special movies on its giant curved screen, stands aglitter against the night sky.

70. Yorkville, a favorite hippie haven of the sixties, is now a more sedate area of chichi cafes and boutiques.

71. Busy Kensington Market purveys exotic foods to the hundreds of thousands of New Torontonians from many distant lands.

72. Ontario Hydro Building, on University Avenue, provides one of the more striking additions to the Toronto scene.

73. The vast Eaton Centre project has brought dramatic change to the area near Toronto's historic downtown crossroads at Yonge and Queen Streets.

74. The Royal Bank Plaza, with its glowing gold-tinted walls of glass constantly changing hue with the passage of the sun, is one of the city's most attractive new buildings.

75. New Massey Hall, home of the Toronto Symphony Orchestra, will replace the grand old auditorium of the same name built in 1894 as a gift to his city from philanthropist Hart A. Massey.

The most spectacular change in the Yonge Street scene has been that provided by the huge new T. Eaton Company development on a 14.5-acre site in the heart of the downtown area. The $200 million first phase of the project includes two tiers of small shops on the Yonge Street frontage between Dundas and Albert Streets. There is a glass-enclosed pedestrian square at Dundas and Yonge Streets, two office towers and a new Eaton's department store. The old store at Queen and Yonge Streets, after holding a final sale that included even its shop fixtures, was torn down. More than 250 individual shops, boutiques and restaurants—some of them open-air cafes—are included in the development plan.

The second phase of the giant project will involve four acres of land with frontage on Bay Street, but work on this section is unlikely to begin until 1981 at the earliest.

Said Robert J. Butler, who was president of the firm when the model for the development was unveiled in 1975: "Eaton's has set out deliberately to play a role in the renewal of the hearts of various cities in Canada. We instructed our architects to build us the best-looking and most efficient store in the world . . ."

The new character of Eaton's will by no means alter its traditional friendliness with its long-time neighbor and competitor, Simpson's. On the contrary, an even closer degree of association between the two great mercantile enterprises will be achieved by a sheltered passageway linking their two premises. Simpson's, content—at least temporarily—with its new tower as a downtown expansion project, embarked upon an extensive refurbishing of its present store, which has officially been classified as a historic building and is therefore protected from demolition. Those Torontonians who prefer the older but more gracious and familiar type of high-class department store, were greatly pleased by the Simpson's decision.

Toronto's downtown area is still sadly lacking in the trees and other stretches of greenery which make the heart of Montreal so pleasant on a sunny afternoon in spring. Some rather forlorn little maples have been planted as a kind of afterthought in the mass of downtown concrete, but it will be a long time before they will offer much shade to Toronto strollers. There are those who accuse Toronto of having always been too preoccupied with crass commercial matters to bother about the more gracious things when its downtown area was being developed, and perhaps this is so. The streets are almost always crowded with automobiles, but when those jam-packed parking lots empty at the close of the day, they contribute their share to the horrendous traffic jams for which Toronto is so renowned that visitors have been known to write shocked poems about them for their home-town newspapers. The cars move fairly steadily most of the time on the city's expressways, but once an innocent motorist strays from such grooves, especially during rush hours, he is likely to find himself trapped and frustrated in a bogged-down line of traffic.

And when are these rush hours? Just about any time from seven o'clock in the morning until ten or from four o'clock in the afternoon until seven that evening. In fact there are some drivers who bitterly complain that there is no longer any such thing as a rush hour in Toronto, but merely three or four comparatively quiet hours, completely surrounded by traffic jams. For years the planners have been trying desperately to get ahead of the swelling hordes of automobiles, but they never quite seem to make it. When the wide dual thoroughfare originally known as Highway 401 was built across the northern edge of the city it was intended to serve as a by-pass for east-west traffic making its way around Toronto. But before it was completed it had already been swallowed by the spreading city and had become just another traffic-choked road where cars often ground to a halt during the rush hour.

One mournful statistician came up with an estimate that enough new cars were being added to Toronto's streets each year to form a line, six abreast and bumper to bumper, all the way from the lakeshore at the foot of Yonge Street right up through the city's main drag to Richmond Hill, seventeen miles north. With an automobile for every three persons, Toronto is said to have the third highest per capita car registration in the world, exceeded only by that of Los Angeles and Detroit.

Toronto's traffic is so heavy that even Metro Roads Commissioner Samuel Cass ruefully admits he hates driving in it. "Driving a car today is no pleasure," he says. But he feels it's only fair play for the Roads Commissioner to suffer like the rest of us. "I have got to experience what other motorists experience," he gamely explains.

It has been estimated that there were approximately 800,000 motor vehicles registered in Metro Toronto in 1977. But they were not the only ones that had to be considered in devising means of untangling Toronto's traffic snarls. Rapid development in suburban districts surrounding the Metro borders provided an additional 300,000 vehicles to contribute their share to the traffic tie-ups when commuters and shoppers and showgoers poured into the downtown section from an ever-expanding radius of built-up areas outside Metro. (So valuable has downtown property become that a pessimistic expert has predicted that by 1986 it will cost a motorist $1800 a year to park his car in the heart of the city.)

But let us drive up University Avenue, which various sets of city fathers have, from time to time, tried to make the most handsome thoroughfare in Toronto. It does have a spacious air about it and it does contain a number of impressive buildings. Still, it is not yet the kind of street that is likely to cause a visitor to shout "Oh boy!" and unlimber his camera, so that its glory can be recorded to show the folks back home. The sad fact seems to be that the efforts to improve the prospect of University Avenue have, like so many of Toronto's recent beautification projects, been a kind of guilty, long-delayed effort to make amends, and some of this shows through.

Sitting there primly at the head of University Avenue, like an aged dowager looking down with mixed feelings upon the changes which have come to Toronto and Ontario, are the buildings of the Provincial Legislature, erected in 1892. They make a great pile of reddish granite, somewhat blackened by the years, and as we drive by them in a half-circle through Queen's Park on the way to Avenue Road we see to the east of them a number of streamlined new buildings which have been erected to house the ever-expanding offices of the Ontario government.

One block north of Bloor Street we leave Avenue Road to enter the modern Yorkville Village. For many years the only reminder of the former separate identity of the hamlet which once stood on Toronto's northern outskirts was a street called Yorkville Avenue. But now the word "Village" has once more been attached to the historic name, although the sturdy residents of the original Yorkville might be aghast if they were to wander again through the modern version of their community. It is dotted with coffeehouses, sidewalk cafes, boutiques and stylish restaurants. One shop with an eye to the history of the locality has painted the original arms of the Yorkville council on one of its outside walls. Houses in what was once a rather beaten-up section of Toronto now command extremely hefty prices. Of a summer's evening Yorkville Avenue is crowded with strollers who watch the customers of the sidewalk cafes, who in turn watch the strollers, as seems to be the custom wherever sidewalk cafes exist.

Although Yorkville Village now appears to be more sedate than many other districts in Toronto—perhaps even more genteel than it was far back in the days when it was a separate community—it wasn't that way during the entire process of its resurrection. For many years it was just another rather run-down street of houses which were plainly showing their age. Then, in the late sixties and early seventies, it became a hangout for hippies, some of whom lived there in "pads" established in some of the seedy houses and others of whom congregated on the streets there from all over the city. Visitors with keen noses claimed they could sometimes detect the heady aroma of marijuana in the coffee shops. Parents of teen-aged offspring began to fear and detest the very name of the area. Others, with a more liberal turn of mind, thought the decidedly bohemian character of the place gave an extra dash of rather weird color to a city that needed something of the sort to help offset its basically rather prim and proper nature.

At any rate, time and rapidly changing tastes managed to smooth out Yorkville and restore its tranquillity. The hippies either grew up to become earnest young business executives or moved off to other localities where they weren't under such constant and disapproving surveillance from various authorities and even mere sightseers.

Restoration of once rather shabby houses such as those which stood in Yorkville is a trend that has now become quite widespread throughout many of the older areas of Toronto, where "white painters," as they are sometimes disdainfully called by neighbors still living in unrestored houses, have undertaken to refurbish old dwellings. Many of these quaint but weather-beaten homes have been converted into quite swanky town houses, which sell at extremely fancy prices to fed-up commuters who have decided to desert the suburbs and move into the central part of the city. It is a trend that is bringing about remarkable changes to many Toronto streets which once looked quite dilapidated and dismal.

Torontonians still get needled now and then about their city, of course. But they don't mind—in fact they've rather grown to take a peculiar kind of pride in the way people in other parts of the country, such as those in Toronto's arch rival Montreal, talk about them. They'd feel a little lost if they weren't occasionally getting a ribbing from someone. Yet, even the needlers are no longer quite so sure about the subject of their jokes as they were a few years ago when Toronto was known far and wide in Canada as Hogtown. The Montreal comedian who once described a contest in which the first prize was a one-week trip to Toronto and the second prize a two-week trip, wouldn't roll 'em in the aisles with this joke today the way he did a few years ago. Something very exciting and profound has happened to Toronto, and it has happened so swiftly that even its own people, leave alone outsiders, are not quite sure of its exact extent or nature.

In many ways, the city is now the financial, industrial, cultural and business center of Canada. More than half of the life insurance companies operating in Canada have their home offices in Toronto, most of them concentrated along a short stretch of Bloor Street between Yonge Street and Mount Pleasant Road. In Toronto are the headquarters of the oil and gas companies which supply two-thirds of the country's needs from these sources of energy. Among its industries serving world-wide markets are such as Massey-Ferguson, which operates thirty branch plants in nine countries and does an annual international business of $772 million. And de Havilland of Canada, which sells airplanes designed and built in

Toronto to countries throughout the world, including the United States. The huge Moore Corporation, leader in the field of business forms, has its head office in Toronto but does 85 per cent of its trade in the United States. The billion-dollar Brazilian Traction Light & Power Company (now called Brascan) in far-off South America has its head office right in Toronto. More people are employed in manufacturing in the Toronto area than in seven of Canada's provinces put together. Of the 4.5 billion dollars' worth of shares traded on Canada's six stock exchanges in one recent year, Toronto's market accounted for 70 per cent.

Agencies selling advertising in the Toronto media have taken to calling that portion of the province served by the city's newspapers and radio stations "Torontario" and claim that within a 100-mile radius of the city lies 44 per cent of the entire buying power of Canada.

But this is business and industry, and Toronto has always been noted for its attention to these matters. In fact, it has sometimes been accused of selling its very soul for the almighty dollar. This may have been true at one time, but in recent years there has been a remarkable change. Almost with a self-conscious blush the city has emerged as a kind of swinger among Canadian communities. You can now dine out for years in Toronto's 2127 restaurants without covering them all. Toronto in recent years has been considered by touring performers to be the jazz center of North America. Some Torontonians, conditioned by the ways of the old city, were horrified when a Henry Moore sculpture called *The Archer*—which looked to many like a huge soup bone—was set up in Nathan Phillips Square in front of the City Hall. But many thousands flocked into the square to admire the city's new acquisition, after Mayor Phil Givens had persuaded private benefactors to buy it.

Toronto's studios stand second only to those of New York and Hollywood in the production of television shows and the city is also the point of origin for most of the nationally broadcast radio programs. Canada's leading magazines and book publishing firms are also concentrated in Toronto and the city contains the headquarters of the Canadian Press, the country's nation-wide news agency.

Toronto's first Metro Chairman, Fred Gardiner, aptly described the exciting new Toronto when he said: "The metropolis is an irresistible magnet. It is where big business is located, where big money, big decisions and big reputations are made. It . . . draws toward it the restless, the energetic, and the ambitious, the young men and women who want to be at the center of things, where opportunity may be just around the corner."

There is a peculiar upbeat something in the Toronto air. People are beginning to display much more sentiment toward their city and more interest in its past—as was witnessed, for instance, in the restoration of the old St. Lawrence Hall in a civic project that involved the donation of their services by architects and construction firms.

When that fine old theater, the Royal Alexandra, was threatened in 1963 with the wrecker's hammer, a merchant named Ed Mirvish, who ran a razzle-dazzle bargain store called Honest Ed's on Bloor Street, astonished his fellow Torontonians by not only purchasing the building, but spending more than $100,000 to restore it to its old grandeur. "Build me the finest theatre on the continent," wealthy Cawthra Mulock had said back in 1905 when he ordered construction of the Royal Alexandra. Ed Mirvish had the great satisfaction of seeing his theater described not long after its restoration, in the U.S. magazine *Showbusiness*, as "The most beautiful theatre on the North American continent." Which, everyone agreed, was a fine thing to happen to the charming old playhouse where, over the years, there had appeared such great performers as Katharine Cornell, Dame Judith Anderson, Ruth Gordon, Paul Robeson, Dame Margot Fonteyn, Anna Pavlova, Sir Harry Lauder, George M. Cohan, Al Jolson, John and Ethel Barrymore, Tallulah Bankhead, Mae West, Beatrice Lillie, Nazimova, George Arliss, Katharine Hepburn, Helen Hayes and Dame Sybil Thorndike.

In such things there is revealed a new kind of heart and soul in the city. Having labored long and hard over the years, in its peculiarly solid and industrious fashion, to make itself wealthy and substantial, Toronto now seems to have reached the point where it has become much more sure of itself and willing to indulge in those intangible human things which so importantly contribute to the true greatness of important cities everywhere.

Chapter 25
1966–1977
AN ERA OF NEW UPS AND DOWNS

The city reaches farther skyward and burrows farther underground. The fabulous CN Tower. The expanding subway. The new promenades down below the city streets. And an attempt to make Toronto's new office buildings a joy to the eye as well as a pain in the neck for those who stare upward at their grandeur. The new Torontonians.

By the year 1966 many jaded Torontonians, having seen the fantastic growth of their city during the previous decade, concluded that the metropolis must surely have reached its full stature. As the song about Kansas City puts it, it seemed that Torontonians had "gone about as fer" as they can go . . .

But, bewildering as it became to many of its residents, Toronto was to continue sprouting outward, upward and even downward in many spectacular and rapid ways during the next ten years. Especially upward. For one thing, the dizzying height of 740 feet achieved by the main tower of the Toronto-Dominion Centre on King Street, which had made it the loftiest building in all of Canada, would soon be surpassed by that of the white and gleaming spire of the Commerce Court building, whose height of 784 feet would in turn soon be eclipsed by the 935 feet of nearby First Canadian Place.

But the most dazzling addition to the already impressive Toronto skyline was undoubtedly to be the CN Tower. Never in the wildest dreams of the most avid civic booster would the inhabitants of a slightly earlier and more staid Toronto have thought they'd ever see the day when such a fantastic landmark would rise above their city.

As it climbed higher and higher, it fascinated some and utterly shocked others. There were those who proudly claimed it would eventually be to

Toronto what the Eiffel Tower is to Paris: a kind of sensational trademark of world renown. But there were others who thought for a while that someone must surely be kidding. What in hell, they wanted to know, was a nice sensible city like Toronto doing with a ridiculously ostentatious thing like *that* rearing up in plain view for miles around?

(A possibly envious Vancouver columnist surmised it was actually a kind of civic phallic symbol, serving to make up for some suspicious lack in the Toronto psyche.)

Others just scratched their heads and admitted they couldn't decide what to think of the thing. Although it couldn't be called the world's highest *building*, it was indeed the world's highest "free-standing structure," topping at last, with its height of 1815 feet, the former champion in this category, Moscow's 1748-foot Ostankino Tower. To make Toronto's new claim really official, Ross McWhirter, associate editor of the Guinness Book of Records, came overseas to Toronto to personally check the height of the CN Tower, a short while before he was shot and killed by an Irish terrorist in 1975.

Excavation work for the fabulous tower began in February of 1973, after a thorough exploration of the underlying soil and bedrock had been conducted by a team of scientists under Dr. Eli Robinsky, of the Unversity of Toronto. First, three holes, measuring only 30 inches in diameter, were drilled down through the soil and bedrock to a depth of 120 feet. It was then the awkward task of Dr. Robinsky and members of his crew to squeeze into narrow cages and be lowered—one at a time, of course—right down to the bottom of these cramped openings, to make firsthand and close-up inspections of the rock and soil composition. These surveys—which must have been a claustrophobe's nightmare if ever there was one—were carried out for three weeks, with the aid of oxygen tanks and special lighting and camera equipment.

The 22-foot-thick concrete and steel foundation was completed without causing much stir in Toronto because people were well accustomed to seeing machines and men in hard hats digging away at spots all over the city. But then a process began which would soon attract almost daily and avid attention in the downtown area. By the use of an ingenious kind of slip form, which allowed the builders to pour concrete twenty-four hours a day five days a week, they were able to raise the height of the tower at an extremely impressive rate, as much as 20 feet in a single day.

Motorists whizzing by along the Gardiner Expressway on their way to and from work began to follow the rapid climb of the CN Tower with almost as much interest as Jack must have displayed while watching the incredible rise of his legendary beanstalk.

While the passing gawkers were discussing the amazing growth of the tower in terms of feet per day, anxious engineers inside the climbing spire were concerned with measurements that had to be precisely checked down to the smallest fraction of an inch. Among other things, they were watching for a rather weird phenomenon called torsional oscillation. It seems that, in the earth's northern hemisphere, matter that moves upward has a tendency to twist in a counterclockwise direction, while that which moves downward twists in a clockwise direction. It has something to do with the earth's rotation and can easily be observed in the clockwise swirl made by water as it descends into the drain of your bathtub. (In the southern hemisphere this spiral is reversed.)

Naturally, the tower's engineers didn't want their tall structure to start twisting around like some giant inverted corkscrew as one batch of soft concrete was being poured on top of another. Their constant vigil against twist was carried out with the aid of three German-made optical plumbs, or "bombsights," purchased for $2400 each and seldom used before on Canadian projects. At two-hour intervals, as the concrete was being poured, one of these instruments was sighted from the main deck of the slip form against a permanent target situated on the foundation at the base of the tower. When twist was detected, it was counteracted by an adjustment to the form.

But possible twist was not the only factor that had to be considered as the tower continued to climb into the sky. There was also the problem of keeping the structure as perfectly perpendicular as modern science could achieve. Anyone who has ever tried to install even a perfectly straight-up-and-down fence post will appreciate the problems involved in accomplishing this with a structure more than a third of a mile high. As it turned out, the engineers didn't have to devise any newfangled tricks of modern science. They decided simply to rely upon a giant version of the old and familiar plumb bob, used by generations of builders.

A 250-pound cyclinder was suspended on a length of airplane cable and lowered inside the open core from a winch as the tower rose. It was hoped that by the time the tower reached its full height of 1815 feet it would not be more than 3 inches out from the absolute vertical. When finished, it was out by only *1.1 inches!*

In August of 1974 the ardent followers of the CN Tower's steady climb noticed that, far up on the formerly smooth face at the 1100-foot level, it appeared to be sprouting something that looked like whiskers. What seemed from the ground to be wayward beard hairs were actually 45-foot-long steel angle brackets, bolted to the tower to support what is called the Sky Pod, a seven-story circular structure containing public observation areas, a revolving dining room and broadcast transmission equipment.

Finally, in the spring of 1975, came the crowning and most spectacular achievement in the erection of the tallest structure of its kind on earth.

P. T. Barnum would have loved to have had the ticket concession for the great show, photos of which shortly appeared in newspapers and on television screens all over the world.

The star of this mighty height-defying act was a huge Sikorsky S64E "Skycrane" helicopter named Olga, which had been flown up for the job from its home base in California. It was capable of lifting a load of eleven tons and its task was to hoist into place, with infinite and delicate care, the 39 sections of the radio and television mast which now tops the structure. The heaviest of these weighed eight tons. And so expert was the helicopter's crew that each section was lowered into place as precisely and dexterously as could be achieved by the most light-fingered domino stacker on a kitchen table.

Thousands of spectators gasped at the marvel of it all. Like a good ham, Olga obliged her enthusiastic audience with an impressive encore, by picking up and safely bringing back down to earth, piece by piece, the large special crane which had been climbing along with the tower all through the process of its construction. This greatly relieved the minds of those who had for months been wondering how in the world the thing would ever be brought back to the ground when its job was done. They hadn't been counting on a helicopter and were constantly worrying about how you could lower such a huge crane with no crane left with which to lower it. Sidewalk superintendents are always stewing about things like that and no building project in Toronto's history had ever been followed by more of the unofficial but enthusiastic experts. After all, thousands of apartment dwellers all over Toronto had for months been able to check the tower's daily progress toward the stars from convenient seats right in their own high-rise bathrooms.

But many of these dedicated tower watchers, it is sad to say, missed one of the most spectacular performances of all, on the afternoon of November 8, 1975. On that historic day an ironworker named William Eustace won a high place, of sorts, in the annals of construction when he calmly walked out on a projecting boom, near the tower's summit, and made a parachute jump. He managed to float down without injury to the ground far below, although he did come dangerously close to a high-tension power line that might have cooked him to a frazzle.

He explained to his understandably agitated bosses that it had been something he *had* to do, because the tower was *there,* just as Sir Edmund Hillary had confessed that he had to climb such mountains as Everest because *they* were there. However, an unromantic judge failed to see things in this way and fined Eustace $50 for jumping his job at the end of the day in such dramatic fashion.

On January 11, 1976, while work on the tower was still proceeding, a foreman discovered, upon reaching the top that morning, one blue sock flying bravely from a staff near the peak. It was later learned that this makeshift banner had been placed there by three adventurous teen-agers who had somehow managed to steal up to the top of the tower during the previous night.

The tower's 335-foot transmission mast is equipped with a smooth outer shell to help prevent ice buildup, which could be a serious problem at such great height. The mast is also equipped with ingenious special "dampering" devices to counteract any sway created by high winds. The antennas installed in this lofty mast have greatly extended the signal range of the various Toronto television and radio stations making use of it.

The tower rises from a parklike setting, with landscaped terraces sloping down to a reflecting pool surrounding the base. Visitors can reach the tower by means of an elevated walkway which carries them from Front Street over the railway tracks. Four glass-faced elevators may be boarded for the ride of slightly more than one minute to the Sky Pod. There are two public observation galleries, one glass-enclosed and the other partly open for the benefit of those more sturdy souls who prefer to face the elements when they are looking out upon the vast panorama spread below them. The galleries are equipped with high-powered telescopes, complete with zoom lenses.

Situated immediately above the observation decks, at the 1150-foot level, is the world's highest revolving dining room, accommodating 450 people. The seating has been arranged to give diners a full 360-degree exposure to the changing view as the room smoothly makes one revolution every 90 minutes.

For those who think they are not really getting high enough in the dining room, there remains one even loftier lookout, called the Eagles' Nest. It is 350 feet higher than the dining room. It is said that on a clear day the view from this 1500-foot level covers a radius of more than 100 miles. This should give even the proudest Torontonian enough neighboring territory upon which to properly look down.

In 1966 the Bloor-Danforth subway was opened from Woodbine Avenue in the east to Keele Street in the west. Two years later it was extended eastward to Warden Avenue and westward to Islington Avenue. A projected further extension of this line is to take it to Kennedy Road in the east and Kipling Avenue in the west.

In the spring of 1973 the Yonge Street subway was pushed an additional three miles north to York Mills, and a year later, on the twentieth anniversary of the opening of the Yonge Street line, the trains were operating over still another extension, to Finch Avenue.

At the Finch station an innovation was provided which soon became known as the "kiss and ride carrousel." At many subway stations a traffic problem is created when wives, arriving with the family car to pick up husbands from work, try to park along the street in front of the stations to await their passengers. At the Finch station, a multi-laned circular driveway is provided so a waiting car can keep moving around and around until the subway rider is picked up. It is then possible to slip into an exit lane and take off for home.

The brand-new six-mile Spadina subway, running from St. George station at Bloor Street to Downsview, opened in 1978 after several delays in its construction. As the building of the new line proceeded, its cost soared tremendously. Although its original estimated price had been set at $155 million, the figure had already passed $220 million by 1976. (Costs of the Toronto Transit Commission's five-year development plan, projected from 1974 to 1979, were originally estimated at $87 million. But galloping inflation and other factors have already made it necessary to revise this figure upward to more than $1 billion.)

One of the effects of this staggering rise in the construction costs was to force the TTC to abandon, temporarily, what was to have been one of the more novel features of the new Spadina line. The commissioners were about to authorize a number of art works of various kinds with which to decorate the eight stations, at a cost of $500,000. These pieces, done by different Toronto artists, ranged all the way from huge murals and a 31-foot-long cotton and dacron blanket depicting caribou in the Barren Lands to a 12-foot-high stack of teacups.

But a deluge of indignant telephone calls and letters from citizens, who had already been warned to brace themselves for still another hike in subway fares, caused the commissioners hastily to reconsider the project.

However, some of Toronto's art lovers finally came galloping to the rescue by launching a campaign to raise funds for the project from private sources. Then the Ontario government decided to match these donations with funds taken from the proceeds of the Wintario lottery, and the subway art program survived after all. The desire to make the new subway line pleasing to the eye as well as fast and efficient has also been manifested in other ways, such as utilizing at one of the stations the façade of a 100-year-old building to make it more in keeping with the surrounding architecture.

Although the generally spick-and-span appearance and the efficiency of the older subway lines and stations have been praised by visitors from all over the world, these stations do now look a bit sterile and utilitarian in an era when the mood seems to be to provide more eye appeal to such public places. As one disappointed Toronto artist rather bitterly remarked, after the Spadina art project appeared to have become bogged down, "Unless you treat the subway as your own home, it becomes a public urinal and a place to get stabbed in."

At any rate, the age of the spectacular but rather boxlike steel and glass structures that have sprung up in Toronto in the past few years—including some of the office towers which have been called "aquariums for people"—seems to be on the wane, if still not actually over and done with. Both developers and civic authorities are becoming more concerned with the appearance of their new structures as well as their usefulness.

In the important matter of making new Toronto buildings more attractive and an extra adornment to the downtown skyline, the Royal Bank Plaza, at Bay and Front Streets, has provided a particularly impressive example of what can be done. Instead of having sheer, straight walls, it is a striking combination of various shapes and angles, with gold-tinted glass panels which change in hue and brightness with the westerly progress of the sun across the city. It thus becomes a kind of vast and glowing sculpture in itself, which does much to relieve the monotony of rather stark and forbidding towers of commerce that surround it. It is perhaps a symbol of things to come, as a result of a new attitude in which Torontonians are no longer satisfied with the marvels of the tall and the big and are now devoting much more attention to that which is more beautiful, or at least not so jarring to the eye of the beholder. There seems to be a growing realization that it takes more than just bigness to achieve greatness in a city. Such is the growing mood of the Toronto of the seventies.

The subterranean passages extending from the lower levels of the new Royal Bank Plaza formed still another link in a network of underground promenades that eventually will make it possible, on the coldest winter day, to board a subway train, travel downtown, spend the whole day shopping in scores of spots in the heart of the city and then return to your home station without ever having once had to venture outside to face the miserable weather.

Before long you may be able, for example, to get off the Yonge subway train and then stroll southward all the way from Dundas Street and the Eaton Centre down to the Union Station, all underground. On the way you will be able to browse through a wide variety of shops or patronize restaurants near such focal points as Simpson's, the Four Seasons Sheraton Hotel, the Richmond Adelaide Centre, Commerce Court, First Canadian Place, the Toronto-Dominion Centre, the Merchants Mall of the Royal Bank Plaza and the Royal York Hotel. And if by that time you're not too footsore to meet Aunt Nellie coming in on the train from London, Ontario, you can just walk through the southernmost passage, under Front

Street to the Union Station, in complete comfort no matter how much the winter gales are blowing the snow around overhead.

Although, at this writing, there are still a few short links in this tunnel system to be completed, the underground shopping malls that already exist are being briskly patronized by as many as 50,000 people on a busy day.

It seems doubtful that any city on the North American continent has changed so quickly and dramatically as has Toronto during the past quarter-century. Even in an age when rapid and often spectacular changes is the rule in virtually all parts of the world, the city's transformation from a rather staid and basically Anglo-Saxon community to a bustling and cosmopolitan metropolis remains a source of wonder to those who have lived in it for any length of time.

The change in its physical appearance, with its forest of tall new apartment buildings and hotels, its soaring office towers and its vast suburban developments, extending for hundreds of square miles from the old city's borders, is impressive enough. But even more startling, perhaps, has been the change in the mood and character of Toronto's people.

Ride in Toronto's subway trains or other public conveyances and you will hear all around you conversations in a dozen different languages. Walk the downtown thoroughfares and you will pass through throngs of strollers who appear to represent almost as many lands as the United Nations.

All in all, the newcomers have added quite a tangy and exciting spice to the city's daily life. There are those who say the newcomers have provided just the extra dash of international flavor that was needed to add some zest to the atmosphere of a city that was once respected for the solidness and God-fearing natures of its citizens but never greatly admired for its liveliness and general *joie de vivre*.

The melding of the old, with its traditional and rather stern regard for law, order and commerce, and the new segments of the population—themselves pioneers of a modern era—has so far worked out quite well. It is as though one influence has nicely balanced the other, to the great benefit of the city as a whole. Today Toronto is exciting but still a fairly safe and pleasant place in which to live, as large North American cities go in these rather volatile times. The new and livelier city, built up on the solid old one, has created a successful combination. However, as the flow of immigrants continues, the balance may become more delicate in the years to come.

Meanwhile, if you want to brush up on any of a number of European languages, there are multilingual radio stations broadcasting in the

Toronto area throughout the day. The main Italian-language newspaper, once a struggling weekly, long ago became a flourishing daily. Every summer the Metro Toronto International Caravan provides an excellent opportunity to take a world tour without ever leaving the city. Each of the numerous ethnic groups taking part in this event has a pavilion of its own, and visitors, carrying a special "passport" that can be purchased to cover the whole tour, may sample the food, music, crafts and culture of the many nations now represented in the Toronto mosaic. The new Torontonians from the West Indies have their own lively carnival each year, complete with a parade through the downtown area to the waterfront, where elaborately costumed performers do their dances and the steel bands throb far into the night.

But for a year-round experience of the city's new international flavor, it is only necessary for the modern Toronto explorer to take a stroll through various parts of the inner city where the newcomers from across the seas congregate to shop or pass the time of day, in the traditional manner of the Old World. The Kensington Market area, just west of Spadina Avenue, is a particularly fertile field for such expeditions. Once it was mainly Jewish in character. Now it caters to the tastes of shoppers from many lands. One store may offer strange and interesting foods imported from the West Indies; another, for the Portuguese, an assortment of fish and other seafood just as varied as would be found in Lisbon. The Italians have their own special stores all over the city, but particularly along the western reaches of such streets as Dundas and Bloor and St. Clair Avenue.

Restaurants offering the cuisine of numerous European and Asian lands can be found almost everywhere in the city. No longer is it necessary to leave the environs of Toronto to experience the kind of gastronomic adventures once available only to those prosperous enough to take a Cook's Tour of "faraway places with strange-sounding names," as the old song goes.

It has been said of Canada itself that one of its more admirable qualities is that the country is made up of so many different cultures, all existing side by side in what has been—theoretically, at least—a large degree of harmony and mutual good will. If this is so, then Toronto today represents perhaps the most dramatic and fascinating example, in a highly concentrated way, of this Canadian characteristic. Which is indeed a far, far, cry from the Toronto of yesterday, where you had to be of good old British stock, a Protestant, and preferably a member of the Loyal Orange Order, if you wanted to get very far in politics, or almost any other pursuit within the earlier community.

Chapter 26

FUTURE MEGALOPOLIS?

A rematch between David and Goliath, as Tiny Perfect Mayor David Crombie fights against more giant buildings in Toronto's downtown. An exciting new plan for the city core. The report of the Robarts Royal Commission on Metro advocates borough boundary changes which bring smiles to some mayors and a cry of outrage from at least one. A Commission recommendation that the government of Metro become closer to its people while the affairs of Metro be further removed from the government of Ontario.

On the evening of January 31, 1976, at the end of a long and hectic debate during which one alderman left his seat and sleepily stretched out on the floor to demonstrate how fed up he was with the proceedings, and another called one of his fellow city fathers a son of a bitch, City Council endorsed a vast and far-reaching plan for Toronto.

It contained wide and sweeping recommendations which may have a profound effect upon the shape and nature of the city's growth for many years to come. If successful, it may establish a pattern for municipal development that will be studied with great interest by other cities all over the North American continent.

The plan, which took several years to prepare, was completed during an interval in which Mayor David Crombie and his supporters in City Council made some rather desperate efforts at least to slow down, if not halt, a runaway building boom in the downtown area until some kind of more orderly scheme could be devised. In February of 1973, shortly after his election, Mayor Crombie asked that a holding by-law be passed to allow the council and the planners time to decide what the rate and the style of growth should be.

In December of that year, City Council approved a controversial by-law limiting the height of all new buildings to 45 feet, which was certainly a startling rule in a community where lofty new skyscrapers seemed to be shooting up almost every other month. In December of 1974 the Ontario Municipal Board (OMB) vetoed the height by-law after hearing objections from some 120 developers who claimed they already had more than $2 billion at stake in previous commitments involving various high-rise projects.

The city then appealed to the Ontario Cabinet, which upheld the decision of the OMB but did allow the Toronto Council to impose another modified and temporary by-law which would remain in effect only until September 30, 1975. When that deadline was reached, Premier William Davis granted Toronto an extra breathing spell, until January 31, 1976, in which to produce a more permanent city plan. It was this plan which City Council finally passed just two and a half hours before the midnight expiration of the time limit.

The concern of Mayor Crombie and some council members over the rapid downtown growth rate—while many other North American cities were worried about the opposite problem of *decline* at their central cores—was fairly well justified. After all, between 1970 and 1973, when the first holding by-law was passed, about 8 million square feet of office space had been added to the downtown area—more than in the previous eight years, which had themselves produced quite fantastic growth in the central areas of the city.

One of the prime objections of the new plan for Toronto is that of bringing more dwellers as well as workers into the downtown section. The new residents would, under the plan, be housed in 30,000 additional living units—many of them incorporated into future commercial structures such as office buildings—right in the central part of the city. Such a move, the planners hope, might quite drastically reverse the trend of the past twenty-five years, in which the population of the inner city has steadily decreased in spite of the erection of numerous new apartment buildings in this area. The planners have estimated that during the next ten years at least 70,000 new downtown residents could be accommodated. Developers of downtown properties would be given added incentive to include living units in their buildings by being allowed to erect an increased number of floors on a given area of land, provided these structures included a certain ratio of residential accommodation.

"The diversity of land uses would be increased," said the planners' report, "providing the city with a centre that offers not only employment but also the full spectrum of urban activities. Provision would be made for a 24-hour activity cycle at the core; an objective to which most American cities aspire . . ."

(The so-called core area has been described as that portion of the city which extends from the Gardiner Expressway to just north of Bloor Street and is bounded on the west by Bathurst Street and on the east by the valley of the Don River.)

One attractive feature of the new plan for downtown Toronto was a proposal that by 1986 at least twenty acres of land should be acquired to provide park areas of various shapes and sizes right in the heart of the city. Under this arrangement, there would be a green oasis of some kind within about 200 yards of all present and future residential areas within the downtown section. In this way the trend of the past few years—to cover every available downtown space with either vertical or horizontal expanses of concrete—would be dramatically reversed and there would once more be grassy spots for people to just sit and read, eat or drowse, under shady boughs, in a downtown which may now be exciting but has become rather sterile and somewhat unsuitable for just spending a tranquil hour or two.

Another recommendation of the planners, and one that brought great encouragement to those who are interested in the aesthetic aspects of the city's growth, was that special consideration be given developers who manage to spare and preserve historic buildings which might otherwise be razed to make way for new construction projects. Many important and interesting Toronto landmarks have already been lost to the city forever as a result of the feverish building boom.

The city planners have suggested that developers who manage to spare any old building designated as being worthy by the Ontario Heritage Foundation be allowed to exceed the specified maximum density normally permitted by the exact size of the structure that has been saved. The increased density the developer would then be allowed on the site would be expected to offset the lost space incurred in saving the historic building.

The new height limitations for buildings in the financial district lying below Queen Street would work out at approximately 450 feet—or about half that of the tallest building now situated in this district. One of the primary considerations behind the setting up of these rather stringent new height rules is that of persuading developers to locate more of their larger office buildings in the suburban boroughs of Metro Toronto. The concept has been called deconcentration and is aimed not only at taking some of the construction pressure off the city's core area, but also at easing some of the burden on Metro's hard-pressed transportation system, by locating more offices closer to the suburban homes of those who work in them.

The planners believe that at present there are already too many people working in downtown areas and living in "dormitory" sections some distance from the central city, and that this trend will increase as more business buildings are erected downtown. It is also with this factor in mind that the planners are attempting to provide more living quarters within the city's downtown core, which would permit those who work there to get to their jobs without having to travel back and forth between the downtown area and the suburban boroughs by GO trains, subways and their own automobiles. Although the planners are not counting much on the financial district as a location for future downtown housing, they do expect to see a marked increase in dwelling units north of Queen Street.

In the flush of victory just after the plan for which he had labored so hard had been passed by City Council, Mayor Crombie had this to say:

"The great debate about Toronto's next ten years is over. It's all about what this city is going to look like, who's going to live and work here and how they'll feel about it all. I think the result is a triumph for the people of Toronto . . .

"First of all, the plan starts by giving us something called deconcentration . . . it means deliberately trying to control and spread out the growth of the office space in Metropolitan Toronto.

"If you go to work by bus, subway or streetcar now, you'll be surprised to learn that some people think there's plenty of room for more riders going in and out of downtown every day.

"Sure, you can adjust the capacity somewhat and stagger some more working hours. But unless you have a day-long rush hour and shrink each passenger 15 per cent, there's not a great deal more room on our subway platforms. And if you live in Scarborough or North York, you've probably wished your work was up there on a lot of chilly mornings. The new plan is a first step to stimulating more growth outside the city core . . .

"Let me spare you all the numbers and put it this way: Under the old official plan, you would have seen downtown office space quadruple. The new plan will slow down office space growth to an average of about a million square feet a year—or roughly 3 per cent a year . . .

"There will be more homes downtown. People who work in offices will be able to buy or rent downtown . . . The same principle of preserving what's good in the present or from the past holds true in the question of preserving historic buildings. For years we've been losing significant old buildings because we haven't had any powers to stop demolitions, any money to buy old buildings, or any tools to negotiate for their preservation. With the new plan, new development rules allow the owners of old buildings to leave them standing without financial loss and build in a more flexible form around them.

"So when you boil it all down, you have a remarkable document—possibly the most enlightened chart ever devised to steer a city through the squalls of urban growth.

"We protect existing neighborhoods and do our share to add new homes in the downtown.

"We make it more lively and livable downtown for everyone.

"We make it possible for everyone to live or work within 200 yards of a green space.

"We save massive new transit costs and prevent total clogging of the system we have now.

"We help to deconcentrate office growth to the areas where it is needed and wanted.

"We control the glut of office building with a smooth and orderly plan, with objective rules for all to understand . . ."

Approval by City Council of the bold new plan for the future Toronto was probably the highlight in the remarkable civic career of the five-foot-five-inch bouncy little man who has been variously dubbed the Tiny Perfect Mayor, the Kewpie Doll and even the Pillsbury Doughboy. With his boyish and ready grin, his tousled hair and his easy manner, he does look a little odd when he's standing there on more formal occasions with the great golden chain of office draped over his shoulders and hanging down almost to his belt. He has been known to leave his running shoes lying on the carpet in front of his City Hall desk, and on one occasion, when an alderman just barged in on him after being told he was in conference, he found the Mayor sitting there in his underwear.

But both those who worked with him and against him came to recognize that David Crombie's casual manner and appearance could be quite misleading. Admiration for his energy and ability soon spread far beyond the boundaries of Toronto, to the extent that in 1974, *Time* magazine's New York editors named him among 150 future world leaders, while some Canadian pundits suggested him as a promising candidate for the leadership of the federal Progressive Conservative Party—and therefore, perhaps, a future Prime Minister of Canada.

His serious interest in urban politics went back to his days as a political science instructor at Toronto's Ryerson Polytechnical Institute. It was while serving in this capacity that he decided to take a try at practical politics by running for the office of alderman in 1964 on a campaign budget of $900. He lost. But when he tried again, in 1969, he won.

Three years later, while still a junior alderman, he startled almost everyone by making a bid for the mayor's chair. Those in City Council who thought this was an extremely brash and foolhardy move were virtually shocked speechless—if such a phenomenon is possible among politicians—when the thirty-six-year-old Crombie went right to the top on his very first try. In the 1974 election he won again, with a much larger majority than before.

It was obvious that a lot of Torontonians liked not only his style but the vision and tenacity he was displaying in his David and Goliath battle to make Toronto, not just big and prosperous, but big and prosperous *and* pleasant to live in. There was a new mood to look at the city's growth in terms of quality as well as quantity, and Crombie seemed to express this new attitude as he took his fight for approval of his new city plan to the powerful Ontario Municipal Board at Queen's Park, from which all such blessings still must flow.

The tremendous and almost explosive growth of Toronto and its five boroughs—not to mention that of a new city of 235,000 called Mississauga on Metro's western boundary—may have been in recent years the object of much admiration and even wonder in other parts of North America. But in Metro itself, swift expansion brought with it such a huge package of headaches that it now seems possible that many years may pass before successive commissions, committees, planning groups and various Metro governments will get the whole bag of problems sorted out. If ever . . .

So complex and interwoven have some of these problems become that a university degree in municipal planning would almost be required even to keep track of all the players, let alone the myriad moves and the actual progress of the game itself. Great stacks of reports from numerous bodies now repose in the municipal files, awaiting further action or study. Various interests, localities and individual neighborhoods in Metro are fiercely defending their own particular pieces of the vast jigsaw puzzle that must be put together to form the ideal city as each group sees it. Once again even the most ardent community boosters have had to admit that there is indeed some truth in the adage that being bigger is not necessarily being better.

There is a gnawing, growing doubt, among many of the residents of the present sprawling Metro complex, about whether bigness ever can be successfully coped with without sacrificing those individual identities of community and neighborhood which have traditionally been cherished by so many generations of Torontonians. It goes back to the days when an unusually large proportion of the residents owned their own homes and jealously preserved the individual character of their particular neighborhoods—so much so that at one time Toronto seemed almost more like a large collection of separate villages than a single, integrated city. It was an attitude that has already disappeared, to a great extent, during the past two decades of Toronto's rapid growth. Yet its passing had been relatively gradual and subtle.

Today the effects of this process of homogenization is becoming much more clear, and many of the residents of Metro Toronto don't like it. Fascination with the spectacular building boom is beginning to fade. The tendency to take a second look at bigness and its true relationship to lifestyle has become more widespread. People want to know just what local representative they should call on the telephone if there's a hole in the sidewalk, instead of having to deal with a growing and sometimes confusing over-all bureaucracy which seems always to become more remote as its size increases. And chances are that it will continue to increase, as galloping growth and a more integrated Metro requires broader and more centralized control if the somewhat ungainly amalgamation of municipalities is not to flounder.

In considering the various problems and suggested remedies bearing upon Metro's future, it must be remembered that actually three levels of government are involved and that the efficient conduct of the area's affairs depends to some degree upon the amount of harmony or discord which exists among them.

At the top of this pyramid is the provincial government, which exerts great authority through its Ontario Municipal Board. Next comes the Metro Council, with authority over the City of Toronto and the five Metro boroughs. Then come the individual governments of the six municipalities that make up the huge Metro complex. To say that these numerous bodies, each of which has some measure of control over Metro, do not always see matters eye to eye would be putting it mildly indeed.

Early in 1976 a second one-man Royal Commission on Metropolitan Toronto concluded its hearings and began to prepare its report. This Commission, conducted by former Ontario Premier John Robarts, was established on September 10, 1974, at the request of Metro Council, to consider what had taken place in Metro in the decade which had elapsed since the Goldenberg Royal Commission's report; to take stock of Metro's current situation and to make recommendations concerning the vital matter of what courses should be followed during the next ten years. The Commission's terms of reference were described as follows:

"The Commissioner is instructed to examine, evaluate and make recommendations on the organization, financing and operations of local governments in the Metropolitan Toronto area, including all municipalities and all local and Metro boards and commissions. Consideration of a single tier or amalgamated form of government is specifically included. Recommendations are to be based on both present and future social and economic conditions and growth patterns. In this connection, the Commission will look at municipal boundaries, the division of responsibilities among various government bodies and the selection and roles of those who govern Metro. It will examine the system of representation in Metro, the relationship between the electors and the elected, the system of administration and the financial well-being of Metro . . ."

Among the numerous briefs presented by various community groups and individual citizens to the Royal Commission were those containing

suggestions for both a single over-all government of a completely amalgamated Toronto and those calling for a more loosely knit system that
would allow greater self-determination to individual localities.

Fred Gardiner, Metro's first chairman, recommended to the Commission that the present borough system be eliminated and replaced by a single, amalgamated Toronto with twenty-four strip wards extending from
Metro's northern boundaries to the lakeshore. It was his belief that such
an arrangement would go a long way toward creating better cross sections
of the populace, holding a wider mixture of interests. This, he thought,
would do away to a considerable extent with the present situation in
which too many concentrated "power groups" in smaller areas were able
to exert far too much self-serving influence upon the general affairs of
Metro.

At the other end of the spectrum were briefs urging that instead of increasing the size and strength of a central municipal government, steps
should be taken to reduce them, permitting greater self-determination for
various localities and much more personal contact between the people and
their representatives. There were also briefs which warned of the dangerous power that could be wielded by one central government of a community as large as Metro Toronto.

In a publication issued by the Royal Commission just before it concluded its hearings, this description was given of Metro's population as it
then existed, with some hints concerning its possible future nature:

"Today Metropolitan Toronto has a population of approximately 2.2
million.* A report on demographic trends prepared for the Commission
revealed the following population patterns:

"At the time of the 1971 census Metro had 2.09 million people, or
slightly less than $\frac{1}{10}$ of Canada's population. The population represented
three quarters of the people living in the Central Ontario Lakeshore
Urban Complex (COLUC), a planning area which includes Metro and
parts of the Regional Municipalities of Peel, York, Durham, Halton and
Hamilton-Wentworth.

"Since 1951, Metro's population has grown at 1½ times the rate of that
of the country. Very little of this growth has been in the inner three municipalities (Toronto, York and East York) but the population of the suburbs (Etobicoke, North York and Scarborough) has mushroomed from
200,000 to 1,100,000.

"Probably because Metro is a major regional and national commercial

* Enumeration records of Metro municipalities in 1975 provided the following population figures for Toronto and the five boroughs: Toronto, 685,333; North York,
556,044; Scarborough, 372,278; Etobicoke, 293,753; York, 140,184; and East York,
104,677. The enumeration also revealed there were 19,000 more females in Toronto
itself than males and that in the five boroughs females outnumber males by 42,000.

centre which attracts those seeking employment, it has a lower proportion of people in nonworking age groups than the national average.

"The City of Toronto has a high proportion of employment relative to other parts of Metro. Retailing jobs are fairly evenly distributed across Metro and well over half the jobs in manufacturing and wholesaling are in the suburbs. However, the suburbs offer fewer opportunities for white collar employment.

"While Metro has a higher birthrate than either Ontario or Canada, undoubtedly because of its age structure, most of its population increase over the last few decades has been due to migration, the largest proportion of which has been international.†

"Metro has been receiving approximately 30 per cent of all immigrants to Canada. It has also gained population from other parts of the province and the country. Metro residents who do leave tend to move to the surrounding regional municipalities as more and more migrants move in. People also migrate from Metro to Alberta and British Columbia. On the other hand, Metro gains people from the Atlantic provinces, the prairies and, more recently, Quebec . . .

"Where immigrants settle in Canada tends to be related to their countries of origin. Americans and Northern Europeans tend to be dispersed in settlement patterns, while immigrants from Southern Europe, Asia and the Caribbean congregate in the large cities. Immigrants also tend to settle in areas of high labour demand and low unemployment.

"Therefore a shift in the immigrant stream away from Asia, the Caribbean and Southern Europe or a decline in Metro's economic position relative to other parts of Canada, would probably result in a significant decline in the number of immigrants settling here.

"Over the last few years growth has been declining in Metro, primarily as a result of decreasing supply of land and affordable housing. By the 1980s, natural increase (births) is expected to be the more important determinant of population growth."

One Metro planning group has predicted that by the year 2000 the population will be between 2.8 million and 3.2 million. It has been suggested that the number of children in Metro will drop and that there will be more elderly people and smaller families.

Although Toronto has been acclaimed far and wide as one of the most orderly big cities on the North American continent, there are growing doubts in some quarters whether the present growth rate will allow it for

† Latest available figures, at this writing, divide Metro Toronto's ethnic groups as follows: British, 1,495,300; French, 91,975; German, 116,640; Italian, 271,755; Jewish, 109,910; Netherlands, 44,430; Polish, 51,180; Scandinavian, 18,360; Ukrainian, 60,750; Asiatic, 71,030; others and unknown, 296,795.

long to maintain this reputation. Some of those who are now engaged in planning its future are of the opinion that violent political groups will almost inevitably threaten the well-being of Metro Toronto sometime in the future. There is even fear that the influence of activities in other parts of the world may eventually bring some degree of rebellion to Metro Toronto in the form of urban guerrilla action. Equality and elimination of poverty, it is believed, are causes which could attract violent support in Metro in the uncertain years which lie ahead.

On July 4, 1977, the Robarts Royal Commission submitted to the Ontario government its long-awaited report and recommendations. Although it suggested numerous changes—both large and small—in the geographical structure and government of Metropolitan Toronto, the most sensational and controversial were those concerning the redrawing of boundaries within Metro and the proposal that a new form of Metro Toronto Council be set up which would consist mainly of members directly elected to this body.

At the time of the report, Metro Council was made up of thirty-seven members, selected from the city and its boroughs in rather haphazard manner, whose main responsibilities were to the councils of their own municipalities. Under the Robarts plan, twenty-seven members of a new Metro Council—although holding seats on their local bodies—would devote their time primarily to Metro affairs and would go before the electors with this special role clearly understood. These members of Metro Council would run for election in twenty-seven newly defined wards, each containing about 80,000 people.

In addition to such councillors, the six Metro mayors would hold membership in a Metro government presided over by a chairman who would first have to be elected to the council of his own municipality before being eligible to head the Metro Council. (Under the original system, the chairman, selected by the Metro Council, was not required to face any kind of public election in order to serve in this capacity.)

Among other proposals of the Robarts Commission was one that Metro elections be held every three years, instead of two years, and in October instead of December, when severe winter weather might make it more difficult for some voters to get to the polls.

But the Commission suggestion that caused the biggest uproar was that the largest borough, North York, should undergo a reduction in size which would result in its losing about 25 per cent of its population and $3 billion of its assessments to the boroughs of York, East York and the City of Toronto.

"I'll fight it to my dying day!" vowed North York Mayor Mel Lastman, and it didn't exactly soothe his worship's indignation when, not long after the Robarts Report came out, prankish Mayor Phillip White of York donned a coonskin hat and stole over to North York territory to plant one of his borough's flags in a flower bed.

Another recommendation of the Royal Commission was that complete control of the Toronto Transit Commission, a semi-autonomous body, be taken over by Metro Council, which also would be empowered to develop a Metro-wide parking policy and set fines for the city and all boroughs. The Metro police force of 6500 would also become responsible directly to Metro Council, instead of to a commission appointed by the province. The Metro School Board would gradually be eliminated and educational responsibilities turned over to the various area boards of education.

During its hearings the Royal Commission had listened to briefs proposing that the widespread boundaries of Metro be extended even more to take in portions of such neighboring counties as Peel and Durham, as well as York. In its report the Commission did recognize some merit in creating a Toronto Region Coordinating Agency, with representation from Metro and five other adjacent areas. Its purpose would be to provide better means of achieving closer co-operation in planning for the future of this whole important section of the province.

But there should be no actual boundary changes for Metro which would expand it into this wider region—yet.

"Governing a megalopolis is as yet an infant and imperfect science," said the report. "At this stage, there does not seem to be an obvious way to address this challenge."

However, although the Robarts Commission did not recommend any increases in the physical boundaries of Metro, it did strongly advise that new and wider powers be given to its council. Because Metro, with a population greater than that of seven of the ten provinces, already had a larger annual budget ($500 million) than all but Quebec, Ontario, British Columbia and Alberta, it "must be treated separately" from any other city in Canada and some of the powers and purse strings held by Ontario should be turned over to Metro Council, said the report.

So much for the efforts of planning boards and Toronto City Council and a Royal Commission to chart a future course for the vast and ever-growing community which now spreads over such a great portion of the northern shore of Lake Ontario.

But the fate of all these brave new plans for a community which has, as the Royal Commission report suggested, become almost a province within a province, still lies firmly in the hands of the Ontario government. It must make the final decision on which, if any, of these numerous proposals shall be adopted, after hearing the pros and cons of it all argued before the Ontario Municipal Board. Such a process is usually a long one, surrounded by many uncertainties. But so has been the progress of Toronto itself, from tiny hamlet to its present huge and complex form.

Mayor Jimmy Walker once said of his fabulous home town: "New York will be a beautiful city, if we ever get her finished."

Today's Torontonians, wending their way through numerous newspaper reports of myriad planning suggestions and past the cement mixers and foundation diggers and road barricades and subway excavations and detour signs and ever-increasing clusters of apartment houses and business buildings soaring steadily skyward, may well echo Jimmy Walker's sentiments as they contemplate the prediction that as early as 1993—just 200 years after Colonel John Graves Simcoe set his Queen's Rangers to work clearing the bush from the site of the tiny new British settlement of York— Metropolitan Toronto may be the home town of more than three million people, a great many of them with comparatively recent roots extending to the farthermost corners of the world.

BIBLIOGRAPHY

ABRAHAMSON, UNA, *Domestic Life in Nineteenth Century Canada*, Burns & MacEachern Ltd. Toronto 1966.

ALLEN, RALPH, *Ordeal by Fire*. Doubleday. Toronto 1961.

ALLEN, ROBERT THOMAS, *When Toronto Was for Kids*. McClelland and Stewart. Toronto 1961.

ARMSTRONG, F. H., *The First Great Fire of Toronto, 1849*. Ontario History, v. 53, p. 201–21. Toronto 1961.

——, *The Rebuilding of Toronto After the Great Fire of 1849*. Ontario History, v. 53, p. 233–50. Toronto 1961.

——, *The Carfrae Family. A Study in Early Toronto Toryism*. Ontario History, v. 54, p. 161–81. Toronto 1962.

ARTHUR, ERIC, *Toronto, No Mean City*. University of Toronto Press. Toronto 1964.

BERTON, PIERRE, *The New City*. Macmillan. Toronto 1961.

BISHOP, WILLIAM ARTHUR, *The Courage of the Early Morning*. McClelland and Stewart. Toronto 1966.

BOYLEN, J. C., *York Township, an Historical Survey, 1850–1954*. Municipal Corporation of the Township of York. Toronto 1954.

BRADDON, RUSSELL, *Roy Thompson of Fleet Street*. Collins. Toronto 1965.

BREBNER, J. BARTLET, *Canada*. University of Michigan Press. Ann Arbor 1960.

BURTON, C. L., *A Sense of Urgency*. Clarke, Irwin. Toronto 1952.

COLLARD, EDGAR A., *Canada's Yesterdays*. Longmans, Green. 2nd ed. Toronto 1963.

CORRELLI, RAE, *The Toronto That Used to Be*. Toronto Star. Toronto 1964.

COSGROVE, EDMUND, *Canada's Fighting Pilots*. Clarke, Irwin. Toronto 1965.

CURRELL, HARVEY, *The Mimico Story*. Published by the Town of Mimico. Toronto 1967.

DRURY, E. C., *All for a Beaver Hat*. Ryerson Press. Toronto 1959.

DUNHAM, AILEEN, *Political Unrest in Upper Canada, 1815–1836.* McClelland and Stewart. Toronto 1963.

ELLIS, FRANK H., *Canada's Flying Heritage.* University of Toronto Press. Toronto 1954.

FIRTH, EDITH G., *The Town of York, 1793–1815. The Town of York, 1815–1834.* University of Toronto Press. Toronto 1962 and 1965.

FRAYNE, TRENT, *The Queen's Plate—The First Hundred Years.* McClelland and Stewart. Toronto 1959.

GRAHAM, W. H., *The Tiger of Canada West.* Clarke, Irwin. Toronto 1962.

GRIFFIN, FREDERICK, *Major General Sir Henry Pellatt—a Gentleman of Toronto.* Ontario Publishing Company. Toronto 1939.

GUILLET, EDWIN C., *Toronto from Trading Post to Great City.* Ontario Publishing Company. Toronto 1934.

HALE, KATHERINE, *Toronto, A Romance of a Great City.* Cassell. Toronto 1956.

HATHAWAY, E. J., *Jesse Ketchum and His Times.* McClelland and Stewart. Toronto 1929.

INNIS, MARY QUAYLE, *Mrs. Simcoe's Diary.* Macmillan. Toronto 1965.

JAMESON, ANNA, *Winter Studies and Summer Rambles in Canada.* Thomas Nelson and Sons. Toronto 1944.

JENNESS, DIAMOND, *The Indians of Canada.* Queen's Printer. Ottawa 1955.

KILBOURN, WILLIAM, *The Firebrand.* Clarke, Irwin. Toronto 1960.

LANCTAT, GUSTAVE, *The Royal Tour of King George VI and Queen Elizabeth in Canada and the United States, 1939.* The E. P. Taylor Foundation. Toronto 1964.

LINDSAY, CHARLES, *William Lyon Mackenzie.* Morang & Company. Toronto 1910.

MACKINTOSH, HONORABLE CHARLES A., *Chronicles of Canada's Diamond Jubilee.* The Ronalds Co. Montreal, Ottawa 1929.

MACPHERSON, MARY ETTA, *The Eatons. Shopkeepers to a Nation.* McClelland and Stewart. Toronto 1963.

MASTERS, D. C., *The Rise of Toronto, 1850–1890.* University of Toronto Press. Toronto 1947.

MCAREE, J. V., *Cabbagetown Store.* Ryerson Press. Toronto 1953.

MCLAREN, JACK, *Let's All Hate Toronto.* Kingswood House. Toronto 1956.

MIDDLETON, J. E., *Municipality of Toronto.* (Three volumes.) Dominion Publishing Company. Toronto 1923.

NEWMAN, PETER C., *Flame of Power.* Longmans, Green. Toronto 1959.

BIBLIOGRAPHY 277

Nicholson, Colonel G. W. L., *Canadian Expeditionary Force 1914–1919*. Queen's Printer. Ottawa 1962.

Pearson, W. H., *Recollections and Records of Toronto of Old*. Briggs. Toronto 1914.

Pound, Arthur, *Lake Ontario*. Bobbs-Merrill Co. New York 1945.

Radcliff, Thomas, *Authentic Letters from Upper Canada*. Macmillan. Toronto 1953.

Raddall, Thomas H., *The Path of Destiny*. Doubleday. Toronto 1954.

Robertson, John Ross, *Landmarks of Toronto*. (Six volumes.) Telegram. Toronto 1894–1914.

Robinson, Percy J., *Toronto During the French Régime 1615–1793*. University of Toronto Press. Toronto 1965.

Rutledge, Joseph Lister, *Century of Conflict*. Doubleday. Toronto 1956.

Scadding, Henry, and John C. Dent, *Toronto Past and Present*. Hunter Rose. Toronto 1884.

Sclater, Lieutenant Commander William, *Haida*. Oxford University Press. Toronto 1955.

Scott, Duncan Campbell, *John Graves Simcoe*. Morang & Company. Toronto 1910.

Slater, Patrick, *The Yellow Briar*. Thomas Allen. Toronto 1933.

Stacey, Colonel C. P., *The Battle of Little York*. General Printers. Toronto 1963.

Taylor, C. C., *Toronto Called Back*. William Briggs. Toronto 1892. *The City of Toronto Municipal Handbooks*, 1909 to 1967.

Toye, William, *A Book of Canada*. Collins. London 1962.

Walker, Frank N., *Sketches of Toronto of Old*. Longmans. Toronto 1965.

Withrow, Dr. Oswald C. J., *The Romance of the Canadian National Exhibition*. Saunders. Toronto 1936.

Files of the *Globe* and the *Globe and Mail*.
Canadian Illustrated News (Montreal 1869–83).
Eaton's Golden Jubilee, 1869–1919 (T. Eaton Co. Toronto 1919).

INDEX

1